Passport Entanglements

The publisher and the University of California Press Foundation gratefully acknowledge the generous support of the Anne G. Lipow Endowment Fund in Social Justice and Human Rights.

Passport Entanglements

PROTECTION, CARE, AND PRECARIOUS
MIGRATIONS

Nicole Constable

UNIVERSITY OF CALIFORNIA PRESS

University of California Press
Oakland, California

© 2022 by Nicole Constable

Library of Congress Cataloging-in-Publication Data

Names: Constable, Nicole, author.
Title: Passport entanglements : protection, care, and precarious
    migrations / Nicole Constable.
Description: Oakland, California : University of California Press, [2022] |
    Includes bibliographical references and index.
Identifiers: LCCN 2022012143 (print) | LCCN 2022012144 (ebook) |
    ISBN 9780520387980 (cloth) | ISBN 9780520387997 (paperback) |
    ISBN 9780520388000 (ebook)
Subjects: LCSH: Foreign workers, Indonesian—Legal status, laws, etc.—
    China—Hong Kong. | Women foreign workers—Legal status, laws, etc.—
    China—Hong Kong. | Passports—Social aspects—China—Hong Kong.
Classification: LCC KNQ9358.A44 c66 2022 (print) | LCC KNQ9358.A44
    (ebook) | DDC 342.5108/2—dc23/eng/20220801
LC record available at https://lccn.loc.gov/2022012143
LC ebook record available at https://lccn.loc.gov/2022012144

31 30 29 28 27 26 25 24 23 22
10 9 8 7 6 5 4 3 2 1

For Sebastian

Contents

Illustrations

Preface

The research upon which this book is based was essentially handed to me on a platter in 2015 by a friendly Indonesian consular official in Hong Kong. He was proud to implement a new biometric passport renewal scheme and thought it would reflect well on Indonesia's modernization and securitization, so he suggested that I write a book about it. The Indonesian migrant workers and migrant worker activists I consulted agreed that it would be a worthy project because they had become aware of some serious problems that the passport renewal project was causing for Indonesians in Hong Kong, including some who were charged with immigration fraud and faced prison sentences.

Passports—especially Indonesian *aspal* or "real but fake" passports— led me down fascinating rabbit holes, including individual, historical, and fictional ones. They took me beyond the migrant workers' experiences and stories I had heard, beyond the perspectives voiced by domestic worker activists, and beyond individual consular officials' views, down socioeconomic, historical, and political pathways that crosscut global, national, and village scales and time periods. Passports are endlessly fascinating, partly because they are full of contradictions. They both facilitate and prevent mobility. They represent the state's unity and equality but reinforce social inequalities and differences. They are instruments of freedom and of control, of protection and exploitation. They represent modernity, rationality, and transparency, but they are entangled with murky and conspiratorial discourses of power, surveillance, and corruption.

This book is about ethnographic and historical entanglements of passports and migrant labor. Passports alone are fascinating, but even more so as an entry point from which to understand migration and the challenges experienced by migrant workers. "Entanglements" provide the analytical framework through which I analyze and criticize many of the binary oppositions that are commonly associated with migration (e.g., migrant and citizen, care and control, free and unfree), with passports (e.g., real and fake), and with ethnography (e.g., ethnographer and interlocutor, researcher and researched).

Passport Entanglements illustrates how new passport technologies and surveillance do not necessarily lead to greater protection, security, or accuracy, as they purport to do. Instead, they produce new vulnerabilities and reveal older ones that are tied to labor control and to the highly profitable migrant labor industry. The Indonesian government's passport renewal project reveals the entanglements of the state with society and with capitalist interests at multiple levels. Together they shape labor migration, sow mistrust, and seriously impact the livelihood and wellbeing of migrant workers. The passport project set in motion new processes of governance that (re)produced the very passports that they sought to eliminate, further revealing the deeper entanglements of real and fake, corruption and care, and free and unfree labor.

Acknowledgments

My annual or biannual travel to Hong Kong from 2015 to 2019 would not have been possible without the time and funding I received from the University of Pittsburgh's Dietrich School of Arts and Sciences, from Yale–NUS College, and from the Asia Research Institute, National University of Singapore.

Acknowledgments are humbling to write, as there are countless people to whom I owe gratitude. I would exceed the book's word limit if I listed them all. I am immensely grateful to the domestic workers, activists and advocates, Indonesian officials, and friends and colleagues in and beyond Hong Kong who provided wisdom, kindness, and infinite patience throughout the project.

At the Indonesian Consulate in Hong Kong, among the many people I talked to, I am most grateful to Andry Indrady, Consul; Charles Christian and Sari Widita, Vice Consuls; and Tri Tharyat and Chalief Akbar, Consuls General. In this book, I use pseudonyms to refer to the many consular staff persons and officials I spoke with, except in relation to news, public events, and public statements. I do this because I don't want their openness about the "passport project" to reflect negatively on them.

For three decades, activist domestic workers (including many who are dear friends) continue to fill me with admiration and awe. They patiently tolerated my endless questions. They welcomed me to rallies, training programs, and social events. We shared feasts and celebrations. I am forever beholden to Eni Lestari Andayani, Chairperson, International Migrants Alliance (IMA); Sringatin, Chairperson, Indonesian Migrant Workers Network (JBMI) and Indonesian Migrant Workers' Union (IMWU); Muthi Hidayati and Maesaroh, leaders of the Association of Indonesian Migrant Workers (ATKI); and dozens of domestic workers and former domestic workers who shared their aspal (real but fake) passport stories with me. Unless otherwise agreed upon, I use pseudonyms to protect their identities.

Local advocates and organizations lent their expertise over the years, including Cynthia Abdon-Tellez of the Mission for Migrant Workers (MFMW); Edwina Antonio-Santoyo of Bethune House; attorneys Melville Boase, Eric M. Y. Ching, and Patricia Ho; Ramon Bultron, Rey Asis, Aaron Ceradoy, and Jun Tellez of Asia Pacific Mission for Migrants (APMM); Nurul Qoirah, International Organization for Migration; and Lia Ngatini, PathFinders Hong Kong. They provided knowledge and companionship in Hong Kong, as have Catherine Cheng, Sealing Cheng and her family, Sikying Ho, Maria Hwang, Venera Khalikova, Anne and Paul Milone, Denise Spitzer, and Kylie Uebergang and her family. Julie Ham generously shared her notes from a passport training session I could not attend. Dolores Baladares Palaez, Janette and Norman Carnay, Father Dwight, Eman and Lalay Villanueva, and countless others have added to the pleasure of working in Hong Kong.

This book benefited from comments on talks presented at the Asia Research Institute, National University of Singapore; the On the Move program, University of Neuchâtel; the Wertheim Institute and the University of Amsterdam; the International Seminar, University of New Hampshire; the Center for Advanced Study and the Center for East Asian and Pacific Studies, University of Illinois at Urbana-Champaign; and the Honors College and Global Studies Center, at the University of Pittsburgh. My thanks to Sunil Amrith, Bridget Anderson, Avie Azis, Michiel Baas, Heath Cabot, Yuchia Chang, Marianne Constable, Teresita Cruz-del Rosario, Janine Dahinden, Michael Goodhart, Kevin Hewison, Pierre

Landry, Tim Liao, Radhika Mongia, Joëlle Moret, Lorenzo Piccoli, Georgina Ramsay, Jonathan Rigg, Lucy Salyer, Jeannie Sowers, You Yenn Teo, and Meredith Weiss. Carol Chan, Gordon Mathews, and anonymous reviewers read the manuscript and offered important and insightful suggestions, which I have tried my best to incorporate. Johan Lindquist provided numerous generous, challenging, and insightful suggestions paired with his deep knowledge of Indonesian migration infrastructures and has made this a better book. Its flaws are my own.

Nancy Abelmann, whom I miss dearly, read drafts of all my previous books. Her voice was often in my head as I wrote this one, reminding me to push the analysis further and to spell out the main points more clearly. Again, I have had the pleasure and privilege of working with Naomi Schneider at UC Press and much appreciate the assistance of Summer Farrah and Richard Earles.

My partner, Joseph S. Alter, continues to motivate me and to center me both in work and in life, offering patience, insight, and support. He and our dog Motu, as well as our dispersed family COVID-19 bubble—Peter, Tory, Tom, Nathaniel, Elizabeth, and Sebastian—helped fill our pandemic-era void with love, good food, companionship, and welcome distraction.

Terms and Abbreviations

asli	Authentic, original, real
aspal	Real but fake (contraction of *asli tapi palsu*)
ATKI	Asosiasi Tenaga Kerja Indonesia (Association of Indonesian Migrant Workers)
BMI	Buruh Migran Indonesia (Indonesian Migrant Worker)
BNP2TKI	Badan Nasional Penempatan dan Perlindungan Tenaga Kerja Indonesia (National Agency for the Placement and Protection of Indonesian Migrant Workers)
BP2MI	Badan Perlindungan Pekerja Migran Indonesia (Agency for the Protection of Indonesian Migrant Workers)
BP3TKI	Balai Pelayanan Penempatan Perlindungan Tenaga Kerja Indonesia (regional agencies for the placement and protection of Indonesian migrant workers)
calo	Recruiter, trafficker (somewhat derogatory)

e-KTP	E-Kartu Tanda Penduduk (Indonesian national electronic identity card)
FDH	Foreign domestic helper (official term used by Hong Kong government)
FDW	Foreign domestic worker (preferred to *FDH* by workers)
G2G	Government to government (implies communication and shared technology)
Imigrasi	Directorate General of Immigration (Indonesian immigration department)
IMWU	Indonesian Migrant Workers' Union
IOM	International Organization for Migration
JBMI	Jaringan Buruh Migran Indonesia (Indonesian Migrant Workers' Network)
KABAR BUMI	Keluarga Besar Buruh Migran Indonesia (Families of Indonesian Migrant Workers)
KJRI	Konsulat Jenderal Republik Indonesia (Indonesian Consulate General)
KK	Kartu Keluarga (family card or household registry)
KKN	*korupsi, kolusi, nepotisme* (corruption, collusion, nepotism)
KTP	Kartu Tanda Penduduk (individual identity card)
MFMW	Mission for Migrant Workers
NGO	Non-governmental organization
palsu	Counterfeit, fraudulent, fake
paspor pungli	A passport that requires illegal fees or extortion (*pungli* is a contraction of *pungutan liar*, illegal fees)
PJTKI	Perusahaan Jasa Tenaga Kerja Indonesia (recruitment agency; older term)
PL	*petugas lapangan* (literally, "field agent" or "labor recruiter")
PMI	Pekerja Migran Indonesia (Indonesian Migrant Worker)

PPTKIS	Pelaksana Penempatan Tenaga Kerja Indonesia Swasta (private and registered recruitment agency; newer term)
PT	Perseroan Terbatas (registered company; refers to a licensed recruitment agency)
SIMKIM	Sistem Informasi Manajemen Keimigrasian (Immigration Information Management System)
TKI	Tenaga Kerja Indonesia (Indonesian Migrant Worker)
TKW	Tenaga Kerja Wanita (Woman Migrant Worker)
transmigrasi	Transmigration policy of the Dutch colonial government, continued by the Indonesian government
USM	Unified Screening Mechanism, Hong Kong
VOC	Dutch East India Company (Dutch: Vereenigde Oostindische Compagnie)

1 Passports and Ethnographic Entanglements

> The passport photograph gives rise to a new kind of anxiety, a new neurosis for the citizen, that our face will be read against us, because the passport photo is always one that doesn't look like us.
>
> Mark Salter (2015, 22)

> It is often the passport's authenticity that is checked and compared to our body and not vice versa. . . . [I]n moments of intended border crossing, the border guards were mostly concerned with the authenticity of the passport and not [with] its authentic relation to the represented body.
>
> Mahmoud Keshavarz (2019, 37)

ARI'S PASSPORT

"My real name is not the one on my passport," Ari said, when I first interviewed her in Hong Kong in 2011. The name on her Indonesian passport, she told me with a smile, was not her own *asli* name, but her older sister's (*asli* means original, authentic, or real in Bahasa Indonesia, the national language). Her passport was that way because when Ari finished middle school and planned to leave her village in East Java to work abroad, she was only sixteen, below Indonesia's required legal age of eighteen for Indonesian migrant workers at that time. Her older sister said that she would never go abroad, so, on the advice of the local sub-recruiter (PL, *petugas lapangan*), who was well regarded in the community and eager to help, and with her family's full knowledge and consent, she gave him her sister's school certificate to begin the process, and the recruiter did the rest. He obtained the various necessary documents for her to acquire a passport, including the letter of permission from her father, an identity card (KTP), a copy of her family/household certificate (KK), and the exit letter required from the police. Then he obtained the passport on her behalf through a regional government office. Several months later, the broker brought her to the PJTKI or recruitment agency (called PPTKIS today), and they arranged for Ari's departure from Indonesia and her travel to Hong Kong, where she would be a "foreign domestic helper" (FDH). At the departure counter at the airport, the recruitment agent distributed their passports to Ari and the other women. Subsequently, every three years, before her passport expired, the agency in Hong Kong renewed it for her at the Indonesian consulate.

Two years or so after her passport was first renewed, as Ari recounted with a laugh, her older sister decided to come to work in Hong Kong after all. She, too, procured a passport with the help of a PL, using her *asli* information, but she used a different recruitment agency. When Ari's sister arrived at the airport in Hong Kong, she was taken aside by Hong Kong immigration officers, brought into a small interview room, and questioned at length. The officers repeatedly asked her name, date of birth, and place of residence. She answered honestly, insisting that her name, date of birth, place of residence, and so on had never changed. She did not mention her sister. They scrutinized her passport. Eventually they let her go, Ari said, "because it was obvious that she was telling the truth." Once, while her sister was still in Hong Kong, Ari had to pass through immigration on her return trip to Hong Kong. She, too, was detained at the airport and questioned at length by Hong Kong immigration officers. They scrutinized her passport and her Hong Kong identity card. Her answers—identical to her sister's—apparently satisfied them. More likely, however, as suggested by the first epigraph above, the officers were convinced that her passport was authentic. Ari's passport was thus stamped, and she was permitted to enter Hong Kong and go back to work.

Beginning in 2015, Ari could potentially have experienced serious trouble. The new Indonesian passport renewal policy required the collection of biometric data and compared all existing passports with the information in a national passport database. If Ari and her sister had not returned to Indonesia before their passports expired, at least one of them could have ended up in prison like a dozen other women I met or knew about who were charged with immigration fraud. According to one unpublished report, around half of the hundreds of Indonesian migrant workers surveyed by an international non-governmental organization (NGO) in 2016 had inconsistencies in their passports, including discrepancies with their names, their dates of birth, and their Indonesian places of residence. Another survey, conducted by members of the Indonesian umbrella organization JBMI (Jaringan Buruh Migran Indonesia, Indonesian Migrant Workers' Network) in 2016, found that almost a third of the five hundred workers surveyed had passport irregularities pertaining to names and/or dates of birth. Given these figures and that there were over 150,000 Indonesian domestic workers in Hong Kong at the time, we could reasonably expect that the passports of tens of thousands of Indonesians in Hong Kong have irregularities of this sort.

This book recounts many stories about Indonesian passports and the migrant workers who carry them, the recruitment brokers and agents who procure them, and the government immigration officials and middlemen who produce them and inspect them. At the core of this study are passports, especially so-called *aspal* passports (*aspal* is a contraction of *asli tapi palsu*, real but fake) and the social entanglements and inequalities they both reflect and produce (Ford and Lyons 2011). Despite the high percentage of likely aspal passports, most passport renewals are "nonevents," in the sense that what *could* happen does not happen.

Although the plan was to eliminate aspal passports, I argue that ultimately *most* aspal passports were simply reproduced because the passport's irregularities were not discovered. In most cases nothing was changed or corrected. Yet such nonevents can be "spectacularly significant" as an indication of a project's failure (Falcone 2012, 155), and because of the questions they raise about why some passport holders had no problems (other than inconvenience, extra expense, time wasted, and perhaps a grumpy employer) whereas others, with similar circumstances, faced life-altering consequences. Some passport corrections resulted in job termination, early departure, court hearings, and prison sentences. This book thus points to the wider importance of studying both the passport nonevents *and* the more serious outcomes. Passports, studied from different angles, reveal key insights about migration and mobility, labor and capital, borders and nation-states. They illustrate deep entanglements of power and money in migration infrastructures, across different temporalities and scales, and in the lives of migrant workers, helping us understand the vulnerabilities of labor migration today, especially in relation to the gray area of migration that combines the illegal and the legal and, ultimately, (re)produces aspal passports.

PASSPORT STORIES

A common saying about passports is that they are "the books that contain the best stories." For some, this saying evokes tales of worldly explorations and adventures of privileged travelers, tourists, entrepreneurs, retirees, exchange students, and others from the wealthier pockets of the so-called developed world. Yet, in this age of global migration and mobility on an unprecedented scale, it is hard not to also think about the stories revealed by the passports (or lack of passports) of less privileged people who often appear in the news and are the topic of scholarly studies, such as refugees who seek to escape countries ravaged by war, violence, and environmental and natural disasters, or temporary migrant workers who seek opportunities to earn better wages abroad than are possible at home.

The passport stories in this book are about Indonesian women who have gone to work in Hong Kong. Some previously worked in other parts of Asia or the Middle East. Most of them grew up in villages in the provinces of Central or East Java and have middle school, and perhaps some high school, education. They worked as caregivers and domestic workers (so-called *helpers* in Hong Kong and Singapore, a term that diminishes the value of their labor). Their explorations and adventures, if they can be called that, relate largely to their experiences as low-paid workers in Hong Kong, "Asia's World City," a British colony from 1841 until 1997, when it became the Hong Kong Special Administrative Region of the People's Republic of China.

Migrant women's Indonesian passports tell fascinating stories of how they were produced and how they came to carry the FDH visa, as part of a

wider, state-supported, profit-driven, capitalist labor-recruitment process. These passports tell of how their holders obtained—or could not
obtain—the required letter of permission from their fathers or husbands
to acquire a passport to work abroad, and of how the *PLs* or *calos* (brokers
or recruiters), often people with higher status or respect in their communities, created a workaround. They tell of how recruitment and placement
agencies, recruiters, Indonesian government bureaucrats, and regional
immigration staff make money from producing or procuring identity documents and new passports, or by validating and amending existing ones.
Such passport stories reveal forms of power, gendered inequality, exploitation, corruption, and illegal recruitment practices that entangle migrant
workers, agencies and recruiters, government bureaucrats, and many others.[1] They also raise questions about "care" for the "little people" (*orang-
orang kesil*), which has a more complicated relationship with corruption
(*korupsi*) than first meets the eye (Tidey 2018). Like all passports, they
document membership in a nation-state as well as individual identities
(Caplan 2001; McKeown 2008). They reveal what it means to be "marked"
as a domestic worker while crossing borders, to have your passport held by
agents or employers, and to be charged with identity fraud.

I have long been fascinated and surprised by the passport stories I heard
since the 1990s, such as Ari's above. This research project officially began
in 2015, however, when I first learned, from a dedicated and enthusiastic
Indonesian consular official, about the newly introduced "passport project"
that was linked to a biometric database project and was being implemented in Hong Kong. The Indonesian consulate's new passport renewal
system subsequently became the main subject of my research. I listened to
many new passport stories and rethought the older ones that I had heard
before. These stories taught me that passports are far more interesting—
and more complicated to study—than they first appear. Passport stories
led me to rethink common analytical dichotomies, including *real and fake*
identities or documents, *citizens and migrants,* and the relationships
between *ethnographer and interlocutor, care and control,* and *state and*

---

1. For key sources on the processes of Indonesian migration and the role of agencies and
recruiters, see Ford and Lyons (2011); Killias (2018); Kloppenburg (2013); Lindquist
(2010, 2012, 2015, 2018a, 2018b); Silvey (2004, 2007).

society. Many assumptions that I brought to this project turned out to be wrong or far too simplistic. The state does not, for example, have a monopoly on issuing passports, and despite the seeming fixity of identities in passports, identities are rarely as simple as real (*asli*) or fake (*palsu*). Even the most common and seemingly simple passport stories reveal subtleties and complexities, illustrating the vast inequalities that are inherent in the labor migration industry, and upon which the industry thrives.

Passports are entangled with global histories of mobility or immobility and labor exploitation in Asia and Africa, from slavery to indentured labor to contemporary labor migration (Mongia 1999, 2018). This history is tied to other documents and forms of identification, from the documentation of slave "ownership" to indenture contracts, to the passports and visas of so-called free laborers. Today's passports are assumed to mark a clear distinction between the unfree labor of the past and the free labor of today. Yet again, this supposed dichotomy involves complicated entanglements of free and unfree labor. Passports and work visas—like their precursors—are closely tied to global capital and the circulation of labor migrants from the global south and still involve disposable labor and exploitation. Today's labor migrations are associated with liberal humanist ideals of the modern period and legal definitions of *consent.* Today's labor migration is assumed to be free and consensual, but as this book illustrates, that is not always the case.

One very common passport story in Hong Kong, concerning workers' freedom, is about employers or employment agents who take domestic workers' passports away from them without consent. A passport is, in fact, the property of the issuing government and should be held only by the person to whom it is issued. Yet the confiscation of passports in Hong Kong is common. Some employers or agents are said to take passports for "safe keeping," because they "care" and do not want the passport to get lost or stolen, while others are said to "confiscate" them to "control" migrant workers and prevent them from running away. Some agents and employers take the workers' passports to "protect" them from taking out devastating loans.

It is sometimes difficult to know which motives drive the seemingly identical practice of taking away a domestic worker's passport. Is the practice indicative of care or control? One worker may experience it as a welcome gesture of care, while another considers it an unwelcome act of control and an indication of her lack of freedom. Whether "my employer/

agent takes my passport for safekeeping because she is looking after me" or "my employer/agent confiscated it to control me" or "so I cannot run away" relates partly to individual subjectivities and social relations. The first instance may be interpreted and experienced by a young and inexperienced domestic worker as care; the second may be considered by a more experienced and independent domestic worker as unwanted control. The consulate might treat such cases differently as well, retrieving the passport for workers who have paid off their loans, but not for those who are still in debt (Palmer 2016, 152–55).[2] As we will see, care and control are not two sides of a coin but are always intertwined and entangled with the process of migration and its inequalities, some of which have deep roots in the global history of labor exploitation, surveillance, and control.[3]

There are some passport stories that many travelers can relate to. At official border crossings at airports, migrant workers' passports—like those of other travelers—usually receive "the look" from immigration officials, who glance quickly up and down from the passport to the holder's face to the passport again and to the computer screen, scrutinizing them for correspondence. As Mahmoud Keshavarz notes in this chapter's second epigraph, the officials are more concerned with the passport's authenticity than with "its authentic relation to the represented body" (2019, 37).

Like the anxiety alluded to by Mark Salter in the other epigraph, I always experience a moment of suspense and a twinge of excitement and anxiety until I ultimately receive the nod and am waved through immigration. Do I resemble the person in my passport photograph, from almost a decade ago, enough that I will be permitted to pass? I am privileged, based on my whiteness and U.S. passport (or earlier UK passport). Migrant workers do not have the same sense of entitlement. Their passports are scrutinized alongside their employment documents, visas, and Hong Kong identity cards (as were Ari's and her sister's). In some cases, they are taken aside for an interview, then forbidden from entering and turned away or detained. Especially after 2015, the anxiety and risk surrounding Indonesian passports grew.

2. One consular official told Palmer that the worker's passport was not "confiscated" but was being held as security for the loan that covered her recruitment fees (2016, 153).

3. On care and control in Asian migration, see Johnson and Lindquist (2020); Constable (2020).

Indonesian domestic worker and migrant activist Eni Lestari, founder of the ATKI (Asosiasi Tenaga Kerja Indonesia, Association of Indonesian Migrant Workers) and chairperson of the International Migrants Alliance (IMA), is a well-known, award-winning leader who has spoken at the United Nations (UN). When I invited her to talk at the University of Pittsburgh in 2019, she described her border-crossing experiences and how she prepares for them. She expects many questions, and worries that she might not be allowed to enter. U.S. immigration officials ask her why she is coming to the United States; when she says she was invited to speak at a university, they ask her occupation. She has come to expect the incredulous expression on their faces and the subsequent questions: Why would a domestic worker be invited to talk at the UN or at a university? Why travel without your employer? She always has her official letters of invitation ready. She dresses up for flights, to not look "like a maid." When Eni described this, my immediate and thoughtless response was "I know what you mean." I grumbled about too often being singled out for extra baggage and security checks. At the time, I failed to recognize the significant difference in our situations. I cross borders with the confidence of a privileged white person carrying a U.S. passport. I dress comfortably for long flights and have never—since becoming a U.S. citizen—worried that I would not be allowed to enter a country. In fact, I have fantasized about what a good story it would make, should I be stopped and questioned about my work or prohibited from entering.[4] Every passport story about crossing (or not crossing) borders is about who you are, about whether you are who you are assumed to be, and about control, privilege, and inequalities of nationality, race, gender, and class (Mongia 2018; Singha 2013).

By late 2015, Indonesian passport stories became an urgent topic of conversation, not only among Indonesian migrant workers. They were the topic of diplomatic "G2G" (government to government) discussions

4. During my early research in Hong Kong before 1997 (as a U.S. "alien" or permanent resident), I used my British passport (based on my birth in England and my father's Scottish nationality). In contrast to a French passport, based on my mother's nationality, the British passport provided me easy entry to Hong Kong. It also meant that (at the time), I paid more for a visa to go to India than my partner, who carried a U.S. passport. Post-2020, with the Chinese National People's Congress in Beijing passing the national security law for Hong Kong, the situation may well change for some U.S. citizens, including journalists and academics.

between Hong Kong immigration and Indonesian consular officials, and between top Hong Kong government officials and their Indonesian ministerial counterparts. The term *G2G* was uttered many times by consular officials and others during my research; they explained that it means more than just intergovernmental communication. It also implies "sharing of electronic data and information systems" between governments or government departments in support of e-initiatives, and thus the term has special relevance to passports and biometrics. Besides G2G settings, passport stories are also set in courtrooms, airports, waiting rooms, parks, shopping malls, and streets where they might have been stolen from backpacks or lost, borrowed, or rented out.[5] Passport stories involve official and unofficial rankings or grades of nation-states and their global networks of visa and visa-free entry policies. They also involve biopolitics and the micro-practices of photographing, fingerprinting, iris scans, and the taking of biometric measurements that are entered into government databases. Such procedures and new technologies are shaped by international and global policies whose stated aims are to prevent trafficking and terrorism, key contemporary concerns; yet they also carry implications and unintended consequences for passport holders.

Passport stories often contrast the present with the recent past. I heard stories about freer times, before biometrics were used, when Japan, Korea, and Taiwan issued migrant workers or entertainers short-term visas (three or six months). The workers would sell their current passports with soon-to-expire visas to someone who had already overstayed and was ready to leave. Later, when they were ready to leave, they would buy a passport from another newcomer for their own use. Passports also evoke earlier historical connections to their precursors, recalling global and colonial histories.

Passports and their precursors are widely understood to have two main functions: to regulate labor mobility and to protect state boundaries, functions that can be traced to the earliest history of passports in the form of travel passes and letters of introduction (Torpey 2000). They have been used to identify and keep track of unwanted people—for example,

---

5. On "identity loans" among migrant workers in California's Central Valley, see Horton (2015).

Romanians in Europe and Jews in Nazi Germany (Keshavarz 2015, 8). Passports construct meanings and identities, although their purpose is to document them—to fix and to define both individual and collective identities (Caplan and Torpey 2001). Passports are especially important in periods of migration. From the perspective of the "receiving" state, passports and their documentation of nationality and place of origin (often as a proxy for race) have historically developed as a means of restricting the entry of non-white or non-European people considered "undesirable" (Mongia 1999).

The issuance of passports is a practice of governmentality, an "apparatus of security," a technique through which well-ordered society is created (Foucault 1991, 103–04). Although passports have changed through time, in form and content, they carry continuities with the past, including echoes of inequalities. Indonesian passports are historically tied to Dutch-era colonial *passen stelsel,* security-related "internal" travel passes. Passen stelsel were designed to keep certain populations—Chinese, "Arabs," and "Natives"—in segregated neighborhoods as part of the *wijkendwang,* a residential zoning system, so that they did not mix with others and cause trouble.[6] Colonial travel passes were tied to security, policing, and taxation. They also helped ensure that local "native" cultivators remained on the land and grew crops, quotas of which were required to be paid as taxes. As such—like passports today—they served to create legibility for the state (Scott 1998). Historically, such passes regulated the movement of traders and merchants, and documents facilitated and regulated the movement of laborers for mines or plantations in regions with labor shortages (Kloppenburg 2013; Lindquist 2018a; Stoler 1985). Indonesian passports today, like all passports, still reinforce specific gendered, classed, and ethnic or racialized patterns of labor movement and control.

Passports create, inscribe, and naturalize not only national identity, but also the presumably true and authentic (*asli*) individual identity of the holder (Caplan and Torpey 2001). They demarcate individual, social, and physical borders as well as global alliances. They produce unequal access of citizens of various sorts and of noncitizens to mobility. They both reflect and

---

6. On *passen stelsel* and *wijkendwang,* see Ahmat (1995, 59–60); Antons and Antons-Sutanto (2017, 410); Barker (1999); Cribb and Kahin (2004, 438); Mobini-Kesheh (1999, 32); Suryadinata (1979, 36–38).

produce, as Keshavarz (2019) argues, inequalities between different types of citizens and noncitizens, based on class, gender, religion, appearance, marital status, age, and so on. Passport identities may appear fixed, singular, or unambiguous, but they are constructed in and by passports and other documents. Until recent passport reforms, Indonesian migrant workers' passports were good for three years (not the usual five), had fewer pages, and had a work permit stamped inside. Some have a recruitment agency sticker on the cover "so the official doesn't even need to open the passport to recognize it as a migrant worker passport" (Kloppenburg 2013, 116).

SOCIAL AND ECONOMIC LIVES OF PASSPORTS

Passports gain different meanings in different contexts and illuminate the contexts through which they pass. Besides thinking about passport stories recounted by migrant workers and other travelers, we can also think about passports in relation to their commoditization and value. Numerous online sites openly offer to sell "real and fake" passports.[7] Moreover, headlines like "How Much Is Your Passport Worth?" that measure the relative value of different passports in terms of their advantages of visa free passage, and the "flexible citizenship" achieved by privileged people who can acquire multiple passports (Ong 1999), suggest the commoditization and value of passports quite apart from the actual cost of obtaining one. Refugees and asylum seekers are also known to purchase or borrow passports and other documents in their efforts to escape the violence of war, oppression, and economic disasters in their home countries (Keshavarz 2019). Given changing technology, it is increasingly difficult and expensive to produce and obtain counterfeit passports.[8] Nonetheless, authentic and official passports and other identity documents can still be obtained, at a cost, in Indonesia and other countries, with the help of middlemen and corrupt government officials.

Arjun Appadurai's writing about "the social life of things" examines the shifting value of things—art objects, heirlooms, carpets, sacred objects—

7. For example, Buy Real and Fake Passports Online n.d.

8. For passport rankings and security, visit Passport Index (www.passportindex.org); see also *Jakarta Post* (2017).

and their commoditization and exchange. He defines a commodity initially as "any thing intended for exchange" (1986, 9). Passports are not normally *intended* for exchange, but they can be produced and bought and sold like commodities—as can citizenship and university admissions (Beck 2017; Keshavarz 2016, 2019). Tracing their social lives and their commoditization, and the different meanings that passports acquire along the way, illuminates the socioeconomic and political contexts they pass through, revealing specific entanglements of passports with states and economies, and with an array of people, well beyond the passport holder.

Scholars of social network analysis and of actor-network theory have described markets and economies as "entangled in a web of relations and connections" with objects, people, and processes (Callon 1998, 8). Michel Callon's work on markets and economic logic builds on ideas of "entangled objects" (Thomas 1991) and "careers of objects" (Appadurai 1986) to argue that it is difficult to disentangle relationships from economic markets, including so-called modern ones. He writes that "if the thing remains entangled, the one who receives it . . . cannot escape from the web of relations" (Callon 1998, 19). Like other "things" such as gifts and commodities, passports—whether real or fake—entangle the holder within a web of attachments to other actors, institutions, and processes through which the passport was produced and validated, amended, corrected, stamped with visas, carried, questioned, examined, confiscated, and canceled or replaced at various points in time. With reference to false distinctions between so-called market and nonmarket economies, Callon writes that "the advantage of this anthropology of entanglement is that it frees us from the irritating and sterile distinctions between *state and market* or between *global economy and national economies*" (1998, 40; my italics). As I argue in this book, the anthropology of entanglement frees us from many other "irritating and sterile" distinctions as well; passports refuse disentanglement from their wider spatial, temporal, political and economic, social and individual contexts and connections and thus provide a fertile entry and focal point for the study of migration. Passports force us to see and to question many common and relevant binaries of us and them, care and control, real and fake, state and society, migrant and citizen, free and unfree—all of which are entangled and not oppositional, as revealed in passport stories, histories, and social relations.

The new Indonesian passport project drew my attention—and eventually my fascination—to the entanglements of passports with migrant workers and many other actors, including migrant worker activists, advocates, lawyers, consular officials, Indonesian and Hong Kong government officials, employers, and recruitment agents and brokers. They also led to bigger-picture questions about history and globalization. The meanings that people attribute to passports are reflected in the stories they tell and their actions. They derive from "human transactions, attributions, and motivations" in relation to use and circulation of things (Appadurai 1986, 5). How passports and other related documents are sold or traded, regulated, and circulated in specific historical, social, and cultural contexts reveals not only a way to understand how value is "sought after," how people find value in things, or how things give value to social relations (Appadurai 1986), but also how passports, as (normally) government-produced documents, represent more than a simple relationship between citizen and state, state and society, or state control of mobility. They also relate to the global labor market and illuminate key aspects of the lucrative labor recruitment industry and the wider migration infrastructure, where travel documents like passports can serve to control and constrain their holders rather than freeing them.[9]

In his innovative study of passports, Keshavarz argues that they articulate "a series of relations which legalize certain bodies while illegalizing other bodies." A passport, by design, "persuades users and the state that passports are given, neutral or merely a product." But passports articulate "possibilities of moving, residing and accessing the world. . . . They shape power relations and orient such relations to certain directions given economic, political and historical tendencies. Thus, material articulations while deriving from certain forms of politics, also form specific politics of movement, inhabitation and emplacement" (Keshavarz 2015, 15). Although often associated with freedom, passports are also linked to immobility and lack of freedom. Gayatri Chakravorty Spivak's experience at London Heathrow airport decades ago, when she was prevented from boarding a flight from London to Canada, is a well-cited example

---

9. On "migration infrastructures," see Lin et al. (2017); Lindquist, Xiang, and Yeoh (2012); Xiang and Lindquist (2014).

(Keshavarz 2015, 9; Salter 2015, 23; Spivak and Gunew 1990). Spivak could travel without a visa from the United States to Canada on Air Canada, but the airline staff in London would not allow her to board her flight to Canada. Surprised, she said, "Look here, I am the same person, the same passport." Yet the visa was necessary, she writes, because Indians from London might "want to jump ship to Canada" (Spivak and Gunew 1990, 65). The politics of mobility, the passport holder's identity, and her relationship to specific locations thus shift depending on where—both figuratively and literally—she is coming from, even when she uses the same passport.[10]

Ari's and her sister's passports make a similar point. They contain seemingly identical information, but the "same" passport is held by two different women; they have the same place of birth, the same name, and the same birth date, but were issued at different times, most likely from the same regional government office, and contain different photographs, FDH visa dates, and passport numbers. The social lives of their passports point to the limitations of identity documentation practices, and to *passport entanglements* with government offices, licit and illicit and legal and illegal processes, labor recruitment, and gendered mobilities. These processes are all part of a wider "migration infrastructure" defined as "the systematically interlinked technologies, institutions, and actors that facilitate and condition mobility" (Xiang and Lindquist 2014, 122) or a wider assemblage of global mobility (Salter 2015). Passports and visas are intertwined with global and historical practices of control and surveillance of mobile people, with older paper records and files and with newer information technologies, electronic archives, and bureaucratic state regulatory systems.

Indonesian immigration officials tell stories about new biometric passports as tools and symbols of a responsible, reliable, and accountable modern state that practices "good governance." In other words, biometric high-tech passports indicate—outwardly to a global audience—that Indonesia is a global player and is following the "right" path to development, adhering to wider measures of the International Organization for Migration, the International Civil Aviation Organization, the World Bank,

10. Mongia's (1999, 2018) study of passports as a way to racially discriminate against Indians who sought entry to Canada in the early 1900s (see chapter 5) is highly relevant to Spivak's experience.

and the International Monetary Fund that judge and offer assistance to regions of the "global south" (using the standards of the West). New biometric passports represent a claim to respect as a "modern nation-state." Immigration officials pointed out the key role of passports in the "global effort" to fight terrorism and prevent trafficking by modernizing and improving the reliability, accuracy, and authenticity of passports and related data and surveillance systems.

Before 2004, the minimum age for Indonesian women to migrate for work was eighteen, but it was well known that many were only in their midteens when they went to work abroad. By the early 2000s, partly due to the annual U.S. Trafficking in Persons (TIP) Report, concerns about "child trafficking" increased, and in 2004, to improve overall migratory care and control and to deter underage migration, the minimum age for Indonesian migrant domestic workers was raised to twenty-one, where it remains today. Accurate passports are widely considered essential in promoting global security, yet they present challenges in locations where corruption and fraudulent documents are commonplace (Bubandt 2008, 2009; Ford and Lyons 2011; Imigrasi 2018; Palmer 2016; Salter 2015; U.S. Department of State 2006). Aspal passports are illegal in Indonesia, but they are widely socially approved, or "licit" (Ford and Lyons 2011). Those who produce and facilitate the acquisition of such documents, at least in some cases, intend to help prospective migrants. By "helping" people get around expensive, complicated, or stultifying state requirements, corruption (or collusion or nepotism) can, "in certain circumstances, ameliorate patterns of exclusion, marginalization, and alienation" (Muir and Gupta 2018, S8).

The "Indonesian passport project" was officially presented (and described to me by Indonesian consular and immigration officials) as part of a government initiative to "protect" women migrant workers in response to public outcries over the physical and emotional violence migrant workers have experienced abroad, including death and rape. A related requirement is that women who want to work abroad as domestic workers must utilize a recruitment agency.[11] Without a letter of support from an agency, they cannot legally go to work in Hong Kong. However, agencies have long

---

11. Indonesian Law no. 39/2004, on the Placement and Protection of Indonesian Migrant Workers, and its later replacement, Law no. 18/2017, both mandate the use of registered recruitment agencies.

been criticized by scholars and by migrant workers and advocates for exploiting migrant workers rather than protecting them (Chan 2018; Constable 2007 [1997]; Killias 2018). The combined efforts of the Indonesian government (including many branches, institutions, and ministries) and recruitment agents are intended to protect Indonesian labor migrants and to ensure the safe passage of workers by creating an "infrastructure of escort" (Lindquist 2018a). Yet, as we will see, the government's "protective" measures can in fact put migrant workers at even greater risk.

Passports offer an ethnographic entry point into the migration infrastructure. The challenge, I argue, is to trace the entangled threads that shape the social lives of passports and the social meanings revealed in individual stories of labor migration. Indonesian women migrant workers' passports are produced within a system in which Indonesian and Hong Kong government migratory agents, policies, and practices are entangled. Although Indonesian passports aim to provide *all* Indonesian citizens with the right of passage to other countries or territories, passports illustrate how opportunities differ according to the gender and class of the passport holder. Superficially alike, passports of domestic workers and of businessmen reflect differently classed and gendered bodies, different itineraries, destinations, and purposes of travel. They reveal a very different politics of movement for different people.

Maria Hwang describes the paternalism of the Philippine government when Filipino women who appear "poor" try to leave the country with tourist visas in their passports. These women can be prevented from leaving through a government policy called offloading (2018, 521). "Those who fail to prove that they are 'real' tourists are labeled 'undocumented workers' or 'tourist workers,'" and are marked as individuals who "intend to obtain [illegal] employment abroad." Hwang shows that gender and class status matter, as "those who 'look poor' and are unemployed are more likely to be flagged for scrutiny" even if they can show they have money (2018, 521–22). Indonesian government agencies respond similarly, with an expanded apparatus of care and protection, directed especially toward women migrant workers. Female would-be migrant workers, according to Indonesian consular officials in Hong Kong, are vulnerable to trafficking (or to child trafficking) and exploitation, which justifies greater control in the name of care and protection.

From the Indonesian government's perspective, reliable passports facilitate and control the movement of migrant workers overseas, so that they can earn money, support their families, and contribute to national development.[12] On the Hong Kong side, individuals' passports and visas allow Hong Kong immigration to regulate temporary migrant workers and to police the borders of the Special Administrative Region. Simple though that might seem, especially given the significant economic contributions of migrant workers to the Indonesian economy through their remittances, and to Hong Kong's economy (doing household labor that allows locals to work for higher pay), the relationship between Hong Kong and Indonesia is not equal, nor do the two governments' interests—especially in identity data exchange—necessarily converge when it comes to administratively useful (but highly problematic) binaries of citizens and migrants (Constable 2021c).

The social lives of passports in relation to labor migration span multiple scales and temporalities and share common themes. New biometric passport policies, for example, are tied to imagined modernity—what Lindquist describes as a particular Indonesian idea, that of *belum* or the "not yet"—a temporality linked to not-yet-completed *merantau* (a type of migration), the not-yet-accumulated savings and remittances, and a "not yet completed . . . development project" (2009, 7).

Government officials and bureaucrats enact new passport policies as part of a wider, more technologically advanced development scheme, aimed at achieving Indonesia's modernity, protecting citizens, or building their careers. The passport project points—like migration more generally—to a hoped-for future, to the "not yet" for the migrant workers. Many migrants accept this promise of development and dream of the possibilities for building a better life, a form of "cruel optimism" (Berlant 2011). To so-called failed migrants, including "passport victims," this hoped-for *not yet* future bespeaks false promises (Chan 2018; Constable 2014, 2015). The agents and agencies, the government offices and policymakers, and the employers benefit most from cheap and flexible migrant labor.

---

12. Indonesia supports both the Global Compact for Safe, Orderly and Regular Migration (see Global Compact for Migration 2018) and the Global Forum on Migration and Development (see Global Forum on Migration and Development n.d.).

ETHNOGRAPHIC RESEARCH

The ethnographic field research upon which this book builds took place over several decades, yet the seed for this specific project was planted in 2015. The project officially started in February 2016 and continued each summer through 2019. Those almost twelve months of fieldwork in Hong Kong were supplemented by online research and almost annual research among migrant workers since the early 1990s. This book also draws from archives of the present, written texts that include passport records, migrant workers' blogs, news releases, immigration files, and legal records related to the social lives of Indonesian passports. A wealth of secondary historical, geographic, and ethnographic studies of Indonesia and Indonesian migration also inform this study.

On my visit to the Indonesian consulate in Hong Kong in 2015, I first learned from the Immigration section of the consulate (not from the Labour division) about the new Indonesian passport renewal project and SIMKIM (Sistem Informasi Manajemen Keimigrasian), the Immigration Management Information System. The passport renewal project required that all Indonesians in Hong Kong appear in person, within a three-year period, to replace their expiring passports with new ones. Their biometric data would be collected, linked to SIMKIM, and used to verify their preexisting data.[13] At that time, there were around 350,000 migrant workers in Hong Kong, half of them Filipino and over 150,000 of them Indonesian.[14]

It is important to note that several Indonesian terms are commonly translated as "Indonesian migrant workers," including BMIs (*Buruh Migran Indonesia*), TKIs (*Tenaga Kerja Indonesia*), and more recently PMIs (*Pekerja Migran Indonesia*). The older Indonesian government-sanctioned term, not often heard in Hong Kong, is TKWs (*Tenaga Kerja*

13. On the implementation of SIMKIM in relation to renewal of passports for Indonesians in Australia, beginning in 2018, see Renaldi (2018). For Germany, see Konsulat Jenderal Republik Indonesia (2018).

14. At the end of 2019, there were just under 400,000 FDWs in Hong Kong; 55 percent were Filipino, 43 percent Indonesian, and the rest were mostly from South and Southeast Asia, including Thailand and India (personal communication, Hong Kong Immigration Department, 2019). The number dropped in subsequent years due to COVID-19 travel restrictions in 2020–21, economic downturns, and anti–extradition law and pro-democracy protests of 2019–20 and a serious COVID-19 outbreak in early 2022, when the total dropped to under 350,000.

Wanita), which specifies *women* workers and the gendered nature of the migration system. By 2016, most activists preferred *BMI* (over *TKI*), because it better corresponds to UN calls regarding the rights of migrant laborers. *BMI* also aims to avoid derogatory implications of *TKI* or *TKW*.[15] The Hong Kong government and most employers use the English term *foreign domestic helper* (*FDH*), but activist workers prefer *foreign domestic worker* (*FDW*), which, like *BMI*, highlights their labor contributions rather than minimizing them as "help."[16] In this book, I often use *BMI* to refer to Indonesian migrant workers and *FDW* to refer to all foreign domestic workers (e.g., Filipinos and other nationalities).

Long before 2015, as noted, Indonesian migrant workers like Ari were surprisingly forthright when they talked about the inconsistencies between their passports and their "real" (*asli*) names and ages. The practice was common and not considered particularly wrong or unethical, and they assumed there was no problem. By 2015 the situation began to change, and women became more guarded. A few were glad to talk about the process, to vent their growing anger and frustration. By then, passport stories about problems in Hong Kong became inextricably tied to workers' stories of their migration trajectories before Hong Kong, their lives and families in Javanese villages, and their labor recruitment experiences in Indonesia. After 2015, when women talked about their passports, it shed new light on the role of PLs, regional Indonesian government offices, and recruitment agencies. Gradually, by asking about passport stories, I heard more about various government ministries, grassroots organizations, and local and international NGOs—all of which are part of a wider assemblage, of which "migration infrastructure" and the "infrastructure of escort" are parts (Xiang and Lindquist 2014; Lindquist 2018a). Connections between global bodies and policies—ranging from the UN's Convention on

15. Indonesian activists prefer the term *BMI* and criticize *TKI* for placing less emphasis on the value of migrant labor and as tied to exploitation, pointing to the (now defunct) Terminal 3 for TKIs in Jakarta airport that was said to "protect" them but facilitated their exploitation (see Silvey 2007). Indonesian laws on the protection of migrant workers have switched from using *TKI* (in Law no. 39/2004) to using *PMI* (in Law no. 18/2017).

16. In contrast to Argentina, where the domestic worker organization AMUMRA rejects the term *domestic worker* (because *domestica* is considered pejorative) and prefers *household worker*, in Hong Kong the English term *helper* has been the focus of criticism (cf. Baiocchi 2020).

the Rights of the Child, to the International Civil Aviation Organization's transportation safety regulations, to the Global Compact on Migration and the objective to "ensure that all migrants have proof of legal identity and adequate documentation," to anti-trafficking and anti-terrorism initiatives, to newer identification technologies such as biometrics—were all part of the entangled assemblage that produced passports and the migration infrastructure that impacts the lives of migrant workers (Collier 2006; Ong and Collier 2005).

ETHNOGRAPHIC ENTANGLEMENTS

Ethnography commonly refers to both anthropological research about people's lives that draws on the researcher's participation and observations and to a type of writing about people's lives that derives from the ethnographer's fieldnotes, thoughts, analytical scribbles, and drafts—and, ideally, results in a published work. *Entanglement* carries various connotations in popular and academic usage. I find that weaving—a hobby of mine—is a compelling metaphor and analytical tool in relation to the study of passports and migration. In weaving, most people see only the neat and tidy end-product: a woven piece of cloth, tied off in clear sections. Ethnographies are similar, as the reader sees mostly a finished book with tidy chapters. Less obvious, though all part of the finished product, are the knots between threads of warp, the tangles of the filaments of transverse weft, the miscellaneous fragments of fluff picked up from the floor (including occasional dog hair), and the *process* of imposing structure and order. Similarly, in ethnography, the messiness and the knots—as well as the imposition of order—are not always made evident in the final product.

Knots, in my experience as a weaver and an ethnographer, can be frustrating, requiring what can seem like wasted time and effort to disentangle, especially when one is impatient to finish. In extreme cases, one may be tempted to simply cut out the tangles (something frowned upon in weaving) and to cover the break to create an appearance of continuity. However, the tangles in ethnography—if not in weaving—often end up revealing the most interesting and challenging parts of ethnographic research. Like weaving, ethnography benefits from patience, focus, concentration, and appreciative attention to the process and tensions between the entangled threads. Creating an impression of effortless continuity can be misleading in weaving, and even more so in ethnographic writing. Discontinuities, gaps, breaks, and unevenness are better seen or acknowledged than smoothed over.

At the risk of wearing the metaphor thin, entanglements in ethnographic research about passports reveal connections, knots, ties, twists, tensions, gaps, breaks, disconnections, and complicated or compromising relationships—especially if we look beyond the seemingly obvious (and too often taken-for-granted) binaries. In weaving, removing the tangles maintains a pattern. In ethnography, spending time with entanglements, observing them, concentrating on them, learning from them, and sometimes picking them apart to understand their constitution, often reveals more complicated patterns (or paths for further research). The point is not complete disentanglement, to create a semblance of neatness and order that does not exist, nor invisibility in the writing. The excitement, for me, comes from learning from the various tensions, interconnections, and messiness of field research and to try to convey it in the writing. In this book, some knots are described and disentangled; others—such as the historical ones—remain messy or fuzzy. Such entanglements are key to my analysis of passports and migrant precarity. Further disentanglement I leave to others.

Scholars have used the term *entanglement* in a variety of ways. Sometimes it refers to social attachments or relationships. As noted above, Callon writes that the "anthropology of entanglement" frees us from sterile binaries (1998, 40). In relation to enduring "webs of relations" pertaining to technologies and goods and their production and consumption, he considers entanglement "very useful, for it is both theoretical and practical" (Callon 1998, 19; Callon and Rabeharisoa 2004). Entanglements often refer to complicated networks of relationships between humans, nonhumans, objects, and technology, both in science and technology studies and in (science) fiction writing (Tosoni and Pinch 2017; Williams 2020).

Rey Chow uses the idea of entanglements in relation to "technologies of capture," such as the reproduction of "copy-images" that "supersede the original" (2012, 4), which is especially appealing when applied to passport photographs that are intended to capture the holder's likeness.[17] Chow observes, counterintuitively and provocatively, that entanglements are "the linkages and enmeshments that keep things apart" and "the voidings and uncoverings that hold things together" (2012, 12). She asks how we might conceive of entanglements beyond the idea of a "tangle of things held together or laid over one another" to also include "partition and partiality, rather than conjunction and intersections, and . . . disparity rather than equivalence" (2012, 1–2). Chow cites Bruno Latour's enlightening view that ideas that are kept segregated can seem to make sense, but when placed next to other ideas their logic may evaporate (Latour 1993; Chow 2012, 10). She calls for "fuzzing up" the order of relationships and concepts that we take for granted. This includes continuing to examine "given" and widely assumed binary oppositions—such as those of nature and culture, woman and man, human and nonhuman, all of which have long been subject to a variety of feminist, post-structural, and anthropological critiques.

ENTANGLED BINARIES

My main arguments about passport entanglements and precarious labor migration relate to six primary analytical pairs or binaries that I aim to "fuzz up." They include *ethnographer and interlocutor, care and control, state and society, real and fake, migrant and citizen,* and *temporalities and scales,* as well as many other associated pairs—such as self and other, free and unfree, state and economy. At first glance, these pairs might seem distinct and oppositional, but I will argue that all of them are entangled. Each pairing attests to both the importance and ubiquity of binaries and dualities in academic and popular thinking, and to their limitations and the problems with focusing on—or looking at or for—dualities in the study of passports and migration. I argue, like Callon, that there is great value in looking for (and at) multiple entanglements, gaps, and frayed threads; and I follow Latour in looking at them together, rather than simply rein-

17. Regarding copy-images, Chow writes, "While the original may remain confined to the particular place of its making, the copy image by virtue of becoming (re)producible in forms that were previously unimaginable, lives a life of versatility and mobility" (Chow 2012, 4).

forcing "sides" in relation to the sociocultural and political-economic study of passports and migration.

Although books necessarily unfold in a linear fashion, page by page, chapter by chapter, I invite the reader to imagine different possible structures. Like a snake swallowing its own tail, a fractal cross-stitch, or an M. C. Escher house of stairways, each of the six primary pairs do not fit neatly within one chapter. Each chapter title refers to one seemingly simple binary, but, as in Abu-Lughod's *Writing Women's Worlds* (1993), each chapter aims to complicate the chapter titles, and in a sense to undo them by highlighting their entanglements and alluding to their relationships with other pairs. Each chapter combines ethnographic anecdotes, excerpts from interviews, and observations or vignettes that relate directly or indirectly to passports in relation to migration, and to the people, policies, and processes that simultaneously "overflow the frame" and resist "disentanglement" (Callon 1998, 18–19).

Chapter 2, "Ethnographer and Interlocutor," serves three purposes. It introduces the reader to the Indonesian consulate's "passport project" and to some of the ethical considerations of this study. It discusses the entanglements of ethnographic research—between the ethnographer and various sorts of interlocutors, and between interlocutors and one another. And it begins to show how the themes of entanglements and binaries came to appear more complicated than I had initially assumed. At first glance, ethnographer and interlocutor—like research and researched, observer and observed, self and other—can seem like a clear and discrete opposition, but in practice, in relation to the passport project, they refused such neat order. The entanglements of interlocutors led me to the idea of entanglements in the first place, and subsequently to key insights about entanglements of passports within the wider context of migration.

Chapter 3, "Care and Control," shows how passports facilitate forms of care, control, and surveillance that are entangled in BMIs' everyday lives, practices, experiences, and relationships in Hong Kong. Care and control are not flip sides of a coin but are both multifaceted and intertwined with the process of migration, which usually requires the help of recruiters and agents and involves going deep into debt to go to work abroad. The stories of Mila, Wali, and Ratna provide examples of giving and receiving care, control, and protection in relation to the wider process of migration. The feminization of Asian labor migration, Hong Kong's policies of "containment" of migrant workers, and Indonesia's practices of "encapsulation" of migrant workers are all tied to passports and to care and control.

Chapter 4, "Real and Fake," illustrates the specifically Indonesian meaning of aspal passports and shows how and why they exist among migrant workers in the first place. It shows how aspal documents cannot be classified simply as "true or false" or "real or fake" but must be understood as licit *and* illegal, corrupt *and* morally justifiable. Stories of Mina, Dwi, Anti, and Ika illustrate how passport irregularities are deeply entangled with the recruitment process, including the PLs who recruit women from villages and small towns, procure their documents and passports from government officials, and accompany them to agencies in larger cities for training before they go to work abroad. Migrant workers' passport experiences and problems in Hong Kong unfold over time, in parks, at the consulate, in courtrooms, and in prisons. The chapter illustrates the entangled roles of recruitment agencies, recruiters, and corrupt government officials at various levels in producing aspal documents, and the consulate's role in producing "passport victims."

Chapter 5, "State and Society," looks at passports in relation to the establishment of the Indonesian nation-state, state discourses about modern and "good governance," and the "duty" of the state and Imigrasi (Directorate General of Immigration) to "modernize" and provide care (or protection) to citizens. It examines the material and symbolic meanings of Indonesian passports and the wider history of passports as identification documents and travel passes in relation to historical concerns about obtaining cheap labor. The chapter shows how state and society are entangled with capital, especially in the profit-driven labor migration industry. Historical threads connect Indonesian passports and Imigrasi to both global and colonial patterns and structures that disrupt any easy distinctions between free and unfree labor, past or present.

Chapter 6, "Migrant and Citizen," criticizes the migrant-citizen binary, showing how migrant worker activists responded to the passport problems as *both* migrant workers *and* Indonesian citizens. It shows how Indonesian consular officials were forced to rethink the passport project after migrant worker activists and their citizen-migrant networks and coalitions—in Hong Kong and Indonesia—presented their demands to

President Widodo and top Indonesian officials. The chapter further complicates the state-society binary, examining the relationship between Hong Kong immigration and their Indonesian counterparts and illustrating the relevance of migrant-citizen activist and state-society entanglements that ultimately led to changes in the Indonesian passport policy, but further underscored the problem of producing real or fake passports.

Chapter 7, "Temporalities and Scales," concludes the book. It returns to the events and nonevents of the passport project and asks why, given the vast numbers of aspal passports and the state concern with "corruption," so few passports were ultimately corrected. The chapter considers temporalities—ranging from the colonial (which is never completely "post" but shapes the present) to the more recent—and scales that span from biometric measurements and embodied experiences to national and international policies and practices that have shaped the passport project and the critical responses to it. It returns to historical and contemporary matters of free and unfree labor, human trafficking, bonded labor, and entanglements of governance and global capital in the production of migratory precarity. It addresses what I call the "afterlives of aspal documents" and the contradictions of the massive (re) production of aspal documents, in the name of good governance, global security, and modernization.

2 Ethnographer and Interlocutor

Subjectivity is multidimensional; so, therefore, is vision.
The knowing self is partial in all its guises, never finished,
whole, simply there and original; it is always constructed
and stitched together imperfectly, and *therefore* able to join
with another, to see together without claiming to be
another.

Donna Haraway (1988, 586)

To study documents, then, is by definition also to study how
ethnographers themselves know. The document becomes at
once an ethnographic object, an analytic category, and a
methodological orientation.

Annelise Riles (2006, 7)

This chapter recounts how my interest in passports began and how entanglements and a critique of binaries became central to my analysis. Two
sets of binaries are addressed below. The first is *ethnographer and interlocutor*, which builds on earlier criticisms of the assumed opposition of
ethnographer and interlocutor—related to binaries of researcher and
researched or self and other. The second, which I had in mind when I
started this research, is *consular officials and migrant workers*, two types
of interlocutors. I assumed that consular officials as state agents (or representatives of the Indonesian government) created the passport problems
and that migrant workers were the victims of the new government policies; I thus assumed that the two categories were oppositional. However,
migrant workers taught me that neither "migrant workers" nor "government agents" is a homogeneous category. Nor do these two groups neces-

sarily see each other as the "opposition." Instead, they are entangled with each other, and with many other sorts of actors in the migration process.

This chapter is built around two seemingly innocuous *ethnographic moments*. On one hand, they serve to introduce the reader to the passport project as I first encountered it, and offer a glimpse of my experiences and methodologies. On the other hand, through a focus on my "productive angst," they reveal an epistemological thread that led me from passport binaries to passport and migratory entanglements. I reflected on my own entangled and multidimensional subjectivity in the field and eventually saw how I could "join with" my interlocutors. In an ethnographic twist on the adage that "what doesn't kill you makes you stronger," the two ethnographic "moments of crisis" described below reveal how my misconceptions yielded a deeper understanding of passport entanglements within the complex structures and relations of migration.[1]

In a famous article, anthropologist Dorinne Kondo described a brief ethnographic experience that led to her "moment of epiphany." She saw the reflection of a Japanese housewife in a shop window, then shockingly realized that it was her own reflection (1986, 80). Not immediately recognizing this Japanese woman as herself, she experienced "fragmentation of the self" and a subsequent "reconstitution of the self" that took place through writing. Kondo writes that fieldwork usually culminates with writing an ethnographic text that draws one away from "the immediacy of the ethnographic encounter" (1986, 82). Writing is "a way of freezing the disturbing flux, encapsulating experience in order to control it. . . . [It] offers the author the opportunity to reencounter the Other 'safely,' to find meaning in the chaos of lived experience through retrospectively ordering the past." Through this quest, "the ethnographer seeks meaning in events whose significance was elusive while they were being lived" (1986, 82).

My moments of epiphany differ from Kondo's encounter with her Japanese American self as unrecognizably "Japanese." Yet her insights about selfhood and epistemology in ethnographic research and about the link between writing and meaning are key. Below, I "reconstitute through writing" two seemingly insignificant but disturbing moments. One

---

1. I have learned not to try to forget or brush aside disturbing experiences or deep discomfort, but to examine them and to take them seriously, for the important insights they often reveal.

I experienced during my first visit to the Indonesian consulate in 2015, when I learned about the new passport project. The second—a smaller echo of the first—took place in summer 2016 at the end of a domestic-worker-organized forum focused on how to address passport problems.

Rather than reinforcing fixed and binary notions of government or consular officials and (or versus) migrant workers, of ethnographer and interlocutor, researcher and researched, self and other, the two moments reveal multiple entangled relationships and identities. They reveal crosscutting, entwined, and complicated categories of interlocutors, their relations with each other and with me, and my relations with them. These relationships were revealed to me because of, and through, passport problems. They also ultimately led to some key victories for migrant workers. Passport problems led me to better understand the critical role of recruitment agents and brokers in the process of migration and in relation to the precarity of Indonesian migrant workers and the accuracy of their identification documents, past and present.

ETHNOGRAPHIC ENTRY

An Indonesian friend in Hong Kong who was familiar with my previous research told me in 2015 that my name came up in her conversation with an Indonesian consular official. He had read my books and wanted to meet me. He asked her to tell me that the next time I was in Hong Kong, I should get in touch with him. I was interested in meeting him, but, given my past experiences, I did not hold my breath.

In 2011 and 2012, while conducting research among migrant mothers and their Hong Kong–born babies, I had tried to interview Indonesian consular officials, without success (Constable 2014). One official had initially agreed to talk to me, but then never responded. I learned later that he had changed his mind for two reasons. One was that I had contacted him by email (when phone calls led nowhere), which meant there was a record of our contact, while he would have preferred that such a meeting remain "off the record." I found this explanation odd but informative. Mistakenly assuming that the meeting would be official and aboveboard,

I had created a traceable link, when he would have preferred plausible deniability. This reflects the power of documentation and of records.

The second reason was that he feared I worked for the CIA. For a long time, I saw this as so far-fetched that it was funny. I was studying migrant mothers and their babies—which, as I joked a few times in academic talks, was so improbable a topic that it might look like a perfect CIA cover. Yet, after reading anthropologist Katherine Verdery's *My Life as a Spy* (2018), the idea no longer seemed so funny or far-fetched. Anthropological practices—using pseudonyms, safeguarding fieldnotes, obscuring sensitive information, encouraging people to share information with us—all resemble the methods of actual spies. Anthropology's colonial history compounds the suspicion of collaboration.

My experience with the Indonesian consulate in 2015 was very different. Consular officials' posts rotate every few years, and the person I had been in touch with was gone. There was a new "KonJen" (Konsul Jenderal, Consul General), and several new and younger consular officials on board. At my friend's suggestion, I sent an email to the official and he promptly arranged a meeting. That visit marked a shift. I had been outside of the Indonesian consulate many times as a participant-observer at migrant worker protests. I had previously entered through the small side door that leads to the service counter and the crowded waiting area for those seeking new passports, visas, and other information, accompanied by my Indonesian migrant worker friends. That day, I entered through the larger main door into a spacious lobby with couches and a well-dressed receptionist behind a counter. She instructed me to register in a ledger with my Hong Kong identity card number or passport number, date and time of arrival, purpose of my visit, and my name and signature. After registering my identity, a common requirement in many offices, the receptionist phoned the consular division to confirm my appointment. She handed me a visitor's tag on a lanyard and directed me to the proper elevator. Exiting the elevator onto a hot and humid landing, I knocked and entered the busy, air-conditioned office space that housed the consulate's immigration section. I asked the first person I saw how to find Mr. Pembasar (a pseudonym), Mr. P for short. The staff member took me down a short hallway to his office and asked me to sit down on the leather couch.

I knew nothing yet about the Indonesian government's passport project or about SIMKIM, but I noticed tall piles of dark green passports stacked on desks and boxes throughout the office suite, each containing multiple large white sheets of paper within their covers (figure 1). I did not understand their importance or that this scene was new. Only later did I fully understand the idea that "reality is what is found in files" and that "any attempt to weaken the file-world, therefore, is obliged to show that the world and files do *not* coincide" (Vismann 2008, 56). "Reality," I later learned, is troubled by lack of correspondence between passports, identity documents, application forms, and data contained in SIMKIM and other files (not to mention their lack of correspondence with bodies and faces).

Mr. P returned from his mid-morning prayer, greeted me with a friendly handshake, offered me tea, and took his seat in a leather armchair. A woman staff member brought us Chinese tea, and I noticed two of my books, *Maid to Order in Hong Kong: Stories of Migrant Workers* (2007) and *Born Out of Place: Migrant Mothers and the Politics of International Labor* (2014), on the coffee table. I presented Mr. P with a (redundant) copy of *Maid to Order* that I had brought as a gift at my friend's suggestion. He thanked me graciously, saying he had wanted another copy for his colleague because it was no longer available in Hong Kong bookshops. He called his colleague in to meet me and asked me to autograph the books. I noticed bookmarked and highlighted sections. His colleague left and Mr. P asked about my views on human trafficking in Hong Kong and about Indonesian workers who had filed non-refoulement claims (popularly called refugee, asylum, or torture claims, part of Hong Kong's Unified Screening Mechanism, or USM) to try to remain in Hong Kong.[2]

Mr. P spoke of his professional background and scholarly interests. He said he had invited me in to tell me about the new Indonesian passport project in Hong Kong and about SIMKIM. He was enthusiastic about the project and his role in implementing it. He explained that it was part of a

---

2. Former FDWs have little chance of having non-refoulement claims approved. Hong Kong has one of the world's lowest approval rates (under 1 percent), and as of this writing only one Filipino and no Indonesians were approved. Former domestic workers know that their cases likely will not be approved, but they can remain in Hong Kong while the claims are in process. During that time, some try to work (although it is illegal), pay back loans, and, if they have children, access education for them (see Constable 2014, 2021b).

Figure 1. Old passports and renewal applications, 2016. Photo credit: N. Constable.

national modernizing project that would eventually contain a database of all Indonesian passports. This required his office to process passport renewal applications for over 150,000 Indonesian domestic workers within a three-year period, an immense task that had already exponentially increased the workload of his small staff.[3]

At that time, many domestic workers' passports (*Paspor TKI*) were twenty-four pages long and valid for only three years, in contrast to the "regular" five-year passports. The three-year passports followed a specific bureaucratic process that shaped and monitored routes of mobility. "FDH" contracts and visas, however, are for two years, so Paspor TKI often expired in the middle of a second two-year contract (as in Ari's case; see chapter 1). These three-year passports were being discontinued and were replaced by "regular" passports.

Until 2015, recruitment agency staff renewed passports for domestic workers (and charged them for it). The new process required that *all passport holders appear in person* at the consulate. Reflecting a global turn and a demand for biometric passports, their new biometric identification was entered into the SIMKIM database and compared with any preexisting data. This new Indonesian effort to verify identities is linked to shifting global technologies and demands for ever newer and more reliable versions of technologies developed over the centuries to improve the identification of those with "suspect identities," including criminals, enemies, religious or ethnic/racial minorities, and, especially, mobile people (Cole 2002; McKeown 2008). Most domestic workers could not afford expensive biometric passports, but the data of regular passport holders was also collected and linked to the national biometric database and to their national identity cards.

At our initial meeting, to my surprise, Mr. P proposed that I write my next book on the passport project. I hesitated and he offered to coauthor such a book with me. I was taken aback and replied noncommittally that it was an interesting idea but that such a collaboration was not possible; as an anthropologist, I could not be a coauthor with a government official,

---

3. Only later did I learn the relevant divisions within the consulate and that this project was initiated by the Immigration section (connected to the Directorate General of Immigration and the Ministry of Law and Human Rights), not the Labour section (under the Ministry of Manpower), which is often more involved with migrant worker issues.

because it would undermine my claim to objectivity. As he likely understood from my previous books, I said, if I were to study the new passport renewal scheme, I would have to explore different sides of the picture—including the experiences and perspectives of domestic workers and domestic worker activists. I did not explicitly say that the notion of coauthoring with a consular official reminded me of disturbing colonial and postcolonial anthropological collaborations with government officials (Rosaldo 1986; Pels 2018). I asked whether, under the circumstances, he would still want me to do such a study. "Yes, of course," he said without hesitation, because the passport project was critically important and deserved recognition.

Whether the passport project was successful or not in the short run, said Mr. P, it was the way of the future, important for Indonesia and its citizens and for the countries they worked in or traveled to. The new passport would create a more reliable and accountable immigration system, protect Indonesian citizens, and possibly advance his career. It was worthwhile to create a scholarly record of the project, he said, similar to what *Born Out of Place* had done in bringing to light the issues of migrant mothers and children and bringing attention to PathFinders Hong Kong (a charity organization that assists migrant mothers and their Hong Kong–born children). He was eager to leave a mark during his three-year post in Hong Kong. He then offered me a tour of the office suite. He pointed out the areas where different passport-related production and verification processes took place.

As we walked through the office, I suddenly found myself looking out from the service counter at several lines of women (figure 2). I immediately, urgently, and viscerally felt that I was on the *wrong* side of the glass windows that separated the consular staff from the lines of Indonesian workers in the service area. I was on the official side, separated from the women who waited to make inquiries or submit their applications and documents for new passports. As I looked out, standing next to the staff, accompanied by consular officials in business attire, I felt deeply self-conscious and exposed. My immediate thought was "I wish I could hide. What if someone I know (e.g., one of the migrant workers or activists) sees me? What will they think?" That part of the tour lasted just a few minutes but left a profound impression on me. At that moment, unknowingly, a seed was planted, one that later sprouted into a probing of sides and

Figure 2. Looking out from the service window at the consulate, 2016. Photo credit: N. Constable.

binaries and that eventually grew into this book's overall analytical theme of passport entanglements.

INSIDE, OUTSIDE, AND THE AWKWARD MOMENT

To understand the significance of that moment, I must describe an earlier visit to the consulate in 2011. During my research with migrant mothers, I often accompanied women and their babies to government offices and registries, such as Hong Kong's immigration department, the birth registry, and the consulate. I was useful, mothers told me, not only because I was an "auntie" or "grandma" who helped with fretful babies and energetic toddlers, but because I offered moral support and was sometimes assumed, by virtue of being a middle-aged white woman, to be an employer, lawyer, or NGO advocate, so they sometimes received better service (Constable 2014, 37). Typically, we waited for my companion's number to be called or to submit or request forms or information from staff members behind glass windows at service counters. During one memorable visit, we entered through the smaller service entrance (not the main entrance I used during the passport project) and waited for my companion's turn at the counter. Despite my presence, the male staffperson spoke harshly and condescendingly, scolding her for having a Hong Kong–born baby. She explained to me that such attitudes are common among consular staff who consider themselves superior to migrant workers in terms of class, education, and morality—especially in relation to women with "out of wedlock" children.

My 2015 consular visit was very different because I was treated like a respected scholar. Yet I felt I was on the wrong side and dreaded being seen there and appearing duplicitous. My reaction felt irrational. I experienced a disturbing "fragmentation" of my sense of self (cf. Kondo 1986, 80). I was accustomed to being outside with protesters or accompanying women through the service entrance. I saw myself as an ally of migrant workers, but I was suddenly alongside state officials. Unlike Kondo's experience, I did not *mistake* myself for someone else, but I saw myself through the eyes of those on the other side of the glass, and it was not the self I recognized. My discomfort did not stem from an unrecognizable transformation (as in Kondo's case), but from the sense of a seemingly duplicitous self—a white researcher, allied with power. Imagining that I looked like a collaborator (not just a pragmatic researcher), I felt embarrassed and exposed by my access to consular officials. Only later did I more fully comprehend, through writing, the significance of my moment of crisis.

I realized that I had worn my earlier rejection by the consulate like a badge of honor, as though it vouched for my credibility, trustworthiness, and alliance with migrant workers. It said (to me, if not to them) that I was on their side. The moment of epiphany revealed the blatant, undeniable fact that no matter how much I empathized with them and supported their causes, I was privileged and had access to those in power (which, I mistakenly assumed at the time, they did not). I was not previously unaware of my privilege; nor, in fact, did domestic workers lack access to power (they could and did access and utilize government and official networks), but my relationship to the consulate was different from theirs. The awkward moment forced me to see my own entangled relationships with variously positioned interlocutors, and eventually to understand theirs with each other. I learned the lessons expressed in this chapter's first epigraph: that subjectivity and vision are multidimensional, and that "the knowing self is . . . constructed and stitched together imperfectly" and is "therefore able to join with another, to see together without claiming to be another" (Haraway 1988, 586).

A LIVELY FORUM AND ANOTHER AWKWARD MOMENT

The second awkward moment (a smaller version of the first) took place at the end of a domestic-worker-organized forum that I attended on Sunday, June 26, 2016. The forum, described below, reveals the mounting problems and growing tensions and criticisms surrounding the passport project during its second year. It also further complicates my assumptions about "sides."

The forum was organized by JBMI (Jaringan Buruh Migran Indonesia, Indonesian Migrant Workers' Network) and led by several well-respected activist BMIs, whom I had known for years, from ATKI and the Indonesian Migrant Workers' Union (IMWU). The event was one of two smaller forums held at the University of Hong Kong (HKU) in anticipation of a larger event on August 7, organized by JBMI and cosponsored by the Centre for Criminology and Sociology at HKU and the Indonesian Consulate General, entitled "Know the Law, Avoid Being Prosecuted: Legal Socialization for Indonesian Migrant Workers in Hong Kong."[4]

The June 26 forum began at 9:30 A.M. and lasted almost five hours. The audience of eighty included leaders and representatives from JBMI member groups and a few academics and advocates. The purpose was to provide updates on the passport project and the problems BMIs had encountered, so that leaders could better advise their group members. Speakers included BMI leaders Sringatin and Maesoro; BMIs who had experienced difficulties with their passport renewals; Jun Tellez, from the advocacy group Mission for Migrant Workers; and, finally, representatives from the Indonesian consulate.

I sat in the back of the lecture hall with HKU sociologist Julie Ham, while Sringatin and Maesoro spoke, and Muthi and Eni Lestari took

---

4. My thanks to Julie Ham for sharing her notes on the August 7 event, where the speakers included Chalief Akbar (consul general), Sri Kuncoro (legal consul), Andry Indrady (immigration consul), Sringatin (JBMI chairperson), and Mark Daly (lawyer, Daly & Associates). See also Ham (2016).

turns translating for the few non-Indonesian-speaking attendees. The presentations included PowerPoint slides illustrating different types of passports, biometrics, and laws related to passports. They described the SIMKIM database and highlighted the problems BMIs had encountered renewing their passports if their data contained "irregularities." They showed a powerful video clip of two domestic workers' emotion-packed stories about how, after having their passports "corrected" by the consulate, they were arrested for immigration fraud and false representation. Fifty-year-old Dwi, in tears, was by then in prison and Minarsih was awaiting her final court hearing (see chapter 4). Sringatin and Maesoro described ten cases of women who were in prison because of changes the consulate had made to their passports. They talked about hundreds of women they had counseled who were frightened and confused, many of whom had left Hong Kong rather than risk having their passports "corrected."

At one point, forum leaders asked the audience to raise their hands if they had ever had a passport with a different name or birth date than their "original" one. Over a third of the attendees raised their hands. This corresponded with the findings of a JBMI research survey of almost five hundred workers that found that 31 percent of BMIs in Hong Kong had changes of birth date and over 15 percent had name changes. The survey showed that "irregular" passport data was most likely among women who had worked in other countries before Hong Kong or had been BMIs for a longer time. The speakers presented various options available to BMIs whose passports were due to expire, and they reviewed the procedures for those with discrepancies between their passports, Hong Kong identity cards, visas, and employment contracts.

Jun Tellez then spoke about "knowing your legal rights" and advised BMIs on how to respond if they are arrested or questioned by immigration (as did human rights lawyer Mark Daly at the August forum). Tellez stressed the importance of not responding if questioned or detained, and about the risks of answering. "Telling the truth" or "saying too much" provides police officers, investigators, or prosecutors with evidence; if they have no proof, they cannot convict you.

Next up was Minarsih, who had expected to be in prison, but whose final hearing was delayed. She wore a black abaya that covered all but her face and spoke briefly. Her passport was changed by the consulate because of a discrepancy in her birth date. When questioned by Hong Kong immigration officers, she took the consulate's advice to "tell the truth." As a result, she was investigated, lost her job, could not send money home to support her family, and now—after months of investigation and repeated court hearings and delays—she expected to be sentenced to prison. She complained that the consulate that should have protected her had failed to help and had made matters worse. She wept (as did some members of the audience) as she described her personal situation. Her employers were supportive at first, but after months of investigation they got angry and impatient and hired someone else. As she finished, two consular officials entered and sat in the front row. She quickly excused herself and left.

Immigration consul Andry Indrady entered with the consular legal representative, Kunjoro (who introduced himself and said he was new to Hong Kong and just getting to know the situation).[5] Andry greeted everyone in a friendly manner and talked about the purpose and process of the passport renewal project and the importance of reliable passport data. He cheerfully said that he prefers the "P2P" (person to person) approach and was very pleased to be there. He acknowledged that the lines at the consulate were too long. His office needed to serve two hundred to three hundred people a day, but desperately needed more staff, more space, and more computer equipment. Indonesia's Ministry of Foreign Affairs (which oversees consulates and embassies) had recently agreed to send some temporary staff and a specialized secure computer to access SIMKIM, so he expected the situation to improve. He urged them to use the new booking app for passport renewal appointments at least six months before their expiration.

Part of the problem, he said, was that passports were issued by many different regional Indonesian immigration offices and thus contained data "irregularities and endorsements [inserted changes, often handwritten and sometimes stamped] that are not compliant." Consular staff "must follow

5. Indonesian consulates and embassies are categorized under the Ministry of Foreign Affairs, while the Directorate General of Immigration (Imigrasi) is part of the Ministry of Law and Human Rights. It is interesting that the immigration consul (or attaché) took charge of the project. The labor attaché is normally responsible for issues pertaining to migrant workers, and immigration staff are responsible for passports and visas. Palmer (2016) points to institutional divisions and to variations in how consulates/embassies in Kuala Lumpur, Singapore, and Hong Kong function.

the law" regarding endorsements. "It is our responsibility to verify and correct everything. Many people ask, 'Why [do so] when you know the consequences [for migrant workers]?'" He said that they had spoken with their Hong Kong immigration counterparts before the renewal process began and they had responded positively. Of the tens of thousands of renewed passports, only thirty-five passports were corrected. Of those, he said, fourteen women were investigated by Hong Kong immigration, two were in prison, and two were in court. (These numbers omitted several cases that had been identified by the activist domestic worker groups and NGOs, including several cases of women who had renewed and corrected their passports in Indonesia and were arrested upon their return to Hong Kong.)

Andry asked rhetorically, "Why were some women approved for visas [by the Hong Kong government] and not others? Why are some charged and not others?" Going forward, the consulate would work more closely with the Hong Kong government. "Please help me when there are differences in your passport. Please properly prepare your documents to correct your data so it can be entered in SIMKIM. I apologize to those who have been charged. We didn't mean for that to happen. We just want a better system in Hong Kong. We need to fix it before it is completely ruined. We need to have the correct data." He stressed that he was there to help them, was on their side, but that he faced financial, logistical, and staffing challenges.

The larger August 7 forum, which I did not attend, was described as "animated" and revealed "numerous accounts of discrepancies between identification documents such as differing dates of birth across documents, or slight variations in name" (Ham 2016). The June 26 session was similar, as BMIs described their passport problems and complained about the renewal process. Some comments elicited loud cheers and applause from the audience, such as "Why do the [consular] staff look so unhappy and angry?" "Why do they never smile at us?" One woman noted that the staff try to look busy but watch YouTube videos on their phones. Another asked about new errors that were introduced to their passports.

Andry replied that many consular staff are "old and incompetent" and set in their ways. Ideas about "friendly service" or that "the customer is king," ideas that "even fast-food restaurant staff know," are foreign to them. He assured those present that he was working to improve service. If BMIs have problems with staff, they should go straight to him. He promised to start an "Employee of the Month" program so that they could vote for the most helpful staff and encourage change.

One woman raised her hand and said that the consulate's new appointment app is inaccessible, even with an Android phone. Others noted that iPhones (and people without smartphones) could not access it at all. Andry spoke enthusiastically about the new easy-to-use app that he had developed, despite his tight budget. He pulled out his phone to demonstrate, but experienced one problem after another. This energized the already spirited audience. He tried to access his mailbox but got his password wrong and was eventually locked out. He tried another account with a humorous username that was projected on the screen and the audience roared with laughter. He joked and chatted with them, walking along the aisles like a talk show host. He gave one woman (dressed in a hijab) a friendly slap on the leg (which produced no visible or audible audience reaction). He exchanged friendly banter with women he recognized from consulate-sponsored programs. He gave the audience his personal mobile phone number, "but only for you— not for the public!" He told them to contact him anytime on WhatsApp.

One woman asked if the new option to receive the new passport by registered mail was free. He said that option was in response to complaints from employers and BMIs about the inconvenience of picking up their passports in person, but that the recipient must "prepay" because he has no budget for it. Another woman asked why the passport was no longer free, and he explained that the Indonesian Ministry of Manpower waives the fee only for first-time BMIs.[6] In response to how to get into the "urgent" queue for soon-to-expire passports, he advised them to simply come to the office in person.

He warmly thanked the JBMI organizers and the HKU cosponsors and reiterated his appreciation of open communication. The consulate was there "to help and protect" them and he was eager to hear their concerns. He asked for patience, saying he could not change everything overnight. He invited them to his office anytime, "but not only with complaints, also with solutions." He said some of them had used "strong language" to criti-

6. The Ministry of Manpower is a major branch of the Indonesian government that is responsible for labor issues, along with the BNP2TKI (National Agency for the Placement and Protection of Indonesian Migrant Workers). See Palmer (2016) for a study of the relationship and conflicts between the Ministry of Manpower and BNP2TKI.

cize the consulate and the passport process on Facebook, "but we want to help." He urged them to come and see him, and said he would even be in his office on Sundays during Ramadan. Several women chanted in unison, "Meet us at Victoria Park!"

At the end of the event, Eni Lestari asked me and Julie Ham to come to the front of the room. Until then, I didn't think that Andry Indrady had seen me; I momentarily experienced another awkward moment. I didn't want to encounter him in that context and wished I was a fly on the wall. Instead, I was formally introduced to him and his colleague. We chatted briefly and agreed to talk again soon.

COMPLICATING THE ETHNOGRAPHER-INTERLOCUTOR BINARY

My research on passports initially made me uncomfortable because of my ability to move back and forth between migrant workers and consular officials. In my earlier work, I felt that I was on the migrant workers' "side" and they were my central focus. Placing passports at the center forced me to move between consular officials and migrant workers. This ultimately led to my better understanding of the disenfranchisement of migrant workers as well as my privilege. The passport project forced me to consider how a wide array of actors along the way to becoming migrant workers—beginning in their home communities—contributed to the gendered precarity of migrant domestic workers. That was clear all along, but repeatedly returning to "passports" drove home the subtleties and complications concerning workers' acquisition of passports, and their ability or inability to control their passport (and its contents), all of which illustrated the precarity that was embedded and entangled in migrant workers' lives. The two moments of crisis created productive anxiety that led me to grapple with more than consular officials and BMIs. The experience reinforced my ethnographic understanding of the importance of trust, humility, and responsibility, and the need for "critical empathy" toward interlocutors, even those with whom I disagreed (Patico 2018).

Whatever groups my interlocutors belonged to, whatever their social affiliations, I came to see their viewpoints and subjectivities as contextual and heterogeneous, not fixed or binary. Their relationships shifted in relation to evolving passport problems. Anthropologists today likely know that we should avoid the "violence of the ethnographic encounter" in which ethnographic inquiry risks reducing interlocutors "to 'data bearers' who provide us with 'information'" (Kondo 1986, 83).[7] Ethnographers are not simply data collectors or information gatherers, and interlocutors (whether consular officials, domestic workers, lawyers, or NGO staff) are never solely data bearers or information providers. With respect to passports, I was also an information broker, an object of study, a data bearer, and a data sharer. BMI organizations and advocates are also researchers; they conducted passport surveys and collected volumes of passport data. They accompanied women to court and studied options and outcomes, which they shared with me, each other, and the consulate. With their consent, I shared what I learned about the passport project and passed on ideas about possible solutions. I was sometimes asked by interlocutors at the consulate, "What do they [BMIs] think of . . .?" Or asked by migrant workers to "tell [the consulate] that they should/should not . . . ."

Interlocutors and Friends

This project benefited from contacts I had established in Hong Kong since my first research there three decades earlier, with foreign domestic workers (FDWs), academics, NGO staff, and advocates for FDWs (Constable 2007, 2014). I have been coming and going to Hong Kong almost annually since the early 1990s, and some of my closest friends and colleagues are (or were) FDWs or employers (occasionally both). It is likely that many of the people I knew longest did not always think of me, first and foremost, as a researcher. Entanglements of research and friendship can complicate the data bearer/data collector relationship in positive ways. Ethnographic research and life are often deeply intertwined, especially for feminist ethnographers. Many people—those I just met as well as those I had known for a long time—readily voiced anger and anxiety about passport risks. Many felt duped and betrayed, stunned that their passports

---

7. Ethnographic violence relates to what other anthropologists have called "symbolic violence" (Rabinow 1977) or "domination" (Crapanzano 1980).

could cause them such problems. In chats with strangers at airports or with friends sharing a birthday meal, a humorous recollection, a rumor, or an anecdote might stay with me and become relevant to my research.

My Hong Kong friends and I do not divide our conversations into friend talk and research talk. For example, one evening, a friend complained that the FDW she had just hired had gone out her first Sunday, bought a new purse, and absentmindedly tossed her old one, containing all her travel documents, down the garbage shoot. My friend, her husband, and the domestic worker sifted through a huge dumpster to retrieve it. By contrast, during scheduled interviews, with a consent script, a request for permission to record or to take notes, and a list of interview questions, I am unambiguously "doing research." Boundaries were clearest with people I hardly knew, including those I met or interviewed only once and the consular officials and staff, whom I rarely saw outside of their work contexts.

Despite the lack of clear boundaries in a lot of ethnographic and qualitative research, there are advantages to having well-established contacts over a *longue durée*. Entangled roles of ethnographer, researcher, advocate, activist, feminist, friend, fictive kin, and perhaps confidant and advisor, and my long-term relationship with Hong Kong, fueled my sense of responsibility and helped to break down the ethnographer-interlocutor and researcher-researched binaries. My sense of responsibility to domestic workers has grown through time—as has my understanding of the challenges they face. Anthropologists cannot simply assume that any research topic is fair game. As Eni Lestari once put it, the research should be "useful, welcome, or at least okay."[8] Given my long-term research and relationships with FDWs and FDW advocates, and knowing of their "research exhaustion" (they are frequently asked for interviews or information by students, academics, and the media), I solicited their opinions about research projects.

After Mr. P proposed that I study the passport project, I asked for BMI activists' and NGO staff friends' opinions. Sringatin, Eni Lestari, and

---

8. Eni Lestari, chairperson of the International Migrants Alliance, and Natividad Obeso, president of the Association of United Migrant and Refugee Women in Argentina, spoke on "Global Migration and Labor Activism" at the University of Pittsburgh on March 26, 2019. Both discussed how the work of scholars and activists can most productively intersect around the issues that matter for migrant women workers.

several other BMIs encouraged me to pursue it. I returned to Hong Kong in February and summer of 2016 with Institutional Review Board (IRB) approval and began to interview consular officials, migrant worker advocates, and Indonesian domestic workers. I observed venues in which Indonesian passports were discussed, including the forums described above.[9] I followed up in the summers of 2017 and 2018, meeting with workers, activists, government representatives, and others. I located Indonesian media reports about SIMKIM and the passport project and did more contextual follow-up work while writing in 2019 and 2020.

Situated Knowledge

Understanding how knowledge is situated in relation to social positions is critical for understanding both ethnographers' and interlocutors' shifting perspectives. As Haraway writes, "The codes of the world are not still, waiting only to be read. The world is not raw material for humanization. . . . [T]he world encountered in knowledge projects is an active entity" (1988, 593). Knowledge about passports shifts with a person's social position and experiences. The obvious ones might seem to be (as I had first assumed) the social positions of domestic worker and consular official, but that is just a simple starting point. There is diversity among Indonesian domestic workers despite some commonalities. As noted, most are from Central or East Java, but they also come from Sumatra and other regions of Indonesia. Most are Muslim, some are Christian, and they express vastly different degrees of religiosity (Constable 2010). Their political views and degree of concern about migrant workers' rights vary. The views and experiences of Indonesian women in Hong Kong depend partly on whether they are current or former BMIs who overstayed or became mothers in Hong Kong, asylum seekers (USM applicants), or are permanent, married residents of Hong Kong. Their views shift through time and circumstances.

BMIs who worked in Hong Kong for decades on repeated two-year contracts are often much more savvy than young new arrivals who may be

---

9. In 2016, I was at Yale–NUS College, Singapore. IRB approval was from the National University of Singapore.

unaware of their rights. Many long-timers and recent arrivals avoid labor activism, and their employers and employment agents tell them to avoid activists. A visible and active minority of BMIs are activists who provide support, advice, and counseling to fellow migrant workers in person and—with the start of Hong Kong's widespread protests and the pandemic of 2019 to 2022—through social media. The memberships of politically active groups such as IMWU and ATKI and other JBMI affiliates are also constantly in flux as members leave Hong Kong and others arrive (Constable 2021a, 2021c). A worker with passport problems might be referred to activists by friends, relatives, neighbors, or other FDW organizations. New members often join after receiving assistance from activist organizations and staying at FDW shelters, where many say their consciousness was raised, and they become empowered. Migrant worker activists are often articulate, knowledgeable, and critical of migration policies and processes. They are well connected with networks of local NGOs, charity organizations, local policies, and legal issues, and local resources as well as networks in Indonesia and other BMI destination countries (Constable 2007, 2010).

A domestic worker's social position in Hong Kong is tied to race or nationality, gender and class, but her position shifts when she moves from being a BMI in good standing who is gainfully employed to someone whose passport is suspect, who is under investigation, whose employment is at risk, who is charged with a crime, and who is sentenced to prison and is subsequently subject to deportation and is deep in debt. BMIs' perspectives change when they perceive that the consulate—rather than protecting them—has put them in grave danger. When activists provide them with care and advice on how to deal with employment problems and teach them about the basis of their exploitation and vulnerability, migrant workers' subjectivity and sense of affiliation can shift. This was especially clear as many BMIs faced passport problems and turned to activist groups for advice and support (see figure 3).

My interlocutors included FDWs, Indonesian government officials and staff, international and local NGO staff, and local and expatriate lawyers, some of whom are long-term FDW advocates. I was interested in the diverse views of Indonesian government bureaucrats, but unlike Wayne Palmer (2012, 2016), who, during his research with Indonesian government

Figure 3. Eni Lestari, a well-known domestic worker activist, talks to workers about passport problems at a rally in Victoria Park, 2016. Photo credit: N. Constable.

officials and bureaucrats, impressively discerned a range of perspectives (especially among the Indonesian Ministry of Manpower, the BNP2TKI, and other Indonesian government offices regarding migration and human trafficking policies), I heard relatively few differing views among the small group of consular officials and staff with whom I spoke in Hong Kong. I spoke mostly to those from the immigration division who were responsible for passports, not those from the labor division (or labor attaché), which is typically responsible for migrant worker issues, although I tried.[10] The two consuls general and various immigration officials I spoke with expressed strong support for SIMKIM and the passport renewal project. Lower-level staff carried out their duties, following the instructions, but mostly presented a "frontstage" viewpoint, expressing respect for national and bureaucratic goals. Occasionally officials made comments "off the record." I located a few dissenting views from other sources that suggested that more critical "back-

10. I had no success arranging a meeting with the consular labor officials. Mr. P approached them on my behalf but conveyed to me that the labor consul said they would have little to add to what Mr. P and the consul general had told me. One labor official attended my meeting with the consul general and Mr. P but did not contribute to the conversation. The labor division was also conspicuously absent at the BMI forums.

stage" views might exist (Goffman 1959).[11] Yet I observed expressions of social difference at the consulate, including some officials' sense of superiority over BMIs and their displays of deference toward employers. Such behaviors were linked to gender, class, educational, and generational differences.

Ethnographic betrayal refers to ways in which ethnographers can betray the trust of their interlocutors, and interlocutors can betray one another's trust by divulging each other's secrets to the ethnographer (Visweswaran 1994). I never revealed individual identities or personal details (especially "irregular" passport data) to other interlocutors. After 2015, people I interviewed for the first time often preferred talking about other people's passport problems. In some such cases, because of someone else's "betrayal," I knew they were referring to themselves, but I did not let on. When I solicited examples of passport problems and how they were handled, I might refer to specific cases as "hypothetical" or to "general problems," or ask about well-known cases from the Indonesian media.

With consular officials, I asked questions but mostly listened. I also became an information broker. Mr. P welcomed information "that will help us know how we are doing" and "helpful suggestions," so, with the approval of BMI activists, lawyers, and other interlocutors, I sometimes relayed passport problems and suggestions. Mr. P and others thanked me politely, even when I knew that BMI activists, NGO staff, or advocate lawyers had already conveyed the same message. Perhaps the voice of a foreign scholar and researcher added some weight or helped Mr. P and his colleagues assess the situation.

Awkward Relationships

The "awkward relationship" between feminism and anthropology, Marilyn Strathern argued, is caused by each having different relationships with "the other" (1987). The anthropologist's other (conventionally) was a foreign "culture." The feminist's other (during second-wave feminism), by contrast, assumed an alliance between women of *all cultures* in relation to

11. Despite several attempts, I failed to arrange a meeting with the labor attaché. The role of the immigration division in relation to passports makes sense and illustrates the consulate's "discretion" to make decisions that differ from those of their counterparts in Singapore or Malaysia (Palmer 2016, 136–64).

an oppressive masculine/patriarchal other. This created tension between anthropologists' search for knowledge and understanding of cultural difference and feminists' more politicized or activist interest in gender equality, and an illusion of a universal alliance between women (regardless of differences). Subsequently, feminist anthropologists voiced criticisms of this view. Feminists (including anthropologists) have long recognized the significance of intersectionality (of nationality, class, race, ethnicity, religion, etc.) that belie any natural alliance between women. Anthropologists (including feminist ones) understand self and other as more complicated than any simple dichotomy, pointing to connections and disconnections, such as "halfie" or "native" anthropologists and the heterogeneities of both anthropologists and those among whom they study (Abu-Lughod 1993; Narayan 1993; Visweswaran 1994). Yet self/other concepts with roots in anthropology's colonial legacy persist despite efforts to decolonize the discipline (Pels 2018). Strathern's work nonetheless promoted critical reflection on illusions of alliance and difference. Selves and others are best understood as culturally and socially constructed, fluid and shifting, not oppositional. Entanglements of nationality, race, class, education, and gender are evident in my relationships with domestic workers and consular officials, and in theirs with each other. For example, consular officials' expressions of "friendliness" toward the migrant workers and BMI leaders at the forum contrasted sharply with the condescending attitudes that consular staff had expressed regarding BMIs in other contexts.

It may seem odd for a veteran ethnographer to struggle over taking sides, given that social science researchers have long stressed the importance of maintaining objectivity and avoiding their own biases. Decades ago, doctoral students were advised not to choose a research topic if they could not maintain objectivity or critical distance toward it. But, as Robert Borofsky puts it, "objectivity doesn't lie in avoiding certain topics. . . . The issue isn't whether one does (or doesn't) have a political agenda. To some degree, everyone has biases of one sort or another. Being a 'disinterested' professional doesn't mean being uninterested in the world outside one's laboratory. It means putting the larger society's interests ahead of one's own interests or the interests of those one works for" (2019, 13).

Feminists have long promoted critical positions on gender inequality and are invested in developing better accounts of the world that reflect on their own and others' expressions of power, privilege, domination, and oppression (Haraway 1988, 579). They do not advocate avoiding topics or groups that they care deeply about. How to understand disagreements, clashing interests, and the causes of "passport problems" from multiple perspectives is the challenge. The anthropological research position of "do no harm" serves mainly to protect research institutions, not our interlocutors (Borofsky 2019). Anthropology should instead be committed to "do good," the basis of an engaged and public anthropology. But "doing good" begs the question of whose idea of "good"—which is especially challenging if anthropological findings conflict with interlocutors' goals.

Beginning in the early 1990s, I conducted research among migrant workers, then marriage migrants and migrant mothers, because I had much to learn from their experiences and I cared about them. My views often corresponded with those of activist domestic workers, but my purpose has been to promote deeper understandings of their lives among a wider audience. I wrote about problems with migrant worker policies and practices. I studied Hong Kong government policies mostly on the basis of written sources—government websites or reports—because labor and immigration officials were unwilling to be interviewed, but often responded to specific written requests for data. They clarified procedures or provided updated figures, but (unsurprisingly) never conveyed opinions or thoughts about contradictions, internal conflicts, unintended policy outcomes, or future directions. I understood the impact of Hong Kong's laws and policies from the experiences of migrant workers or of people who were familiar with their cases (social workers, NGO staff, academics, or lawyers). By not talking to me, government officials conveyed official information (not their opinions); conversely, I did not develop a *personal* sense of obligation toward them.[12] In contrast to my lack of direct access to Hong Kong government officials, some Indonesian consular officials were very willing to talk to me, which heightened my sense of responsibility and my concern with fairness toward them.

---

12. I spoke to one Hong Kong immigration officer (a colleague's former student) by phone at the height of the passport problems in summer 2016. He was completely unaware of any Indonesian passport problems and asked if perhaps I was misinformed.

Empathy and Shared Narratives

Attachments to long-term interlocutors, as noted, can produce a deeper sense of responsibility and understanding than one-time interviews or surveys, but ethnographic materials can create greater risk of betrayal or alienation of interlocutors (Stacey 1988; Visweswaran 1994). They can lead to one-sided views of those with whom we identify most. How to navigate these risks is often left implicit.

Edward Bruner once argued that ethnographers are drawn to interlocutors who share their primary "narrative" or view of the world (1986). He thought that such narratives exist independently and shift through time. During his research among Native Americans, such narratives shifted from themes of "assimilation" to "resistance." An ethnographer interested in resistance, he posited, would seek out (or respond best to) interlocutors who voiced that narrative. Bruner's point is appealing, but feminists and anthropologists have long criticized the idea of single, homogeneous narratives and explicitly consider multiple, competing, or counterhegemonic narratives and perspectives (Marcus and Fischer 1986; Marcus and Cushman 1982; Haraway 1988).

Domestic workers' resistance was one focus of my first book and was a popular anthropological topic at the time (Constable 2007; first edition published in 1997). But I also wrote about accommodation, self-discipline, and migrant workers who opposed political activism and protest, and about employers' supportive and critical views of FDWs. Although I largely shared activist migrant workers' prognosis of the problem of global capitalism and labor exploitation, that was not the only "narrative" in the book, nor did my academic understandings and analyses of power, drawing in part from Foucault, completely mesh with theirs.

Despite the shortcomings, "shared narratives" help explain my sense that there were "sides" in relation to the passport project, especially as the situation heated up and migrant workers became increasingly critical of the consulate and its handling of passport renewals. The awkwardness was not because I agreed with the consular officials' position, especially when I learned more about the impact of the passport project on migrant workers, but because I appreciated their input into the research, and I felt awkward being critical of it. I listened carefully as officials emphasized the role of passports in protecting Indonesian migrant workers and citizens, but I heard and saw the contradictions as BMIs' lives were upended because of their passports. Consular officials often referred to the "bigger picture" of what is ultimately good for "the country" or our "citizens." I also heard their condescension, criticism, and blame of migrant workers—whom they saw as naive, uneducated, and unsophisticated—revealing their gender and class biases. I observed conversations in which consular officials allied themselves with Hong Kong employers, acting polite and obsequious toward the employers while ignoring the BMI, who was present but seemingly invisible. Talked about but left out of the conversation, she constituted the "grounds" upon which the discussion was based but had no agency or voice in that context (Mani 1987).

ENTANGLEMENTS OF INTERLOCUTORS

As this chapter shows, at first, I saw my interlocutors as falling into two discrete and opposed camps: Indonesian migrant workers (BMIs) and consular/government officials, in relation to the passport renewal project. I assumed that the criticisms and disagreements I heard reflected a clear division. Despite my concerns about being seen with the "opposing" group, I was *never* pressured to pick sides. I seemed to be the only one who was uncomfortable with my position. Interlocutors understood my role as a researcher better than I did. They encouraged me to meet and talk to a variety of people. I eventually saw that neither "side" was homogeneous, fixed, or static. Moreover, I could express critical empathy without supporting a position I disagreed with (Patico 2018).

Migrant workers have heterogeneous views, experiences, and politics. Not all BMIs were concerned about the passport project, and most had no passport problems. Activists were open about their friendly encounters and relatively easy access to consular officials. I witnessed many friendly and joking interactions between them. Activists explained the importance of maintaining such relationships and keeping the avenues of communication open, even though they complained that *they* often did the research and work of protecting the interests of BMIs that the consulate *should* be doing. BMI activists emphasized the issues that were relevant to them, rather than criticizing specific individuals, politics, political factions, or candidates. I came to see the BMI focus on shared *issues,* rather than *sides,* as critically important. As they explained, it helped prevent creating or exacerbating divisions between BMI groups with different political affiliations. It meant that their interactions and discussions with consular/ government officials were issue-oriented, not personalized. This point struck me especially hard during the Trump era from 2017 to 2021.

My awkward moments taught me the extent to which I had constructed and experienced the world of migrant workers (and their passport problems) in terms of two sides. Being attuned to conflicts and sides serves to reinforce ideas about dividing walls and barricades that are conceived of as firm and fixed. The risk is to overlook or minimize the *connections* between individuals and groups and the figurative bridges, ladders, and tunnels that help circumvent the walls and barricades—as well as more subtle, shifting, and short-term pathways and permeable entrances. Some migrant worker leaders had direct access to the various consuls general (over the course of this research) and to other officials, such as Andry Indrady and Mr. P (by phone, text, WhatsApp). Some officials were more receptive to their concerns than others. My being allowed "in" to (parts of) the consulate *and* among migrant workers was an indication of porous divisions and possible alliances. Migrant worker activist friends talked about alliances with sympathetic consular and other government officials and about shifting alliances between/among FDW organizations and networks, but it took the awkward moments at the consular window and at the forum, and their aftermath—during which time I was neither shunned nor turned to stone—to fully comprehend what that meant in terms of passport-related entanglements and my misconceptions of binaries.

Ethnographic research can involve productive anxieties that enrich our analyses. Dichotomies—of self and other, consular official and migrant worker, citizen and migrant, state and society, and so on—initially obstructed my view of the more complicated entanglements of lived realities that are revealed by a sustained focus on passports. This project and my previous ones have convinced me that the most difficult ethnographic experiences, the ones that make us feel torn, uncomfortable, and closest to failure, are often the most productive.

In sum, this chapter has shown how I began to "know"—in the sense of the chapter's epigraph, by Annelise Riles—what I know about passport entanglements, and how I came to focus on entanglements and tensions surrounding the government's passport project (rather than on simple binaries), which provided a picture of social processes that do not neatly align with a dichotomy of (state) power and (migrant) resistance. My first impression was that migrant worker activists and consular officials stood in opposition to each other. Eventually I realized that, because they knew me primarily as a researcher, neither government officials nor migrant workers were concerned about my talking with the "other side" about passports. Partly through the writing, I came to see a range of differently positioned interlocutors who revealed a more entangled, richer, more complex picture—a promising and productive, passport-centered one. The consulate may utilize authoritative *strategies* from above, and migrant workers may utilize *tactics* from below (Certeau 1984) and "weapons of the weak" (Scott 1987). However, such terms and labels risk simply (re)creating further binary divisions. My aim is to consider the importance of entanglements that are overlooked if we are too focused on such pairs. Strategies and tactics depicted in this book are entangled in productive and impactful ways.

Domestic workers' and government officials' entanglements (with each other and one another) can be antagonistic or unsympathetic, as illustrated by the 2016 forum. Simultaneously, their relations can be productive, collaborative, and constructive. Their relationships are multifaceted, complex, and linked in different ways to the elephants in the room during my conversations with migrant workers and consular officials: the recruitment agents, brokers, and employment agencies in Hong Kong and Indonesia. Brokers and agents play a huge role in passport stories. Structuralists of old might consider them "mediators" between the binary of government and migrant workers, but this would be far too simplistic, as the subsequent chapters show. Entanglements (rather than binary oppositions) reveal complex and unexpected negotiations and compromises. They can also be a source of hope if they constitute an "ethics of care" (Puig de la Bellacasa 2017).

3 Care and Control

> The pairing of care and control offers an entry-point for describing how migration takes shape through the historical development of entangled relationships—ranging from the supportive to the coercive—rather than strictly through dyadic relationships, social networks, structural forces, or as an effect of push-pull factors.
>
> Mark Johnson and Johan Lindquist (2020, 195)

I began drafting this chapter in Hong Kong in May 2019, at a little café with a window that overlooked a busy intersection of Nathan Road, in the crowded Yaumatei area of Kowloon. From there I could see young and middle-aged Filipino and Indonesian FDWs in t-shirts, with short hair or ponytails and occasionally hijabs, as they pushed strollers or wheelchairs, held the elbows of their elderly charges, and carefully crossed the busy intersection. Some held umbrellas to shield their charges from the intermittent drizzle and tropical sun. Such forms of *caregiving* were visible everywhere: on sidewalks and in teahouses, markets, playgrounds, public libraries, and the waiting rooms of doctor's offices. A few months later, back in the United States, half a world and a twelve-hour time difference away, I would witness—in the same area, via live feed from the *Hong Kong Free Press*—seemingly opposite acts of violent *control,* as Hong Kong police in riot gear cracked down on anti-extradition-law and pro-democracy demonstrators, using baton charges, tear gas, rubber bullets,

Epigraph: Johnson, Mark, and Johan Lindquist. 2020. Care and Control in Asian Migrations. *Ethnos* 85, no. 2: 195–207. DOI: 10.1080/00141844.2018.1543342. Reprinted with permission of Taylor & Francis LTD.

and pepper spray, while protesters chanted, among other things, "Hong Kong lives matter."

Anthropologists have long studied the provision of "care" in society. Functionalists and structural functionalists a century ago were especially interested in how social institutions, including kinship, politics, economics, and religion, helped fulfill people's basic needs for food, shelter, protection, and reproduction. A more recent anthropological definition of *care* refers to "cultivated body-knowledges and sensibilities by which creatures come to attend to one another's needs," which more specifically includes the embodied acts and feelings of care (Boke 2016). Care, moreover, "does not follow universal principles" but must be situated and understood in specific contexts (Yates-Doerr 2014; Mol 2008, 63).

Care work, the paid and unpaid feminized labor of care, is of interest to feminist and migration scholars. It encompasses *reproductive labor,* including biological reproduction and the labor necessary to feed, clothe, shelter, and protect people, as well as other feminized, affective, and emotional forms of labor. It also raises questions about the casualties, ethics, or violence of care (Mulla 2014; Puig de la Bellacasa 2017; Ticktin 2011). Care work done by FDWs in Hong Kong is often *intimate* labor that is—or gives the impression of being—"physically and/or emotionally close, personal, sexually intimate, private, caring, or loving" (Constable 2009a, 50). Intimate labor includes commodified reproductive work, such as paid "childcare, nursing, and hospice care" (Constable 2007, 2009a, 2014; Ehrenreich and Hochschild 2003; Parreñas 2001, 2008; Weeks 2011; Zelizer 2005). As a form of caregiving, domestic work often requires *emotional labor* or the work of performing the required demeanor, making oneself smile and act pleasant when feeling tired or in a bad mood (Hochschild 1983). Hong Kong employers sometimes complain about domestic workers' "long faces," and they expect to be obeyed without question (Constable 2007; Palmer 2020a). Refraining from expressing anger or impatience and appearing pleasant, cheerful, submissive, or neutral requires emotional labor.

FDWs do a wide range of labor: washing bodies and clothing; cleaning floors, dishes, and dwellings; marketing, cooking, and feeding; accompanying the elderly to appointments; transporting children to school; entertaining; organizing and supervising activities; teaching and helping with homework; dressing wounds and giving medicine; and so on. Mopping the floor does not usually require emotional labor unless someone is watching (in person or via a webcam). Intimate labor such as bathing, massaging, changing diapers, or feeding a child or elderly person often involves both emotional labor and affective labor. While *emotional labor* refers to the work done to appear pleasant, *affective labor* is the related work that is done to create a positive feeling (or affect) among *others*, to help the elderly charge feel less frustrated or the infant feel safe and comfortable (Hardt 1999; Lukacs 2020).

Returning to the domestic workers crossing the busy road with their charges in 2019, caregiving was evident, but so was *control*, as they led or guided their charges through the crowds, safely to the other side of the road. Control was also at times evident in the actions of the children and elderly, who might resist, pull, or shout impatiently, perhaps preferring a different pace or a different route or destination. At the nearby street market, I also saw domestic workers shopping alone or with their employers. Employers exerted control, telling domestic workers what to do and how to do it. Workers often appeared poker-faced, infinitely patient, perhaps daydreaming or doing emotional work. Watching them reminded me of the many stories I had heard from FDWs about endurance, loneliness, patience, and the provision of care without complaint and with a great deal of emotional labor and self-control, while hiding their own worries—about a sick child or parent at home, a failing marriage, a relative's request for money, or overdue loans and mounting debts.

Control, within this context, includes both self-control and control as influence, authority, or power over others. FDWs are controlled not only by their employers, but also by laws, regulations, policies, and hegemonic practices that are tied to their recruitment and their regulation, beginning with their passports. Control *of* workers takes place on multiple scales and in different spaces, through laws and through minute day-to-day practices, from the global level of international agreements that shape their passports (and visas and identity cards) to that of the micropolitics of regulating an FDW's clothing, hairstyle, timetable, and food intake (Constable 2007, 90–118). Care and control can be experienced as mutually exclusive, yet in many circumstances they are deeply entangled. The domestic worker who holds a child's hand to cross the road simultaneously exerts care for and control of the child. Without control she would literally be careless. The employer who tells the FDW, on her day off, not to go out "because of the protests" or "because of COVID-19" can be understood as expressing care, control, or both. Again, the specific context and social relations matter.

Social scientists are interested in power and social control, and in the ability to exert power or influence over others, in relation to the provision of care. In both Hong Kong and the United States in 2019, 2020, and 2021, people grappled with the issue of police violence. During the murder of George Floyd, a watershed moment of the #BlackLivesMatter movement, the need for "care"—or its masculine version of state or police "protection"—was said to justify violent forms of control. In Hong Kong, care is entangled with the diverging histories of China and Hong Kong, and with China's desire—with support from its HK government allies and the opposition of protesters—for greater control of Hong Kong.[1] In the United States, violence is entangled with the history of slavery and its deep entanglement with systemic anti-Black racism. In both cases, police violence and crackdowns were said to be justified because of the police duty to protect society from supposedly violent protesters.[2] In both cases, this claim was widely challenged and the question raised: Care and control of, by, and for whom?

Passports are at the foundation of the structures that permit FDWs to labor abroad. Their low-wage labor—which is essential to the highly profitable labor industry, in both the sending countries and the destination countries—would not exist without passports. As a form of registration and identification, passports can facilitate access to care for passport holders, assuring citizens of assistance from their consulate or embassy while away from home. They simultaneously serve—along with the Hong Kong visa and ID card—as a means of control and surveillance. The word *surveillance* comes from the French *sur* (over) and *veiller* (literally to "watch over" or "oversee"), both of which can imply an act of care or protection. Protectors or caregivers watch over their charges, which can imply,

1. Hong Kong was a British Colony from 1841 to 1997. The British had a ninety-nine-year lease of the New Territories from 1898 to 1997. Hong Kong's Basic Law specified that after 1997, as a Special Administrative Region of China, it would maintain its own independent administration and economy ("One Country, Two Systems") for fifty years. Protesters have opposed China's increasing encroachment as contrary to the Basic Law.

2. In both cases the term *riot* (rather than *protest*) was used to justify police violence.

depending on the context, a hierarchical relationship and the authority of the caregiver over the recipient of care. FDWs are theoretically "cared for" and protected by the passport and visa, and by the rights that they purportedly guarantee. FDWs are both givers and receivers of care, and both exert and are subject to various forms of control and surveillance.

"Protecting our citizens abroad" is a phrase I often heard and read in relation to the Indonesian consulate and Imigrasi's sense of duty to their citizens. It was often uttered with pride by consular officials and as a complaint by migrant workers who spoke of what their government or consulate did not provide but should have. From the officials' perspective, the passport is a tool for the provision of protection (a masculine form of care) and a form of registration and official identification that allows a person to claim or receive benefits (Breckenridge and Szreter 2012). But for BMIs, passports could be—somewhat counterintuitively—at the root of their problems, especially after the new passport renewal policy. The passport project reveals how passports, like governance and surveillance more broadly, can be double-edged swords, entangling care and control and mutually justifying each other's existence.

Passports and other identity documents facilitate government surveillance and control. Yet passports are not only instruments of state control (of both the Indonesian state and the Hong Kong government) over FDWs; they are also used as means of control by employment agencies and employers. Passports illustrate how care and control are entangled in complex, irregular, and context-specific ways in relation to migration and governance. The problems created by the passport project are, in one sense, specific to Indonesian workers in Hong Kong in relation to processes of migration that began in Indonesia, but some of their problems and challenges are more widespread among migrant workers in general.

BMIs are historically part of a late twentieth-century wave of feminized Asian migration and the growing labor recruitment industry. In this chapter, Ratna's story illustrates how the "encapsulation" of migrant workers in Indonesia during the recruitment process is intended to protect workers, but in fact often subjects them to further risk and exploitation (Killias 2018; Lindquist 2017, 2018b; Kloppenburg 2013), and Mila's interview illustrates how the care she gives in Hong Kong is tied to the provision of care in Indonesia. Rules and policies in Hong Kong (e.g., the employment contract, the two-week rule, and the live-in requirement) are also tied to care and control of migrant workers, especially in conjunction with Indonesian workers' high levels of economic debt. This chapter shows how migrant workers who provide valuable care are controlled in Hong Kong and Indonesia (often in the name of care and protection). Such care and control are tied directly and indirectly to passports—directly by employers, agents, and loan sharks who confiscate workers' passports, and indirectly by the necessity of obtaining passports through brokers and intermediaries in the first place.

GENDERED MIGRATIONS

In a special issue of *Ethnos* on "Care and Control in Asian Migration," Johnson and Lindquist (2020) locate contemporary Asian migrations historically. The first major increase in the scale of Asian labor migration took place at the height of colonialism, during the growth of industrialization in the second half of the nineteenth century, with the rising demand for "coolie" labor (Johnson and Lindquist 2020, 196; Amrith 2011; Stoler 1985). Labor migration then slowed in Asia during the first half of the twentieth century with the Great Depression, the two world wars, and the struggles for decolonization and independence. A second large increase took place in the later decades of the twentieth century, fueled by the growth of the East Asian "tiger" economies, the oil boom in the Middle East and Gulf States, and economic growth in China and India (Johnson and Lindquist 2020; Amrith 2011). Later twentieth-century migration is characterized by the feminization of migration, the importance of brokerage, and new forms of communication and surveillance technologies (Johnson and Lindquist 2020, 196).

The coolie labor migrations of the earlier period did not usually require or utilize individual passports, nor do some recent "undocumented" forms of labor migration from Indonesia to Malaysia. A major shift that distinguishes migrations of the mid-twentieth and twenty-first centuries is the heightened importance of proper documentation, especially passports, including the more recent biometric technologies. The growing international labor migration industry, first of men and then increasingly of women, led to greater public concerns about the need for government oversight and regulation of migration, including the utilization of improved technology, more reliable identification systems, and better care and protection of migrant workers against trafficking and exploitation through processes including "encapsulation and escort" (described below).

Filipino and Indonesian women who migrated to Hong Kong, Singapore, Taiwan, the Middle East, the Gulf States, and elsewhere to do domestic work are an important sector of this recent wave of gendered migration.[3] The increase in FDWs in Hong Kong is explained partly by the growing need for household workers as local women preferred being factory workers to being domestic workers, extended households became less common, and Hong Kong women became more educated and eager to work outside the home (Constable 2007, 23–28). Indonesian labor migration policies also shifted after the Asian financial crisis of late 1997, following President Suharto's resignation in 1998 and during the subsequent Reform Era (Reformasi), actively promoting women's labor migration beyond Saudi Arabia and Malaysia and into non-Muslim regions of Asia such as Hong Kong, Taiwan, and Singapore (Chang 2021; Constable 2014, 71; Hugo 2005, 2007; Robinson 2000; Silvey 2004).

Filipino women first went to work as FDWs in Hong Kong for English-speaking expatriates in the 1970s and early 1980s. Hong Kong Chinese employers gradually began hiring them in the 1980s and 1990s, and their numbers grew from the hundreds to thousands (Constable 2007).[4] Until the late nineties, the numbers of Indonesian FDWs in Hong Kong and Taiwan were small. In the late 1990s, following the Asian financial crisis of 1997, their numbers rapidly increased. In 1993, there were 6,000 Indonesians and 105,000 Filipinos in Hong Kong; by 2001, there were 155,000 Filipinos and the number of Indonesians had multiplied over tenfold to 69,000 (Constable 2007, 4).

Domestic work is one type of "feminized" migrant labor. Others include nurses, entertainers, sex workers, hostesses, and wives.[5] As of the end of

---

3. See Constable (2011) on domestic workers and "Inter-Asian" migrations.

4. See Parreñas's (2001) early work on Filipino domestic workers in Italy, and Lan (2006) on Filipinos in Taiwan.

5. For further reading, see Amrith (2020); Constable (2003); Parreñas (2011); Boris and Parreñas (2010); Chin (1998); Lan (2006).

2019, among almost 400,000 FDWs in Hong Kong, only 6,040 were men (80 percent of them Filipino).[6] Many male FDWs work as gardeners and drivers for wealthier employers, thus doing more "masculine" work. A few Filipino women are drivers, many of them self-defined "tomboys." Drivers are usually paid significantly more than FDWs who do "feminine" household labor.

Approaching Asian migration "as a socio-political field that is shaped through emerging forms of care and control," Johnson and Lindquist (2020, 195) consider it a type of "expansion" through "the use of connections" (Yates-Doerr 2014) that are shaped and constrained by various factors, including the state, the market, brokers, and others. As noted, Indonesian women who go to work in Hong Kong are mostly from parts of Central and East Java, and some are from Sumatra, especially regions that were impoverished and overpopulated during the Dutch colonial period. The global demand for cheap labor fuels the recruitment industry that became increasingly lucrative in the 1990s. It creates profitable jobs for agency owners, managers, agents, and various sorts of brokers (Killias 2018; Lindquist et al. 2012; Lindquist 2018b; Palmer 2016; McKeown 2012).

Growing numbers of licensed recruitment agencies (the legal designation is *Perseroan Terbatas,* or *PTs*) and recruitment agents or brokers (*petugas lapangan,* or *PLs*) in Indonesia, and of placement agencies abroad, facilitate the expansion of migration opportunities for mostly young and rural Indonesians (men and women). Agents or brokers help them obtain the documents they need to get passports, and they help them access recruitment agencies that are required for working abroad. PLs are key players in the "social lives" of the passports of migrant workers. They are intermediaries who recruit prospective migrant workers and connect the pieces—facilitating the creation of the passport that links the would-be worker to the passport-issuing offices, to agencies in Indonesia and in Hong Kong (or elsewhere), and also (as in many of the cases below) to the Indonesian consular staff in Hong Kong who (at the time of my research) decided whether to renew the passport with the same data, correct it, or send the holder home.

---

6. These figures were provided by email by the Hong Kong Immigration Department in 2019 and 2021.

INFRASTRUCTURES OF ESCORT

In colonial times and in the present, the "politics of connection" and "infrastructures of escort" play an important role in migration to and from Indonesia (Lindquist 2018a). Traveling alone is considered dangerous and unusual for men and women in many parts of Southeast Asia and is especially inappropriate and dangerous for women (Lindquist 2018a, 79). This helps explain the need in Indonesia for escort and for "encapsulation—or isolation—of migrants during the migration process" (Lindquist 2018a, 81; Kloppenburg 2013). This encapsulation of prospective migrants and the use of PLs as "escorts" in the process leading up to departure from and return to their home villages is "written into government directives, ostensibly in the name of protection from bad actors, such as *preman* (thugs, gangsters)," thus illustrating the "Indonesian state's enduring and paternalistic concern" over migrant mobility (Lindquist 2018a, 81–82). Escort helps to produce "a form of *jalur*, a channel" through which migrants are transported "from the village, to employment abroad, and back to the village again" (2018a, 95).

The need for escort is more important for women because they are thought to require greater protection from coercion and exploitation or from dangerous thugs whom they might encounter along the way. Escort has become part of the "modern" labor recruitment process. Unlike disreputable brokers of the past known as *calos* or *taikong* (smugglers) who are associated with undocumented migration, PLs are "figures of Indonesian modernity" that emerged in relation to state-sanctioned efforts to formalize and legitimize labor migration in the 1970s and 1980s (Lindquist 2009, 55–57). PLs lack contracts or licenses but are paid by the agency for each recruit. They serve as necessary and trusted connecting links between recruitment agencies (PTs) and villages in which prospective migrant workers reside (Lindquist 2018a, 80). The process of escort, and the politics of connection of which it is a part, involves a "relationship between comfort and coercion"—or between care and control—that can subject migrants to risks as they are targeted for forms of revenue (Lindquist 2018a, 78; Silvey 2007).

A prime example of how encapsulation can lead to exploitation (not protection) is the infamous (former) Terminal 3 at the Jakarta international airport, which channeled and segregated migrant workers and served as a prime site of extortion, exploitation, and corruption rather than protection (Silvey 2007; Ananta 2009).[7] Indonesia's migration infrastructure is a regulatory apparatus that helps extract labor and manage a particular population. It is also a "historically embedded cultural form" (Lindquist 2018a, 79; Xiang and Lindquist 2014). PLs may coerce prospective workers who depend on them, but Lindquist argues that they ought not simply be demonized as exploitative, because they also serve as advocates and mediators between workers and agencies, and their relationships are often based on trust and a sense of responsibility (Lindquist 2012, 89; 2015, 173; 2018a, 78).

RATNA: ESCORT AND ENCAPSULATION

Ratna was in her mid-thirties when I interviewed her in 2016. When she was eighteen, before Indonesia raised the minimum age from eighteen to twenty-one in 2004, she was planning to go to work in Hong Kong. (Hong Kong, notably, has no age requirement for FDWs but specifies that they must have two years of work experience, and its general labor laws prohibit children under fifteen from working.) As a high school graduate, Ratna was more educated than most Indonesian BMIs, but her family could not afford her further education, so she wanted to work abroad and help them. Like many Indonesians in Hong Kong, she was from a rural village in East Java (Jawa Timur), outside of the city of Surabaya, and was introduced to a PL by a well-known sub-PL who was a trusted and respected person in her region. Her experience largely echoes Lindquist's brief description of the process and provides some interesting details and differences:

> Once a PL and prospective migrant have agreed to proceed, a process of documentation is initiated in order to apply for a special migrant passport. At this point, the migrant usually has no contact with the recruitment

7. Kloppenburg describes how, even after Terminal 3 was closed, returning migrant workers are recognized and channeled through the airport and often required to take compulsory minibus rides home (2013, 116–19).

agency and the PL transports the migrant to and from the different govern-ment offices. For the prospective migrant, it would be an arduous and expensive process to gain access to all of the necessary documents on his or her own, and it is therefore nearly impossible not to use a PL, even for migrants who have previously been PL themselves and thus understand the process. If a prospective migrant were to turn directly to the agency, in fact, he or she would be asked to access those documents by way of a PL, or some-one within the office would act as the broker at the same charge. (Lindquist 2012, 82–83)

When I asked Ratna how she had obtained her first passport, she said, "Oh, it was so long ago, too long ago, before 2000!" She recalled:

First, I gave all my documents to the broker [PL]—the school certificate. Umm, I didn't have an I.D. [card yet] at that time, so only the school certifi-cate and—I can't remember—oh, and the letter from the family, and the letter from the local head of the village. And then the broker took me to the agency. I think within one month they brought many, many of us—I don't remember how many, twelve to fifteen of us—to the immigration office in Surabaya together. And there they just took a photo, asked us to sign on a blank passport page, and then we left. Then we only saw our documents again when we go to check in at the airport [to go to Hong Kong].

Ratna remembered being brought to the agency by the PL. The agent held on to all their passports and handed them out, one by one, to the official at the check-in and emigration counter at the airport for their departure to Hong Kong. I asked if there were any surprises in her passport.

Yes! Because they put my father's name [first] and they changed my birth-day to make me older. But I am not even underage! I was already nineteen, legal age at that time under Indonesian law. And then they just—and I did not ask a question at that time. I think I was able to pay attention to that only when we were [already] on the flight. During the check-in it was very tight, and they still hold all the passports like this [she indicates a very heavy/thick pile] and then check in, and at that time it was the agency that checked in for us, and they call names, one by one. And they show the pass-port to the person at the counter and then they keep the passport. And then, only before we enter, they give us all the passports. I remember I don't have time to check. I only saw [it] when I went to the plane. I ask [myself], 'Hmm. Why like this?' So, when we arrived, they—the agency—took the passport from me [again]. So, there is not really time [to look].

Most interesting in her account is how the passport is passed from one agent to another, Ratna seeing the document only briefly when it was her turn in line at the airport and when she boarded the plane. After passing through Hong Kong immigration, the representative from the agency took her passport.

Ratna had several different employers during her time in Hong Kong. She never renewed her passport because the Hong Kong agency did it for her, four times, without a problem. Once she tried to renew it herself in Indonesia, but the immigration office told her she must use an agent and turned her away. Forcing her to use an agent undoubtedly allowed the passport office to maintain its mutually beneficial relationship with PLs, and for them to demand more money than the official cost of the passport.

Like all FDWs, Ratna had a two-year renewable "FDH visa" and (at the time) a three-year migrant worker passport, so the passport and the visa needed to be renewed with almost every contract. The Hong Kong agent gave Ratna's passport to her first employer, who confiscated it to prevent Ratna from running away. It was common for employers to tell workers, "I have your passport, so you cannot run away." This caused Ratna problems because her employer was abusive; she wanted to leave but felt trapped without her passport. With subsequent employers, Ratna insisted on keeping her own passport. Keeping it, she said, would make it easier to leave a bad employer, should she ever need to do so again.

The Hong Kong employment agency had refused to retrieve Ratna's passport from her first employer until a year after she had left. An NGO that advocated for migrant workers pressured the agency to do so. The consulate, I was repeatedly told, was not very helpful at retrieving passports from employers, and considered it the agency's responsibility, while agencies often refused to respond. Ratna had also asked a well-known migrant advocate NGO for advice about removing her father's name from her passport and using only her own. Given the NGO's experience with Filipino workers, they said it was not a good idea to make changes, "because Hong Kong immigration will just review it as a criminal issue." So, "since then, I have to stick to that identity." When we spoke, I knew she had recently returned from Indonesia and had renewed her passport there. Asked why she hadn't renewed it in Hong Kong, she said, "I don't have a choice. Well, mainly I will be safe anyway, because everything [in it] is the same. But it was—who knows—because the [Indonesian] government already said that in the next three to five years they will integrate all the data back home with the passport identity [data]. So that would be a problem for many of us."

"Because the data is different?" I ask.

"Yes, because maybe you are safe now, but not in the years to come." Over the many years she had spent in Hong Kong, Ratna had seen many workers leave to get married or to rejoin their families in Indonesia, but in 2016 many were leaving out of fear of what would happen if they renewed their passports in Hong Kong. Some renewed their passports in Indonesia and then returned, but many did not. She speculated, "This is a forced soft deportation policy that they created to encourage migrants to go home. The [Indonesian] government has been saying [to BMIs], 'Oh, just go home, you don't have to be here.' For the government it is an easy answer. 'Just go home!' 'You can still work abroad. Just go home!' But [what they don't say is that] you cannot enter Hong Kong again."

"But you were able to come back?" I say.

"Yes, with the same [identity] information as before. They checked my ID, but I was able to get some [of the] same documents, but some had to be changed. That's very difficult. Many of them [fellow BMIs] have to pay the brokers. Some of them contact the agency [PT] in Indonesia—the agency that falsified the documents [in the first place]—and they [the agents] say, 'Oh don't worry, you just come home and pay me this HK$8,000 [over US$1,000, almost two months' salary], and we'll give you—we'll make sure you have same passport.' And it becomes a business for some agencies."

"Are these businesses connected with Indonesian Imigrasi?" I ask.

"Yes, of course they are connected to Immigration! You cannot fake the passport! So, who else will make the passport? So, [it is] still the same. Even in the past it was issued by Immigration. Except that [now] the bribing has to do with the identity and [is] to speed it up. It's just a cycle of problems! As long as the government pushes people to the agencies, many people will face this problem." The agencies and their PLs encouraged women to work abroad and facilitated the acquisitions of necessary documents to procure a passport. As in Ari's case (chapter 1), they escort and encapsulate them (or control them) through the process of obtaining the passport, to the migrant worker training centers, and to their overseas departing flights, all in the name of care and protection.

The main outlines of Ratna's story resemble the stories I heard from dozens of Indonesian women, especially with regard to (1) having a "school certificate" and few or no other forms of identification when they first considered working abroad; (2) playing very little role in the process of obtaining the passport and other documents, other than following the PL's instructions; (3) being accompanied by the PL (with a group of recruits) to the local immigration passport issuing office to have her photograph taken and to sign the passport; and (4) rarely having "control" or possession of her own passport either during the period of "encapsulation" before leaving for Hong Kong, or after arriving in Hong Kong. Most women, like Ratna, who had been in Hong Kong for multiple two-year contracts, barely saw the passport the first time they traveled. When, sooner or later, they noticed the discrepancies in their names and/or birth dates, most thought (or were told) it was too late to do anything about it, since the same information appeared in their employment contracts, their visas, and their Hong Kong identity cards, all of which reproduced that identity as the official one.

Strangely enough, Ratna's birth date was changed, although she was over eighteen and could legally work abroad. I had heard many times about women's birth dates that were altered by only days or months. It was more common for birth dates to be altered because women were underage, or because they were well into their thirties and might be considered "too old" by employers. Making an underage teenager older could raise concerns about "child trafficking" in the early 2000s in Indonesia, but it was not a significant concern among the women I talked to who wanted to work abroad after middle school in their mid-teens. Early on, it was common practice to have their ages adjusted. Women said that they had wanted to work abroad, and that the PL had "helped them" to do so. This did not seem problematic to them, coming from communities where women often worked and married in their teens, and where some went to work abroad to avoid marriage.

Ratna's recollections differed in some ways from those of other women. Many women described going to the immigration office with the broker and having only a fingerprint taken for the passport. Some only remembered having the passport photograph taken at the passport office, but not signing anything. There were other small variations in women's stories, especially regarding how they acquired the necessary documents, obtained their father's or husband's permission to work abroad (sometimes with help from the PL), and adjusted their age. There were many things they could not clearly recall, especially for women who obtained their first passports and first went abroad more than a decade earlier, a point I return to at the end of the chapter.

Escort of migrant workers today—from the village to the passport issuing office, the agency, the training center, and the airport—echoes elements of Indonesia's colonial history of labor mobility, in which workers were also carefully encapsulated and controlled. One rationale for escort and encapsulation of migrant worker recruits, like coolies and indentured workers of the past, is to protect the recruiter's or broker's investment. If workers run away or change their minds, brokers receive less compensation.[8] The domestic and international migration infrastructure creates a channel through which rural migrants like Mila, Ratna, and Ari (chapter 1) pass. Today's migrant workers require PLs or *calo* (the latter a derogatory term today) to escort and "protect" them as they make their way from their home villages to urban training camps and agencies, whose staff or agents escort them to departure airports.[9] As brokers or intermediaries, PLs of recent decades are usually in respectable social positions that enable them to mediate between prospective migrant workers (and their parents or husbands), recruitment agencies, and government offices (Lindquist 2012, 82; 2015). The encapsulation of migrant workers—in the name of protection and care—involves informal brokers and sub-brokers, employment agencies, and government offices, and it is reinforced by legal assemblages, state legal regulations, and policing intended to protect migrant workers (Killias 2018; Lindquist 2018a, 2018b; Palmer 2016; Silvey 2007). Both "Indonesian government and nongovernmental organizations warn prospective migrants, through media and outreach

8. Lindquist (2018, 95) notes that the "indirect rule of the Dutch colonial state . . . relied on a wide range of intermediaries to mediate between villages and urban centers of power."

9. Both *PL* and *calo* are used to refer to recruitment brokers and sub-brokers. *Calo* is sometimes used to refer to informal brokers, but Lindquist argues that it is impossible to distinguish between formal and informal brokers, all of whom he refers to as "PL" (2012, 84; 2015).

campaigns, about the importance of using formal recruitment channels" (Lindquist 2018a, 79). Multiple actors are involved in regulating, aiding, and profiting from migrant mobility and form "the basis for the development of a migration infrastructure—a socio-technical platform for mobility—of recruitment, documentation, transport, temporary housing, reception, and physical encapsulation centered on the 'protection' (*per-lindungan*) of the migrant" (2018a, 78). This encapsulation controls migrant workers for the supposed sake of "protection" but, as noted, it also turns returning workers into targets of extortion. Ultimately, this protective encapsulation did nothing to protect women from passport problems and criminal charges of immigration fraud in Hong Kong. In fact, the PLs, agencies, and government passport agents *produced* women's passport problems, as Ratna and other workers well understood.

DOMESTIC WORKERS AND GLOBAL CAPITALISM

Passports are necessary for migrant workers to work "legally" abroad. They facilitate their entry into—and their participation in—a global and transnational capitalist and neoliberal system that thrives on and deepens socioeconomic inequalities, especially those tied to class, gender, race/ethnicity, and nationality, through the extraction and exploitation of cheap and flexible labor (Constable 2007, 2014). Passports are the "tickets" that permit workers entry into a marketplace where care and control are entangled. Contrary to earlier assumptions that time-saving household technologies (washing machines, vacuum cleaners, etc.) would reduce the need for paid household workers, the market for FDWs has grown rapidly in Asia, especially in Hong Kong, Singapore, Malaysia, and Taiwan, where extended households are no longer the norm, child-care and elder-care facilities are rare or too expensive, and local women must or prefer to go out and work. These regions often compete for Indonesian migrant domestic workers (Chang 2021).

The promotion and purchase of migrant labor (in origin and destination countries) is rationalized and justified through international and national notions of development that promote the idea that migrant labor is a win-win, a part of free trade that benefits all. This is a fallacy, but many workers nonetheless place their hopes in it and many employers buy into it (literally). The discourse of fairness and mutual benefit, and related neoliberal ideals of individual responsibility, allow workers and their family members, employers, agents, recruiters, government bureaucrats, and others to justify a fundamentally exploitative practice.

Under this system, so-called unskilled workers from poorer countries are considered fortunate to get jobs abroad. PLs and agents claim to care and to help, while employers often consider FDWs poor, unskilled, and lucky to work abroad. FDWs are not usually seen as valuable laborers who contribute significantly to the local economy and deserve greater rights, privileges, and remuneration. Undervalued gendered household work, especially feminized elder care and child care, was once done in Hong Kong (and many parts of the world) for free by women family members. Although such care work is indispensable and essential to many families (as clearly illustrated during the COVID-19 pandemic in the United States), in most parts of the world it is still poorly paid and undervalued.

Filipinos and Indonesians represent 96 percent of the roughly four hundred thousand foreign domestic workers in Hong Kong in 2019. Over half were from the Philippines, and slightly under half were from Indonesia, with an additional almost ten thousand workers from other South and Southeast Asian countries, mostly Thailand, as well as India, Bangladesh, and Sri Lanka. Most such workers are women who provide child care, elder care, and household work. As in many societies, these jobs are low-paid but are economically important to the societies in which they work. Roughly one-third of Hong Kong households with children hire an FDW (LegCo 2017). In 2019, almost four hundred thousand foreign domestic workers—equaling the total population numbers of some midsize U.S. cities—worked in this relatively small area of 427 square miles. FDWs represent almost 10 percent of Hong Kong's total workforce. As Hong Kong's elderly population rapidly grows, the need for FDWs is projected to reach six hundred thousand by 2047 (Enrich/Experion 2019; LegCo 2017).[10]

10. In 2020, during the Hong Kong protests and COVID-19 pandemic, the numbers of Filipinos and Indonesians each decreased by approximately twelve thousand (Hong Kong Immigration Department, personal communication, June 1, 2021). By 2022, news sources report that the number had dropped further, to under 350,000.

In a 2019 report, "The Value of Care: Key Contributions of Migrant Domestic Workers to Economic Growth and Family Well-Being in Asia," Experion (a research firm) and Enrich HK (an NGO that provides financial and other training for domestic workers) quantify the value of such labor, documenting and assigning monetary figures to the labor of FDWs in Hong Kong, Singapore, and Malaysia (the Experion/Enrich project calculates the value of the various sorts of labor occurring in each of the three locations). It is well known that FDWs do mostly feminized labor that allows *women* employers to enter the paid workforce or have more leisure time, but the report shows that Hong Kong's high female labor-force-participation rate of 78 percent would plummet to 49 percent without FDWs. Calculating the cost of child care and elder care outside the home, and cost savings from laundry and food preparation, they calculate that FDWs contributed US$12.8 billion to Hong Kong's economy in 2018. The same year, combined remittances from FDWs in Hong Kong, Singapore, and Malaysia contributed US$1.1 billion to the Indonesian economy and US$1.1 billion to the Philippine economy (Enrich/Experion 2019). Despite their low salaries, their economic contributions are significant.[11]

Hong Kong is one of the most expensive cities in the world, but FDWs were paid only HK$4,520 (US$575) per month in 2018. Hong Kong's standard minimum hourly wage, which does not apply to FDWs, is very low, at HK$37.50 (US$4.80) in 2019. Given that most domestic workers labor sixty hours a week or more, if they were paid the minimum hourly wage, they would earn around HK$9,000 per month (US$1,150); instead, they earn roughly half that. A common rationale is that their compensation includes room and board.[12] Hong Kong's Standard Employment Contract specifies that FDWs must "live in" with their employers, and that employers must provide them with "suitable housing," "reasonable privacy," and food. Employers who do not provide food must provide HK$1,075 per month (US$4.50 a day), which is low by contemporary urban standards.

11. See Zelizer (2005) on how monetary value is legally assigned to domestic work or care work.

12. Local full-time domestic workers paid hourly earn approximately HK$8,000 per month and "live out."

FDWs provide Hong Kong employers with labor that is otherwise unavailable or unaffordable locally but is considered essential to maintain or attain a middle-class standing. Given Hong Kong's "workaholic" lifestyle, with long and fast-paced workdays and workweeks, many locals have little time for household responsibilities. FDWs are especially necessary for families with small children or sick or elderly members. Surprisingly, not all employers are middle class or wealthy. Some live in extremely poor and crowded conditions. To qualify to hire an FDW, a household must earn a minimum monthly salary of HK$15,000 (US$2,000) per month. This figure is shockingly low for one of the most expensive cities in the world and had not been adjusted for over fifteen years at the time of my research. The "poverty line" for a household of three in Hong Kong is HK$15,000 (US$2,000), "calculated as 50 per cent of median monthly household income before taxation and the government's policy intervention" (Chiu 2018).[13] Low-paid Hong Kong locals thus can hire even lower-paid FDWs, which helps to placate them while they perform other types of low-paid work.[14] Those below the poverty line may be most in need of FDWs, as they cannot afford to hire locals. They help the government justify FDWs' low wages. A cheaper but riskier option is for employers to hire hourly "undocumented" workers, such as FDW "overstayers" (whose contracts have expired) or asylum seekers (who are prohibited from working legally). Individuals without valid passports may be willing to work for less than "documented" FDWs but are more vulnerable to underpayment and abuse, and workers and employers are liable if they are caught.

FDW wages are considered fair in Hong Kong because they are higher than the wages FDWs would earn in their home countries. On a day-to-day and experiential level, this system thrives on the illusion of benefits and "care for all." Migrant-receiving states consider inexpensive foreign workers an affordable solution to local labor needs. However, more Hong

13. The article explains: "The poverty line is set at 50 per cent of median monthly household income before taxation and the government's policy intervention, which includes social welfare payments, such as allowances for the elderly and low-income families. In real terms that means a single person with a monthly income of HK$4,000, a two-person household earning HK$9,800, while the threshold for a three-person household is HK$15,000" (Chiu 2018).

14. Hong Kong's working poor are increasingly disgruntled with skyrocketing housing and living costs but are forced to work long hours for a low wage.

Kong locals and recent mainland immigrants would likely do such work if it offered better remuneration, work conditions, and work hours. Indeed, "documented" *local* domestic workers and caregivers demand more than the local minimum wage, work shorter hours, and mostly refuse to live in. The Hong Kong government recognizes the needs of local families, and FDWs are the cheapest and easiest way to meet demands. Moreover, the labor recruitment industry is highly profitable and powerful in both sending and receiving countries.

The promise of "economic development" in migrant-sending countries aims to justify the growing number of recruitment agencies and expanding migration infrastructures in sending and receiving states. Migratory and recruitment infrastructures create jobs and profits for government bureaucrats in immigration and labor offices, for employment agents and recruiters, for training staff, for lenders and banks, for insurance and remittance businesses, and for many others (Chang 2021; Killias 2018; Lindquist 2018a; Palmer 2016; Silvey 2007, 2018). In the immensely profitable recruitment industry, owners and managers—some with relatives in powerful Indonesian ministries—make money from prospective migrant workers who want to work abroad and support their families. Income and profits from this industry reach local and regional recruiters and trainers, some of whom are former migrant workers, teachers, or leaders with close ties to local and regional government functionaries. Agencies, in turn, pay for licenses, and government agents are paid for inspections and approvals. Banks and loan agencies benefit from remittances and interest payments. Migrant workers borrow money (directly or indirectly through the agency) to obtain their documents and to cover the costs of training, physical examinations, and so on (see chapter 4). For the migrant workers themselves, the benefits rarely amount to what they hope or expect (Chan 2018; Constable 2015).

In the early 1990s, almost two-thirds of Filipino domestic workers had college or university degrees or advanced training, but they went abroad as FDWs because of the unemployment and underemployment in the Philippines (Constable 2007, 82). They worked abroad to provide their children with better opportunities. Some told me they worked abroad so that their daughters would not need to. Yet some FDWs I met in recent decades are daughters of former FDWs. I have met children of FDWs who went to Canada or the United States to earn university degrees, but for most their remittances barely cover consumer goods and routine daily expenses. They cover the family's short-term needs, not investment in long-term goals (Allerton 2020). Remittances are used for food, education, health care, and home improvements. Dirt floors might be replaced with concrete ones, or wooden or split bamboo walls replaced with bricks. A better toilet, a television, a refrigerator, or a mobile phone are common purchases. Some buy land or livestock or otherwise invest in farming. However, such improvements rarely produce the significant or sustainable life improvements imagined or hoped for, because of the high costs of migration and the fundamental inequalities that are reinforced and perpetuated by the migratory infrastructure.

Entangled concepts of care and control—ranging from the "supportive to the coercive," as noted in this chapter's epigraph—are tied to a system in which migrant workers labor to benefit themselves and their families, to escape poverty and change their lives, but often fail to do so because their interests are subordinate to the interests of employers and others who profit from the trade in migrant workers. Meanwhile, FDWs' situations can improve incrementally in some cases. Yet the situation is fundamentally unfair because global capitalist-fueled labor migration is profit-driven, unequal, and exploitative, regardless of the worker's consent, the employer's best intentions, or the agency's and PLs' desire to "help." Exploitation is camouflaged in part by the entanglements of care and control.

MILA: CAREGIVING

N: *How old were you when you first left Indonesia and went away to work?*

I went to work in Singapore when I was, umm, eighteen, and worked there for six years.[15] Then I went home and got married, then had my daughter. I went to work in Hong Kong when she was only fifteen months old. When I go back [home] the first time, my daugh-

---

15. Specific dates are omitted in such examples for anonymity.

ter does not remember me. And my husband found another woman. So now I am a single mother. He never helps us. I go back to Hong Kong because I need to support my daughter.

N: *Who took care of her?*
My mother is the one who has been taking care of her all these years. My mother alone now, after my father died.

N: *How long have you worked here?*
I have worked in Hong Kong for thirteen years. For my same employer twelve years now, six contracts. I take care of my employer's children, but now they are mostly grown and now two are gone away to college. [She smiles and sighs.] So quiet now they are gone.

N: *Is it different now?*
Yes, work is easier now but still cooking, cleaning, laundry, everything for ma'am, sir, and youngest daughter, and helping with the popoh [grandma]. She is getting old.

N: *Are they good employers?*
Yes, they are very good, but it was not always easy. At first [it was] very hard. The difference with Singapore and Hong Kong [pause]. One thing is better in Singapore—is that there you eat with your employers and you eat what they eat. Here they give you very little food, or you have to get your own food, and they give you very little money. Yes, salary here is higher [than in Singapore] but I have to spend a lot of my salary here. I send some of my salary home to take care of my daughter and my mother. I need some of it here for food and transportation and other things, and I have to save some of my salary for me for later [old age]. I took the seminar on what is it called financial—uh, literacy.

N: *With Enrich?*
Yes, you know Enrich? I almost finished the training. Almost graduated. I open a bank account and try to save for my future. Already have been here a long time. I take care of my employer's children when the youngest was very little and now they are already grown . . . two already in college. My daughter is very good. She is in special—what you call it—religious school for Islam. She wants to

be a teacher, a religious teacher who will teach children. She is learning about the Koran and many things. . . . Here I also like to help other domestic helpers in this organization.

Mila is part of the pattern of feminized labor migration that creates international "chains of care" (Parreñas 2001) as women leave their own children in the care of others (often other female family members) and provide care for people in wealthier destination countries (Constable 2007, 2016; Hochschild 2000; Silvey 2007). When I interviewed Mila in 2018, she was in her late thirties and had spent eighteen years working in Singapore and Hong Kong. She described interconnected manifestations of care across time and geographic divides. Each form of care is tied to different social relationships. Mila's mother cares for (looks after) Mila's child in Indonesia while Mila cares for her employer's children and elderly kin in Hong Kong (Constable 2018a, 2018b). Meanwhile, Mila provides care to her mother and daughter by way of sending regular monthly financial remittances. Mila also takes part in forms of self-care, taking financial management classes with Enrich, saving some of her earnings and participating in a support group for migrant workers that meets in Victoria Park most Sundays. In this group, she and other women both give and receive care in the form of emotional support and as they learn and teach about healthy lifestyles and conduct outreach work on migrants' rights.

ENTANGLED FORMS OF CONTROL IN HONG KONG

Hong Kong is often referred to as the "best destination in Asia" for FDWs because it has a standard employment contract and offers greater "freedom" than other destinations. The FDH employment contract guarantees the worker a minimum monthly wage (nearly US$600 per month in 2020) and a mandatory weekly day off or "holiday" (usually Sundays). The "two-week rule" mandates their rapid departure when their contracts end or if they are terminated early. The mandatory live-in rule, noted above, requires FDWs to live with their employers. These policies, alongside FDWs' debts, especially when they first arrive, are tied to the care and control of workers and to passports. Passports are tied to their visas and Hong Kong identification. Their debts are also tied to their passports.

FDWs' indebtedness, paired with their financial responsibilities and obligations back home, forces them to tolerate physical and emotional maltreatment or poor or dangerous work conditions, for fear of termination. If they could simply leave a bad employer and find a better one, it would not be as much of a problem. However, the two-week rule obligates them to leave Hong Kong within two weeks, so they do not have time to change employers.[16] If FDWs complain or do not maintain the employer's expected cheerful and submissive demeanor, they risk losing their jobs and having to return home with no means of repaying their debts. If they file complaints with the Labour Tribunal, the outcome is often stacked in the employer's favor, and FDWs are not permitted to work in the meantime, but depend on charity (Constable 2007; Palmer 2020a).

According to the Enrich report (above), Hong Kong FDWs accrue higher debts than workers in either Singapore or Malaysia, and they are least likely to have their own bank accounts. In Hong Kong, 83 percent of study respondents were in debt, in Malaysia 65 percent, and in Singapore 34 percent (Enrich 2019). Hong Kong law specifies that FDHs cannot be charged recruitment fees over 10 percent of a month's salary; however, Hong Kong agents and officials claim that there is little they can do because the problem is in Indonesia (see also Palmer 2016).

Researchers have noted the difference between Indonesian factory workers (mostly men), who must pay migration fees "up front" before they migrate for work, and Indonesian women domestic workers, whose employers are said to pay the recruitment fee (Chang 2021). In fact, the situation in Hong Kong is often more complicated. BMIs end up paying their own fees and expenses by way of obligatory loans and salary deductions (of as much as seven months' wages), especially during their first contract. Although Hong Kong law prohibits charging more than 10 percent of a month's salary, Hong Kong agencies commonly require BMIs to sign loan agreements with lending agencies upon arrival. This ensures that the loan will be repaid by automatic salary deduction. Some Hong

16. The two-week rule was temporarily suspended during the COVID-19 pandemic because of the growing shortage of FDWs.

Kong agencies hold workers' passports as collateral until recruitment debts are repaid (Palmer 2016). During those months of salary deduction, if they are desperate to send money home, they might be tempted to borrow money from informal loan sharks (illegal moneylenders) who charge exorbitant interest rates and often demand passports as collateral (Lo 2018; Ng 2018). Aware of such practices, some employers preemptively confiscate the worker's passport to "prevent such trouble."

Other employers, like Ratna's first employer, simply take the passport to prevent workers from leaving. Debt and passport confiscation are key factors in workers' reluctance or inability to leave abusive employers. Justified as "encapsulation" that is intended to take "care" of workers, such practices justify and facilitate exploitation. Women must use a PL and an agency, which in turn means that they must take out loans to repay their debts (including costs of training, transportation, medical examinations, passports, and other documents). Prospective BMIs are legally required to utilize an agency. In theory, they can apply for their own passports in Indonesia, but in practice, as in Ratna's case, they must use a PL. Local government offices issue passports and other documents and receive payment from the PL (Ford and Lyons 2011). The PL is paid by the agency, and the agency indirectly recoups money from the partner agency abroad, which further "escorts and encapsulates" the worker.

The employment contract is intended to protect workers, employers, and Hong Kong at large, but in practice several factors make the situation worse for workers. The contracts stipulate, for example, a weekly twenty-four-hour rest period (which is why many workers prefer Hong Kong to Taiwan). But many women do not have twenty-four hours off. Often employers institute early-evening curfews, perhaps intended as an expression of care or protection, to ensure the FDW is back before dark, or that she has a good night's sleep. This can be experienced as unwanted control or exploitation or as infantilizing. In the 1990s, several FDWs discussed the "freedom" of Hong Kong, and a young Filipino woman said that she preferred working in "Saudi" (a term often used to refer to Saudi Arabia or the Middle East in general) with no day off. She appreciated staying at home because her employers "cared" about her and looked after her. Her Hong Kong employers expected her to go out on Sundays, which made her feel unwelcome and uncared for. Her preference for the Middle East was uncommon, but workers understood feeling unwelcome in employers' homes, or being obligated to work if they remained there on their day off. The ability to "rest" at the employer's home was often difficult, given sleeping arrangements, so women rested outside. FDWs routinely worked when they returned home. Employers might think that workers "freely choose" to work on their day off, but workers often feel they must, otherwise a mess awaits them the next day.

Care and control are contextual, related to the giver and recipient and the power relationship between them. *Allowing* or *requiring* a domestic worker to live in or live out, to go out on Sunday or not, or permitting her to come and go as she pleases versus dictating a curfew, have different implications with regard to care (as consideration and concern) or control (as domination, exploitation, or condescension). Some employers clean up on Sundays or teach their children to do chores and appreciate the domestic worker's contributions. Many go out to eat and some leave a mess, conveying a lack of care or a sense of disregard that can be experienced as coercive by a domestic worker.

WALI: LIVE-IN REQUIREMENTS

"Suitable housing" and "reasonable privacy" are required by the employment contract, but they are not clearly defined, nor had anyone I knew ever heard of housing inspections by employment agents or Hong Kong, Filipino, or Indonesian government representatives (only by the Thai consulate). Employers whose incomes are near or under the poverty line likely interpret the contractual requirement to provide an FDW with suitable housing and reasonable privacy in relation to their own living conditions.

Wali compared her 2018 work situation with her previous one. She previously worked for a family of four who lived in a tiny (under 350 square feet) flat in a densely populated Kowloon neighborhood. The five of them (including Wali) ate together on a food budget of HK$500 (US$65) per week. They shared a tiny bathroom. Wali's "living space" was minuscule, like that of the other family members. Despite the contract, she had no privacy. She slept on a bedroll in the combined living/dining area, after a small table was folded. Calculating the household's monthly expenditure for meals at home (HK$2,000, which is extremely low) plus the domestic worker's monthly salary (HK$4,500), this left them approximately HK$8,500 (just over US$1,000) per month to cover rent, transportation, the two children's school costs, and all other expenses.

Wali's current employer's household included two adults and their small child in a spacious flat in an upper-middle-class neighborhood of Hong Kong Island. Wali does the grocery shopping and is instructed to buy organic produce, imported products, and expensive cuts of meat. Groceries for a single dinner at home regularly cost over HK$700 (more than her first employers' weekly food budget). Wali's living space includes her own room with an air conditioner that she controls, and an adjoining private bathroom with a toilet, sink, and shower. (Her room alone is larger than many subdivided flats where migrant workers, poor locals, and asylum seekers live.) Wali's employers pay her HK$200 above the minimum monthly wage and provide her with a food allowance.

Contractually, these two living-working spaces are "equivalent" despite their differences. The living space (regardless of quality) is officially what makes up the difference between an FDW's monthly salary and what she might earn if she received Hong Kong's hourly minimum wage (or what she would need to pay for housing). In the first case, were it permitted, Wali might have preferred an additional HK$4,000 per month (which her employers could not afford) to secure her own lodging.

Yet Hong Kong is an expensive and densely populated region, and many locals struggle to find decent affordable housing. Hong Kong newspapers often report on shortages of affordable government-subsidized housing, and on the public criticism of new private housing estates, parks, and golf courses that utilize space that could be used for public housing. Hong Kong residents who qualify for subsidized housing enter lotteries and wait many years to qualify for tiny flats. As a result, many employers' living conditions are cramped, and those of FDWs even worse. Although many employers of domestic workers are middle class or wealthy, crowding, expensive housing, and lower-income employers help explain the inadequate food and housing of FDWs who share the hardships of less fortunate Hong Kong residents.[17]

Calls to do away with the live-in requirement are often voiced by activist workers and NGOs. Campaigns are reenergized following tragic, publicized cases of FDW abuse, where workers were isolated and virtually imprisoned in their employers' homes, such as the famous case of Erwiana (Constable 2016). The Mission for Migrant Workers (MFMW 2017) published a report on domestic workers' living conditions, including photographs of bed mats that are unrolled each night on the porch, on the roof, in the bathroom, or on the kitchen floor, after household members have gone to bed. Activists and media have drawn attention to the issue of inadequate housing for FDWs, and reports and images of substandard housing have gone viral on social media.[18]

A Chinese migrant worker activist showed me a photograph of a space that an architectural designer had proposed in 2018 after seeing pictures of inadequate FDW housing. It resembled an IKEA cabinet that one might use to display dishes, mounted horizontally on the wall a few feet off the ground in a fancy living room. It was a rectangular box, coffin-length but slightly higher and deeper—with tiny windows and shutters. It resembled a fancy-living-room version of Hong Kong's squalid "coffin apartments." As a BMI friend and I looked at the photograph, we laughed uncomfortably. She said, "Oh my god! Would they want their children to sleep in such a box?" Yet it was a serious proposal by a well-meaning local designer who "cared about" FDWs and their "bad sleeping conditions."

Despite the documented link between physical, sexual, or emotional abuse of FDWs and the constraints of living and working in isolated

---

17. Some Hong Kong locals oppose increases in FDW salaries because of employers' poverty. However, maintaining low household incomes and low FDW wages can be a race to the bottom. Instead, the HK government should ensure that the working poor earn an adequate living wage, with shorter work hours and benefits including subsidized child care and elder care.

18. After sleeping in a domestic worker space for one night, journalist Rachel Blundy (2017) writes that "trying to sleep like a foreign domestic worker in Hong Kong left me irritable and groggy." See also Hincks (2017), "In the World's Most Expensive City, 1 in 10 Maids Sleeps in a Kitchen, Toilet, or Corner of the Living Room"; and Hollingsworth (2017), "Sleepless in Hong Kong . . . on Fridges and in Toilets: Worst Places City's Domestic Helpers Have Called a Bed."

private households where workers have little choice but to tolerate abuse, abolishing the live-in requirement has been widely opposed. Proponents say the live-in rule provides protection, care, and control of workers, and that their labor is required all day and night. Some argue that allowing FDWs to live out would increase competition for local low-cost housing and transportation, both of which are very crowded (Palmer 2020a).

A long-standing justification for hiring foreign (versus local) FDWs is that locals will not live in, and allowing FDWs to live out would create competition with local workers. Yet allowing the option of living out could benefit both foreign and local workers. Many employers and workers would not opt to do so, but for employers who can afford it and desire it, there would be greater family space and privacy. If employers need twenty-four-hour help (common justification for hiring a live-in worker), they could hire two shifts of live-out workers. Allowing FDWs to live out might decrease the overall dependence on them, which could mean shorter work hours and better work conditions for both local and foreign workers. The argument that FDWs can be better "protected" by living in ignores the fact that most of the abuse they experience takes place in the employer's home. Live-in and two-week rules may be part of the protective "encapsulation" of workers, but these policies, combined with passport confiscation, hefty debts workers incur to get a job, and maltreatment, are forms of control that can resemble forced labor and debt bondage. The system helps assure the agency and the employer that their "investment" in a worker fulfills the contractual agreement, but it often falls short of protecting the worker herself.[19]

MIGRATORY CONTROL AND SURVEILLANCE

A wide range of regulations and restrictions on multiple scales, including Indonesian and Hong Kong laws and local practices, and more subtle micro-level social practices, are linked to the care and control of migrant

19. Abuse of domestic workers and their disposability was especially evident during the February and March 2022 outbreak of COVID-19 in Hong Kong, when domestic workers who tested positive were locked out of their employers' flats and forced to take refuge in parks and at domestic shelters (Magramo 2022).

workers. Passports and visas are part of a "migration apparatus" of surveillance. Acquiring a passport is at the foundation of migratory control. Passports help construct and regulate national borders, determining who can cross borders and for how long (Feldman 2012; Torpey 2000).[20] Writings about surveillance often draw from Foucault's work on the disciplining forces of governmentality—especially Bentham's image of the panopticon and self-discipline in response to the all-seeing eye (Foucault 1977). Foucault's work has fueled a perspective on regimes of biopolitics that is largely negative, imposing ideals that "bring stigma, impose self-control, impose uniformity, and seduce individuals to embrace social ideals that are not necessarily in their own interest" (Borovoy and Zhang 2017, 2).

Mistrust and criticism of surveillance is characteristic of growing concerns about the protection of privacy and the ability to track our whereabouts and consumer practices through mobile phones, computers, Facebook, facial recognition technologies, and DNA testing, especially in the West. In Silicon Valley, California, some nannies' contracts stipulate that they must "hide phones, tablets, computers and TVs" from the children they look after to protect them from harmful media (Bowles 2018). In many parts of Asia, especially Singapore, surveillance is viewed more positively, as helping to ensure safety and law and order. But serious concerns echo older ones, such as post–World War II British objections to national identity cards, which were considered a threat to individual privacy and freedom (Agar 2001).

Despite widespread negative views of surveillance as a form of control, especially in the West, some scholars warn against tossing out the baby with the bathwater. Breckenridge and Szreter (2012) emphasize the importance of registration as a tool and a requirement for acquiring benefits (care), in contrast to the potential danger and destructiveness of surveillance. Similarly, Borovoy and Zhang (2017), building on Foucault's work, are careful not to automatically equate governmentality (or surveillance and control) with oppression, and to point instead to the potential

---

20. See Rodriguez (2010) and Tyner (2004) on the migration and recruitment industry in the Philippines.

benefits of registration in relation to recognition, care, and access to benefits (see also Ferguson 2012; Johnson et al. 2020; Lyon 2001).

As FDWs well know, certain forms of digital technology, especially smartphones, allow for greater communication and expressions of care—between workers, friends, and faraway family members. Yet phones, cameras, and new biometric technologies used in passports and other forms of identification can have a more ambivalent relationship to care and can facilitate greater control and surveillance by states, employers, and family members (Johnson and Lindquist 2020; Madianou and Miller 2012; McKay 2012, 2016). In a study of the video surveillance of FDWs by their employers in Hong Kong, Johnson et al. (2020) argue that domestic workers can use the surveillance intended to observe and control them in the workplace as a means to reclaim a degree of control or power over their work conditions. The study shows that domestic workers use their knowledge of such surveillance cameras to their own benefit. For example, one domestic worker had stayed up all night caring for a sleepless charge. When her employer criticized her for sleeping in too late in the morning, she urged them to look at the videocam to see that she worked all night. This illustrates the complicated relationship between care and control, as the employers' surveillance of the worker becomes a worker's tool for self-care in the context of migration.

Such research engages with the complex relationship between care and control. Foucault is often credited for critiques of surveillance and governmentality, but he noted the "fine lines between productive and repressive power" (Borovoy and Zhang 2017, 2). He recognized that "punitive measures are not simply 'negative' mechanisms that make it possible to repress, to prevent, to exclude, to eliminate; but they are linked to a whole series of positive and useful effects which it is their task to support" (Foucault 1977, 24). Foucault's ideas about governmentality, moreover, "shed light on the fine line between care or nurturance and control, repression, and manipulation" (Borovoy and Zhang 2017, 2). Yet I would argue that even a "fine line" between care and control warrants further attention, because it can be a thread that connects, as I think Foucault intended, rather than a line that divides them.

Care and control are interrelated—connected to nurturance, protection, repression, and coercion—and not easily divided (Constable 2021c;

Johnson et al. 2020). "A fine line" may begin to break down the binary, but it does not go far enough. It fails to adequately capture the complicated multiple entanglements. What one person experiences as care another can experience as control. Shifting views and situational experiences of care and control can change through the life cycle. What a child experiences as care, a teenager or adult might experience as control. A sixteen-year-old prospective domestic worker's trust in, appreciation of, and dependence on a PL can shift to anger and criticism a decade later when she faces the consequences of the aspal passport that she was assured was "no problem" and loses her job or goes to jail.

Obtaining a passport is a major precursor to obtaining an employment contract, "FDH visa," and Hong Kong identity card, all of which are tools of governmentality that function as means of surveillance and control but can also serve the more positive purpose of "registration" (Breckenridge and Szreter 2012). Ideally, they offer rights to care in the form of protection and benefits including a minimum salary, housing, food allowance, and medical benefits. A major challenge is how to implement and guarantee such rights when workers live and work in individual homes with hundreds of thousands of different employers (Baiocchi 2020). Mandatory live-in policies not only facilitate poorer Hong Kong residents' ability to hire FDWs, but allow employers to control workers' everyday lives and labor, justifying low wages for their undervalued feminized labor.

This chapter has shown that care and control of FDWs in Indonesia and in Hong Kong—including the care work they provide to their employers, the care they give to their own families as remittances, and the self-care among domestic workers—rely on obtaining passports. Passports provide a connection to processes of encapsulation and escort by the migratory infrastructure, which simultaneously promises care and protection of workers and serves to control them, target them, and profit from their labor. The process of migration begins with recruitment and obtaining the necessary documents. Chapter 4 builds on the entanglements of care and control through the stories of aspal passports that eventually created major problems for migrant workers.

4 Real and Fake

> When fakes are successful, even when they are revealed as
> fakes, there is clearly a relationship between both power
> and authority, and deception and authenticity, worth
> pursuing.
>
> Nils Bubandt (2009, 557)

> Identity photography is rooted in the state's faith in the
> camera's powers of indexical transcription and its own abil-
> ity to map appearances reliably onto "identity." During the
> New Order, the identity photograph became a widespread
> visual idiom for legitimate belonging within the state-
> authorized national community, but the state's fetishization
> of "proof" of identity also gave rise to doubt and irreverence
> about documentary truths.
>
> Karen Strassler (2010, 20–21)

In the era of "fake news," we often question what is real or true and what
is false or made up. *Real* gold is authentic or genuine, not counterfeit,
fake, or imitation. A *real* threat means that danger is significant. *Real* is
equated with truth and authenticity—like real name-brand products, as
opposed to imitations or reproductions, which might carry a specter of the
real thing but are not the same. *Fake* is equated with deception or fraud—
a "fake" hundred-dollar bill was presumably not issued by the U.S. Mint.
But Indonesian *aspal*—real but fake—passports and their logics beautifully complicate this seeming binary.

  As noted in chapter 1, the colloquial term *aspal* is a contraction of
the phrase *asli tapi palsu. Asli* means "authentic," "original," "real," or

"genuine"; *tapi* means "but"; *palsu,* as an adjective, means "fake," "phony," "false," or "counterfeit." As a noun, *palsu* can also mean "ghost," "haunting specter," or "illusion," which seems especially apt in the case of passport identities.[1] Aspal documents are simultaneously real *and* fake. They are authentic, or "real," government-produced documents. Unlike dollar bills produced on a copying machine, aspal passports are *not* counterfeit— although, given the slipperiness of language and translation, they are often spoken of as such. It might be tempting to simply assume that aspal passports contain "fake identities" and leave it at that. But that would ignore the contextual logic of aspal documents and the truths they produce. What makes you the person on your identity card or your passport, and is that who you really are?

As Cornelia Vismann wrote in her book on files and the law, "reality is what is found in files. Any attempt to weaken the file-world, therefore, is obliged to show that files and world do not coincide. . . . Which reality is strong enough to contradict files, if files alone pave the legally acceptable way to reality? . . . The law operates not *in mundo* but in the medium of literality; it believes only what is written—more precisely, what it has itself written down" (2008, 56–57). Similarly, Mahmoud Keshavarz suggests that passports have agency, as they come to define a "reality" or a "truth" even if they (or the photographs within them) do not (or no longer) resemble the "body" of the person they are said to document (2019, 37).[2] Aspal documents can thus define a reality.

Nils Bubandt and Karen Strassler, quoted in this chapter's epigraphs, both write about the specific Indonesian contexts of mistrust of government, during and after the New Order, and about the Indonesian state's "fetishization of 'proof' of identity" that "gave rise to doubt and irreverence about documentary truths" in Indonesia (Strassler 2010, 21). In an analysis of politically charged "fake letters" that circulated after the downfall of Suharto in 1998, Bubandt argues that the fake letters he studied were an

1. *Palsu* is also defined as "a mental representation of some haunting experience," with the synonyms "ghost, shade, spook, wraith, specter, spectre," at https://dictionary.lana .school/word/palsu (accessed May 26, 2021).

2. See Freeman (2011, 191–92) on how "fake documents" can be more successful than "real ones" in documenting kinship relations and facilitating migration to South Korea. See Friedman (2015) on Taiwan immigration bureaucrats' concerns about fake documents of mainland Chinese wives of local men.

"extension of a state" and ultimately "'proof' (*bukti*) of a fundamental inauthenticity and illegitimacy" (2009, 559). Such "fake-but-authentic documents" are read within a particularly Indonesian context in which there exists "a fundamental distrust of official forms of veracity and a deep sense that the state forms of authority that provide a measure of authenticity to the fake letters may themselves be counterfeit." Thus, "the social life of 'truthful fakes' emerges from their dual reality of both seeming fact and seeming fake" (2009, 561). Similar to the "specter" of reality that echoes the idea of photographic copies, and tied to technologies of "capture" (Chow 2012), fake letters and aspal documents involve "conspiratorial realities, and epistemic murk" that evoke "a flip side of technological innovation, rational governance, and the politics of transparency" (Bubandt 2009, 556). Aspal documents utilize official stamps, signatures, photographs, and insignia that conjure "a particular kind of empathy in a constellation that can be traced through Indonesian and global forms of political practice and imaginary" (2009, 556).

To focus on the entanglement of real and fake in seemingly official passports is not to argue that "anything goes" or that there are no fundamental truths or facts (in this era of questioning the truth value of science).[3] It is to recognize that the realities and truths produced by aspal documents are meaningful. Identities are produced through laws and through official identification, signatures, and documentation. State-produced identities are real to many migrant workers. If their documents are (mis)understood as fake outside of the world in which they were produced, they may face criminal prosecution, prison sentences, mounting debt, deportation, and loss of their right to work, as illustrated in the stories below. Fake news is based on fundamental lies, but aspal documents contain and produce real—and true—identities and lived experiences; their reality is without question. Aspal passports exist in a context where the distinction between real and fake collapses through Indonesian "semi-legal" practices and understandings of government and the "signatures of power" that constitute its authority over "truthful fakes."

---

3. Singapore passed legislation against "fake news" in 2020. Some criticized the law because new scientific ideas are often considered "fake" before they are accepted (e.g., the idea that Earth is round).

ASPAL PASSPORTS

Michele Ford and Lenore Lyons write insightfully about the "aspal route" in the early 2000s—the process of semi-legal "grey migration" set up and operated by local agents *and* the state, running between the Indonesian border region of the Riau Islands and the neighboring countries of Singapore and Malaysia. Aspal documents became an "established part of the migration process" for prospective migrant workers going to the Riau Islands and traveling from there to Singapore and Malaysia and back (Ford and Lyons 2011, 116). The remarkable thing, they write, is not that aspal documents and the aspal route exist, but rather "the high level of institutionalization and public acceptance of this alternative system" (2011, 116). Their interviews and observations document the knowledge, acceptance, and understanding of these processes in Riau Islands towns that are saturated with migration and travel-related enterprises. "The aspal route has become such an entrenched part of local life that most locals know how the system works and who to contact to obtain the necessary paperwork. By contrast, few understand the steps involved in the official process, or could explain how or why the aspal system is 'illegal' beyond the fact that it may involve payment of bribes to officials" (2011, 116).

The aspal route—or aspal elements of migration—is often significantly faster and less bureaucratic than the "official" one (Lindquist 2012; Ford and Lyons 2011). Although the aspal route to work in Malaysia through the Riau Islands was officially illegal, it was widely considered "licit"—that is, defined as wrong by law, but socially condoned and considered a widespread, reasonable, and valuable alternative (Ford and Lyons 2011). Many authors have contributed insights into the common and widespread recruitment practices in Indonesia, focusing especially on agencies, recruiters, or brokers involved in facilitating and profiting from men's and women's migrations to Malaysia and elsewhere.[4] In a study of the recruitment of men and women from Lombok, Lindquist writes, "Ideally, the potential migrant presents the necessary documents before the agency handles the rest of the paperwork together with the migrant," but in practice "labour

---

4. In addition to Ford and Lyons (2011), these include Killias (2018); Lindquist (2010, 2012, 2015, 2018a, 2018b); Palmer (2016); Rudnyckyj (2004); Spaan (1994).

recruitment does not follow this process. Migrants almost never approach the agency directly." Rather, they use a PL (*petugas lapangan*, field agent or labor recruiter) who "approaches—or is approached by—the migrant directly, either in the area where he or she lives or through other forms of social relations, such as friends, family or a local figure of authority" (Lindquist 2010, 125; see also Killias 2018; Silvey 2004).

Indonesian migrant workers I knew had all used recruitment agencies, and most relied on PLs or sub-PLs to obtain their documents and introduce them to the agency (some obtained passports after being taken to the agency, others beforehand). Some blurred the roles of PLs (recruiters) and PTs (*Perseroan Terbatas*, registered agencies), as all are "agents" of sorts, but there are differences. Recruitment agencies usually rely on many PLs who are, in a sense, freelancers or sponsors who recruit for multiple agencies, depending partly on the prospective migrants' expected destinations (Lindquist 2012). The typical pattern for recruiting Indonesian domestic workers is that agencies located in big cities, such as Jakarta, or Surabaya in East Java, have branch offices in smaller towns and cities. Since the agencies are not legally permitted to approach prospective recruits and lack ties to rural communities, they rely on PLs who may rely on sub-PLs to recruit workers from rural areas and villages. Sub-PLs make themselves available to prospective migrant workers from their own or neighboring villages and are paid for each recruit, usually by the PL who has the contacts with agencies and stands to earn a significant amount from the agency, especially for women recruits (Agustinanto and Davis 2003, 57; Killias 2018, ch. 3; Lindquist 2010, 2012). Local-level PLs are often trusted and respected neighbors, village leaders, or family friends who "help" young women and their families by facilitating their migrations, as they had in some cases done with their own family members (Davis 2003; Ford and Lyons 2011; Lindquist 2012, 2018a). Some PLs and sub-PLs may be unaware of "abuses or deception inflicted on the workers" and may not be directly "involved or assist in the falsification of documents" (Misra and Rosenberg 2003, 53). However, PLs often help prospective workers obtain at least the initial necessary identity and permission documents, and the physical examination, before they take them to the agency or agency training center, where other procedures are followed, and government permits, training, and passports are obtained (Killias 2018). The whole time, "migrants are often unaware that the informal brokers' practices, and therefore their own migrations, are illegal" (Silvey 2004, 257).

Ari (chapter 1) and Ratna (chapter 3) had aspal passports but managed to avoid renewal problems in Hong Kong, in Ari's case by returning home, and in Ratna's by obtaining aspal documents to match her passport and to renew it in Indonesia. This chapter recounts the passport stories of Dwi Murahati, Minarsih (Mina for short), and Ika and Anti, all of whom were much less fortunate and faced criminal charges in Hong Kong. Dwi's, Mina's, Ika's, and Anti's aspal passports were based on aspal documents from their PLs and agencies. Their stories illustrate the idea of "encapsulation and escort" (Lindquist 2018a) and the idea of "documentary citizenship," a phrase that captures the importance of documents "in acquiring citizenship, *whether documents are legal or not*" (Sadiq 2009, 8; my italics). Although these women's legal citizenship was never in question, their problems resemble those of people with unverified, unrecognized, or undocumented "citizenship claims" in developing parts of Asia. Indonesian women from poorer rural regions of Java who seek to migrate rarely have the documentation required to obtain passports and exercise the right to travel. The state "confers the right to have rights" through documents (Sadiq 2009, 16; Arendt 1968). The documentary nature of citizenship (aspal or not) is what establishes the need for legible identity documents to claim one's citizenship rights. Such documentation is often linked to corrupt practices in so-called developing states (Ford and Lyons 2011; Sadiq 2009; see also Freeman 2011; Friedman 2015). This corruption was highly normalized and licit, at least when many of the women I knew first acquired their aspal passports during the first decade of the 2000s. This notion of what is illegal but licit resembles the idea of "corruption" among lower-level government officials and civil servants in Indonesia, where helping family or community members may be considered "corrupt" (and legally wrong) but can also be justified, on the local level, as ethical and as helping the "little people" (Tidey 2016, 663; 2018).

Aspal documents are produced through collaboration between recruitment agencies, recruiters, and lower-level government bureaucrats, all of whom profit from them. Ultimately, however, it is the migrant workers— and not those who recruit them, who help them procure the aspal passports, and who profit most from their labor migrations—who face the greatest risks. A key question raised by Ford and Lyons is how "a system that has been established ostensibly to assist and protect hundreds of thousands of low-skilled workers in fact makes criminals out of those same workers and officials who try to help them" (2011, 121). Regardless of the intentions of PLs, agencies, or lower-level government officials to help or protect migrant workers, blame, responsibility, and criminality is placed on the workers, as the examples below will illustrate.

PASSPORT INCONSISTENCIES

I was fascinated by Indonesian passport "inconsistencies" before 2015 but did not know about aspal routes and documents. I knew that many passports, like Ari's, contained information that women openly said was not "real"—especially names and birth dates. I was also unaware that criticisms of Imigrasi and its corruption were circulating in Indonesia around the same time (chapter 5). Passport discrepancies appeared to be a widespread nonissue among Indonesian workers in Hong Kong, until 2015.

Indonesian women I interviewed in 2011 and 2012, when asked their names and ages, replied, "Do you want my real [*asli* or original] name or the one in my passport?" "My passport says I am twenty-seven but my real age is twenty-three." "My passport says I was born in 1981 but I was born in 1985." One woman said it was so difficult to get used to or respond to her new name that her first employers thought she was deaf or daydreaming all the time. Several former domestic workers who had married Hong Kong residents had sought advice from the Indonesian consulate (KJRI) regarding their documents. One woman recalled that the KJRI official in 2010 advised her to obtain aspal documents from Indonesia to match her current Hong Kong identity card and Indonesian passport and to simply accept that name and birth date from now on as her "real" ones. Many women used their "real" name in daily life, like a nickname, even if it did not match the passport.[5] This resembles having a formal or professional name and an informal one for everyday use. Chinese employers were well

---

5. In my earlier research, I asked women to choose pseudonyms. In some cases, they picked their "real" or original names.

aware of how different names are used in different contexts, so it likely would not have raised any issues with them (Watson 1986).

Since the 1990s, Filipino FDWs never casually volunteered to me any information about inconsistent names or birth dates, but some said they had heard of such cases. Filipino community leaders and NGO staff confirmed that similar passport inconsistencies existed among Filipinos, not only in Hong Kong but in other parts of Asia. Yet Filipino FDWs knew the legal risks and ramifications and treated their passport identities as their sole identities. They occasionally spoke about earlier times, before airports used fingerprints and biometrics, when there was a lot more passport flexibility.

By 2015 and 2016, the Indonesian situation had changed. Only women I already knew or whom I met through trusted friends talked openly about their aspal passports. They mentioned friends who had returned to Indonesia for fear of encountering problems in Hong Kong. Some could not renew their passports in Indonesia because of the prohibitive cost of aspal documents. Some did not return to Hong Kong at all, but went to work somewhere else, where they had no immigration history. Little news about the passport project or aspal documents made it to the Hong Kong media, but the topic received attention and criticism in the Indonesian media. The first time I said "aspal" in a conversation with Mr. P in 2016, he laughed uncomfortably, raised his eyebrows, and said, "Hmm, you know that term, do you?" His response was shaped by the link between aspal documents and state corruption in the post-Suharto Reformasi period, amid national goals of democratization and anticorruption.

Ford and Lyons describe an owner-operator of a "passport bureau" in the Riau Islands town of Tanjung Uban who "specialized in providing passports for domestic workers planning to go to Malaysia and Singapore" (2011, 114). He provided passports for licensed and unlicensed recruitment agencies. He "obtained 'real' passports . . . through a contact in the local immigration office who was able to supply him with official passports using local identity cards supplied to him by his clients" (2011, 115). One longtime domestic worker said that she had easily obtained identity cards (*Kartu Tanda Penduduk*, or *KTP*) in each of the provinces she had lived in, and at one point she held three of them. As a worker told Ford and Lyons, "In each place we can be a different person" (2011, 116). In the aspal passport cases I knew, names, birth dates, and places of origin varied. According to activist migrant workers, aspal passports are produced by corrupt and profit-driven brokers, agencies, and government bureaucrats. Many BMIs blamed the consulate or the recruitment agencies. Scholars have argued that at least some PLs' motives are complicated (not solely profit driven) and that not all PLs are aware of the illegality or the long-term risks for their recruits (Ford and Lyons 2011; Davis 2003; Lindquist 2010, 2012).

BIRTH CERTIFICATES AND OTHER ASPAL DOCUMENTS

Several documents are required to obtain an Indonesian passport, and even more are required to go abroad as a domestic worker. Few, if any, residents of poor regions of Indonesia would have them all before they plan to work abroad. They include the family card (*Kartu Keluarga,* or *KK*), birth certificate, school certificate for many domestic workers, KTP (more recently an e-KTP), and, for women, a letter of permission from the father or husband.[6] Many women have only school certificates. Experts widely consider the lack of birth documents as being at the root of many problems, ranging from human trafficking to children's health and education. Yet the lack of birth documents alone did not create the need for aspal documents in Indonesia. Also responsible is the complicated, expensive, time-consuming (and corrupt) bureaucratic process of obtaining official documents, especially for people who live far from areas where the requisite offices are located. As one migrant worker explained, "if one recruiter says to the woman [prospective recruit], 'I'll take care of the documents' and another says, 'You need to travel many hours to apply for these documents from this office and that office and wait a long time,' then which will you pick?" The recruiters, she explained, are in competition

---

6. A few do have access to the KK, a registry that lists place of residence, household head, family members, and relationships. The household head, the head of the neighborhood association (*ketua RT*), and the village head (*kapala desa*) should have copies.

with each other and will lose their recruits if they cannot "hook them" quickly.[7]

The lack of birth certificates in Indonesia—or "Indonesia's missing millions"—is widely known. In 2000, Indonesia had one of the world's lowest rates of birth registration, with approximately 70 percent of Indonesians unregistered (AIPJ 2013; Sadiq 2009, 92; Sumner 2015). Rural residence doubles people's chances of being unregistered (Ball, Butt, and Beazley 2017, 309). Few women I knew had birth certificates before planning to migrate. Reasons include being born not in a hospital but at home with local midwives. Some parents do not know how to register the birth, are deterred by the cost, or are unaware of the value of having a birth certificate. Others fear that government officials will demand bribes for the registration (Davis 2003, 121). Parents might think that there is no benefit, since documented children still have difficulty accessing benefits (Butt and Ball 2017, 2018; Ball et al. 2017). Birth registration is also complicated by whether the parents are married and whether it is a religious or civil marriage (both are legal in Indonesia, but religious marriage requires different documentation).

Costs and bureaucratic requirements to acquire official documents, like birth certificates, create a market for aspal papers. In poorer, remote rural regions of South and Southeast Asia, "the lack of birth registration and possession of identity documentation among rural and poor people fosters an environment of corruption and manipulation where illegal immigration, trafficking, and human smuggling become possible" (Sadiq 2009, 97; Butt and Ball 2017, 2018; Ball et al. 2017). Recruitment agents can take advantage of the lack of birth certificates to obtain them and to falsify the ages of women who are too young to work overseas. In West Kalimantan, "both legal and illegal agents use the immigration office in Entikong . . . to process fake passports for underage girls," and the immigration office issues them passports, "despite how young the girls look, because they cannot question an identity card issued by the district office" (Davis 2003, 121). The district office, in turn, said they were obligated to

7. They do this partly by giving them "shopping money," which adds to the debt (Constable 2014, 62; Lindquist 2012, 79; Palmer 2010).

issue an identity card "if the young girl has a letter of birth date from the head of the village," and "village heads often issue letters with false birth dates in order to help young girls migrate" (2003, 121).

Given the long-term normalizing and widespread acceptance of aspal documents as licit (but not legal) in Indonesia, "cleaning up" (*pemutihan*, literally "bleaching") the passport system can create serious problems for passport holders. The English terms *bleaching, cleaning,* and *correcting* were used interchangeably by consular staff to refer to correcting passport data, but women often referred to the KJRI's "bleaching." Interestingly, in Nunukan, a regency in East Kalimantan, from which many Indonesians go to work in Malaysia, *bleaching* took on "an additional meaning as authorities furnished intending migrant workers with new birth certificates, identity cards and passports that hid the fact that they were from another jurisdiction, in some cases also changing their personal details" (Palmer 2016, 128). In other words, consular officials in Hong Kong could be perceived as doing the same thing as brokers and agents who "bleached" or changed workers' identities in Indonesia. The consulate's "correcting" of passports seemed similar, until it was interpreted very differently by Hong Kong immigration officials. Renewing Indonesian aspal passports in Hong Kong was easy before passport holders had to come in person and have their passport data verified against the data in SIMKIM. If the data matched (or there was none in SIMKIM's database), the new passport data remained the same. If discrepancies were discovered, the applicant had to submit additional documentation attesting to their "true" identity. Serious problems occurred when the "new identity" differed from their prior Hong Kong identity.

The "nonevent" is also important. Since over 30 percent of BMIs likely had aspal passports, why were most passports renewed without a hitch? Why, eighteen months after the project began, had only thirty-five passports been corrected? Most such passports were probably renewed either because SIMKIM had no record or because the existing record was consistent (albeit aspal). In some cases, BMIs with inconsistencies returned home for good, like Ari and some of Ratna's friends. Others, like Ratna, went back to Indonesia (at great expense) to obtain aspal documents attesting to their "true identity" in order to renew their existing aspal passports. In such cases, *aspal* appears or becomes *asli*. Some BMIs who renewed their passports in Indonesia encountered problems with Hong

Kong immigration when they returned, because the passport no longer matched their Hong Kong identification. Others, like Dwi, Mina, Anti, and Ika, whose passports were "corrected" in Hong Kong, fared worst.

DWI MURAHATI, A.K.A. NUR AINI

Dwi worked in Malaysia for three years, then in Hong Kong for thirteen. She was known by her friends and peers and by consular staff as a kind, honest, well-meaning, very pious woman who regularly took part in consulate-sponsored community activities. Dwi was born in 1965 in a small village near Blitar, East Java. In 1995, her husband and eldest child were both killed in a tragic accident and Dwi was hospitalized and in a coma for days. She survived with a serious leg injury that made it difficult for her to work in the fields. She was the sole breadwinner for her two surviving daughters but struggled to support them. From 2000 to 2003, she worked as a domestic worker in Malaysia but was determined to go to Hong Kong, where she could earn more and thereby send her daughters to college. In a 2017 interview, after leaving prison in Hong Kong, she reported that her daughters "finished college and succeeded in working, even without a father figure" (Apakabar Online 2017).[8]

Dwi was one of thirteen Indonesian women migrant workers I knew of who, by mid-2016, were arrested, charged with immigration fraud, and given a prison sentence. She was fifty-one years old when she was convicted of giving "false representation" to an immigration officer and sentenced to five months in Lo Wu women's prison. Her sentence was initially longer but was reduced because she agreed to plead guilty at the advice of her court-appointed lawyer. In a 2017 news article titled "Nama Nur Aini, Berkah Sekaligus Petaka bagi Dwi Murahati" (The Name Nur Aini, Blessings and Disasters for Dwi Murahati), she described her passport ordeal (Apakabar Online 2017):[9]

8. Several sources exist regarding Dwi Murahati. Besides interviews with people who knew her, I read the consulate's mitigation letter for her. She is the subject of several Indonesian news reports, BMI blogs, and news releases (De-Yuan.com 2016) and was interviewed after her return to Indonesia (Apakabar Online 2017).

9. My translation.

The PT told me to use the name Nur Aini. That was 2003 when I first wanted to work in Hong Kong. I was taken to the Srengat immigration office (in Blitar) and told to change my name. I asked, "Why should I change my name?" He said, [I should] because I already had a passport with my real [*asli*] name. I had been to Malaysia with a passport with my real name. I didn't want to use the fake [*palsu*] name Nur Aini because I felt it was wrong. Finally, the immigration person was angry. So, I decided not to go instead of changing names.

The next day I got a call from the PT. I was scolded. But I wanted to stay home instead of changing names. The PT said, "You can stay home but you have to pay IDR 2.5 million [around US$270 at that time]." I [agreed to] pay and then I went back home. But *they did not return my original documents:* KK, KTP, marriage certificate, SMEA [middle school] diploma, certificate of husband's death, *all of my personal documents are held by the PT.*

Two months later, Dwi was in Blitar visiting her husband's tomb and she encountered someone from the agency by chance. He said, "Your passport is waiting."

I was confused. I didn't make a passport. Finally, out of curiosity, I went to the PT and asked about the passport. Uh, it says "Nur Aini," I protested. The [person at the] PT said, "If you want to work and get lots of money, use this passport. If you don't want it, you will get charged." I ask, "What charges?" and he said, "You have to pay Rp. 21 million [over US$2,500] to reimburse us for the cost of the passport and related things." I'm confused. I ask for time and am given two weeks, but still I could not get that kind of money. Finally, I was forced to go to Hong Kong.

At the Hong Kong agency, I asked for my name on the passport to be changed to my real name. I was scolded again by the agent. They said, "You are new. Don't do anything. *You have to use the data that you have now.*"

In Hong Kong I first worked in Sheung Shui. My passport was taken by either the agent or by my employer, I don't know. I never saw my passport for two years. After I finished that employment contract, I changed jobs and I also changed to a different agency.

At that time, I asked my friends about changing the name on my passport. Someone suggested asking the agency for help, but the agency couldn't help. Someone suggested asking the Indonesian Consulate General. I met with Bu Sendra Utami [former labor consul, deceased]. He said, "I can't, ma'am. You just use the data from the PT. Later, if you want to go home, then just change it [there]." It was 2006. After that I finally let it go. I never tried to change it again.

Until then [2015], the agency took care of the renewals. I never even filled out the forms. I just picked it up at the KJRI, thank you. They renewed the passport three times with the name Nur Aini. In 2015 there was a new regulation from KJRI for Immigration. To renew the passport, you had to come in and fill out the form yourself. You cannot have anyone else represent you. When I filled it out myself, I wrote my real name, Dwi Murahati, because I am used to writing it everywhere.

At the consulate, Dwi was photographed for biometric measurements and her fingerprints were collected. She was interviewed by a staff member and by a consular official.

I told the whole story. I said I felt it was wrong to write Nur Aini. At that time, Mr. Andry (Andry Indrady, Immigration Consul) suggested that I use my real name, Dwi Murahati. Mr. Andry said, "This is a document cleaning [*pemutihan*] program from the Indonesian government. Everything wrong will be fixed, not only Ms. Dwi's, but all of them." Mr. Andry patted my shoulder and assured me, "There will be no prison for Ms. Dwi."

On October 4, 2015, my [new] passport was made with the name Dwi Murahati. I went to Hong Kong Immigration because I needed to replace my HKID [HK identity card] because it says Nur Aini. From there it all starts. . . . In November I was called to the HK immigration office in Kowloon Bay, interrogated, and required to pay [HK$1,000] bail.

On March 5, 2016, I finally had the first court hearing in Shatin. During the interrogation and the trial, it felt like living but not [being] alive, [being] dead but not [having] died ["hidup tapi enggak hidup, mati tapi enggak mati"]. After three court hearings, I was finally sent to prison. On June 3, 2016, I entered Lo Wu prison.

If not for the new Indonesian passport renewal process in Hong Kong in 2015, Dwi Murahati would not have gone to prison. It was her fourth passport renewal in Hong Kong, and the three renewals handled by the Hong Kong agency were problem free. All they needed to submit, at that time, was the renewal form, the current passport, and a copy of her Hong Kong identity card.

Absentmindedly, or not wanting to be dishonest, she wrote "Dwi Murahati," the name that she had always considered her real (*asli*) name, rather than Nur Aini, the name she had been assigned. One consular staff person I talked to blamed Dwi for her troubles, not for having an aspal passport, but for foolishly acknowledging it. Had she not done so, there would have been no problem, since SIMKIM had no evidence of any other identity. The problem, in other words, was that Dwi was honest, so her passport *had to be* corrected. This raises questions about the real goal of the project. Was it in fact to correct passports or to produce an *impression* that they were all reliable and true? Dwi had tried to "correct" the passport several times years earlier, but the Hong Kong agency and the consulate had said to "let it go." In 2015, she trusted the consulate's goals and their assurances.

PASSPORT VICTIMS

Dwi's case was interesting because she possessed the required documents to obtain a passport with her original name and had used them to get her passport to go to Malaysia (most likely with the help of a PL). Yet the agency and their contact at the immigration office insisted that she use the name Nur Aini, probably because it was available. Many agencies typically did not return the original identity documents to their owners, perhaps to force them to pay to retrieve them or to deter them from using a different agency in the future.

Like others, Dwi was criminalized although the agency had pressured her to use aspal documents and she had tried to change them. Migrant worker activists refer to those with aspal documents (or palsu data) as "passport victims," asserting that they are victims of recruitment agencies and corrupt agents and of the consulate's mishandling of the situation. Activists argue that the consulate (and the Indonesian government) places increasing responsibility on the agencies for the protection of workers, but that the agencies are often responsible for trafficking workers. Dwi's case shows that repaying the recruitment costs was impossible unless she went to work in Hong Kong. She was thus forced or coerced to migrate with a new name and aspal passport.

Dwi's case illustrates the problems with the passport renewal project in Hong Kong. The consulate's advice and their "mitigation" letters for women who were being investigated by Hong Kong immigration made the situation worse. Dwi and others were given one sort of letter to give to

Hong Kong immigration after their passports were corrected, when they applied for a new HK identity card. The letter described the passport "corrections" (but made no mention of the role of agencies or PLs). Another letter, signed by the consul general, was intended to reduce women's prison sentences. One such letter, addressed to the Hong Kong court magistrate, advocated "lenience" in sentencing a BMI who was charged with making false representation to immigration officials. At Mina's hearing, described below, her court-appointed duty lawyer read the letter and refused to use it because, in his words, it "could only hurt" her case, as it presumed her guilt and appeared to document it. Some of the boilerplate text, written in English, was shared with me by domestic workers:

> Ms. ___ was born to a rural peasant family in the little village of ___. Her family was poor. . . . Ms. ___ has a very rudimentary education and . . . we understand that she *must have been in a state of confusion* when she made the declaration to the immigration officer. . . .
>
> We strongly believe Ms. ___ *did not have the planning or [fore]thought to use a passport in a different date of birth, and given her naïve and simple mind, she most regrettably committed the Index Offense out of momentary folly* [my italics].

The letter condescendingly describes the domestic worker as rural, uneducated, naive, and simpleminded. Unable to read English, most women obediently presented the letter to immigration as instructed. The letters documented passport discrepancies and corrections and thus constituted evidence in women's immigration interviews. The consulate claimed that their letter and Dwi's admission of guilt resulted in her reduced sentence, but the letter did more harm than good, and the consulate's critics saw Dwi and others like her as innocent "passport victims." The real culprits, BMIs argued, were the agencies (PTs), the recruiters (PLs), and corrupt immigration officials in Indonesia who produced aspal documents and made money from migrant workers. Those guilty parties faced no penalties at all.

From the Hong Kong government's perspective, the legally relevant point was that Dwi knew that the name on her passport was not hers, yet she entered and left Hong Kong with it, thus misrepresenting herself to immigration, so she was guilty of immigration fraud. The "how and why" of aspal documents in Indonesia and the role of other, more powerful players were legally irrelevant to them. Because the consular officials advised Dwi to "tell the truth" in her immigration interview, she admitted that she knew that "Nur Aini" was not her real name, which constituted evidence and admission of immigration fraud. That Dwi had tried to correct her passport on several occasions (but eventually gave up) helped to reduce her sentence but did not mitigate the judge's finding of guilt.

Advocate lawyers and legal advisors to the activist BMIs criticized the court's logic and the consulate's advice. Attorney Melville Boase, a long-time supporter of migrant workers, said that the consulate should have simply sent a very short letter saying "this is now her true legal identity" and "it replaces the previous one." Since the state is responsible for documenting a person's identity, he explained, it must be assumed that any document they provide (as opposed to one that is forged by someone else) *is* the "true identity." Government-produced passports produce legal identity. The idea of a "false identity" or "fake document" is wrong, he explained. One's name can change through one's lifetime, as do many Hong Kong Chinese and Indonesian names.[10] Echoing Vismann's ideas about files, one does not in fact "know" one's birth date. We may assume that we know, but the date is based on documents. The state officially establishes one's name and birth date through its documentation. Mr. Boase explained that even the Queen of England has two birth dates. The British royals' website says that if a royal's birthday is in the winter (when the weather is bad), they often have a second one that is celebrated during the summer.[11]

Birth dates and names in Indonesia can vary in village, family, and school records or in memory—especially when children's naming ceremonies, and the actual registration, can take place long after the birth.[12] Several KKs that I looked at listed both parents' and older siblings' birth dates as "January 1." Lindquist observed an agency where most birth dates

10. Indonesian fiction reflects the logic and ease with which Indonesians change their names, including those who sought to escape their past, such as "Saman" in the novel of the same name (Utami 2005).

11. Queen Elizabeth II celebrates two birthdays, her actual birthday on April 21 and her official birthday on (usually) the second Saturday in June. See www.royal.uk/queens-birthday (accessed July 7, 2020).

12. On Javanese naming patterns, single names, and related problems, see Kuipers and Askuri (2017), Widodo and Saddhono (2012), and Widodo (2014).

were listed as "December 31" (2010, 121), indicating that many people do not have records of their exact birth dates. Mr. Boase and others pointed out that names can be legally changed, and he advised women to accept the name and birth date in their passports or to legally establish a different one. He advised BMIs to say, "This is my identity as given to me by the government in my passport," or "My government put it in my passport so it must be true." Such advice, or to say as little as possible in consular or immigration interviews, was passed along by activists and their networks.

As in Dwi's case, however, the consulate gave different advice. The women who had the most problems followed the consulate's advice and answered the Hong Kong immigration officials' questions rather than saying, "I prefer not to answer." Without evidence of fraud, cases were dismissed (as in Ika's case below). By summer 2016, however, it was already too late for Mina.

MINARSIH

Minarsih, or Mina, is an Indonesian woman in her late thirties. I met and interviewed her in June and July 2016, attended her trial, and heard her speak at a migrant worker forum (chapter 2). I talked to people who knew her and read about her in the *Jakarta Post*, in which—to spare her elderly parents the knowledge of her situation and the stress and shame it would cause for them—she adopted the pseudonym also used here (Salim 2016b; JBMI 2016a, 2016b).

Mina was well known in the Indonesian community as a "passport victim," on trial for passport fraud because of the passport project. She had applied for a new passport in fall 2015, was charged by immigration in February 2016, and was scheduled for a second hearing at which her sentencing was expected in June 2016. Certain that she would go to jail, Mina took out a loan and arranged for the money to be sent monthly to her elderly parents and young daughter. She told them she would be traveling abroad with her employers and not to worry if she was out of touch for many months.

My first interview with Mina took place in Victoria Park on June 12, 2016 (about a week before her court date), in the pouring rain on a steamy hot Sunday. She was overcome with emotion at times during the interview but insisted that we continue, sometimes asking our mutual friend Ayu to take over. Ayu was a migrant worker and activist, a member of ATKI (a JBMI affiliate), which was on the front lines of assisting workers with passport problems. We sat under our umbrellas as I listened to Mina's story. To help her parents, Mina first went to work in Singapore in 1999.

> The agency helped me to make the first passport. I just bring my ID . . . and family card and have the birth certificate. All are original [*asli*], and high school certificate and they make it. They tell me they will just put together my name and my father's name and they say, "No problem." And I say, "Okay," because I don't know. The agency combined his name "X" and mine and put it together [X Minasarih] even though I have only the one name on my birth certificate.
>
> There was no problem then. I go to Singapore. I finished my contract— two years. Then renew my contract and finish that contract and go back to Indonesia after four years in Singapore. In 2003, I want to go to Hong Kong. I go to the agency, and the same as the first time I bring my family card, family certificate, my ID card, and school certificate and they made a new passport.
>
> I went to the passport office with the PL just for taking the photo and then go. The photo is just "Okay, sit down, look at camera. Okay, done." No interview or anything. I never filled in any forms. Everything, the agency does it. Someone does it for me. I never even signed anything. If you ask anything, the agent gets angry. You cannot ask. You must follow the group.
>
> The agency only gives me the passport one hour before I go on the plane, and I see the birth year is different. I say, "What happened, it's different?"
>
> "No problem," they say.
>
> "But why is my birth year changed? I'm already twenty-four, twenty-five. Why is my birth date not the same [as in my first passport]?"
>
> They say, "Oh, go away! Don't ask anymore! If you cancel you must pay HK$21,000." It means that if I delay going to Hong Kong, I must pay the agency. My name is the same as [in my] old passport. Just the date has changed.

Mina arrived in Hong Kong in 2003. For the first seven months of her contract, as with most new hires, most of her salary was deducted to (re) pay the recruitment fees. The agency then renewed her passport in 2006. Her photograph was new, but her passport data was the same. She returned to Indonesia in 2009, gave birth to her daughter, and returned to Hong Kong in 2010. The agency renewed her passport again. In 2015 the renewal procedure changed, and she went to the consulate in person.

> I filled in the form with the same data as my last passport and with my Hong Kong ID [year of birth 1978]. Then I queue up at the KJRI. The staff called me, and she asked, "Which one is your real document?" because the KJRI has [a record in SIMKIM of] two documents. The first is from when I went to Singapore [and read 1979], and the one for Hong Kong [that read 1978]. I answered that the true one is 1979. The passport says 1978 but the corrected date [in an endorsement attached to the passport] is 1979. Then the staff says, "Do you have any proof that this [1979] is the correct one?" I have a school certificate and family certificate, but I know the Hong Kong government is very strong and strict. I have a friend who has [similar] problems and I know they will have problems with me [so she hesitated]. Then the staff says, "We are [all] Indonesian people. We want to help you. Believe me."

Recalling the consular staff member's appeal to Mina's trust as a fellow Indonesian, Mina's voice cracked, and her eyes filled with tears. Ayu continued for her:

> The staff said the KJRI will change the document, but Mina said no, because in Hong Kong now this is difficult, and Hong Kong is very strict. The staff said, "No, we are the KJRI. *We came here from Indonesia to take care of you all here.* So, believe me. Just believe us. In [HK] immigration you just say what is true, and you can say that the agency changed your document, not you. You can say it truly." But she [Mina] is still against it. She said, "No, no, no." And by then her visa is almost done [expired]. But the KJRI staff said they don't want to make the new passport like her current one [i.e., they want to change it]. So, Mina didn't want to change the documents from the ones she came to Hong Kong [with], but the KJRI insists.

When Mina told the staff member that she did not want them to alter her year of birth, she was taken to a higher consular official's office. He said, "Believe me, we are here to take care of you"—and, like other consular staff and officials at the time, he likely believed what he said. Like Dwi, Mina was told, "You are never going to jail. No problem, no problem, you are going to be okay!" Since her visa was nearly expired, she felt she had no choice but to do as the consulate advised. Like many BMIs, Mina grew up thinking that those "above" her (in terms of class, education, and authority) must be obeyed and respected, even when her instincts told her otherwise.

Mina received her new passport and was instructed to renew her visa at the nearby immigration office in Wanchai. Before going, she talked to a friend with similar problems who said the consulate had given her a letter to bring to immigration. Mina returned to the consulate and asked for a letter. They would provide it only if she had a birth certificate documenting her 1979 birth date, so she obtained it from Indonesia. "I go to KJRI again with my birth certificate and then I get the letter. Then, November 2015, last year, I go with my employer to Wanchai, but immigration cannot take me because the quota is full. The next day, the last day before my visa expires, I go again. Then, after two weeks immigration called me and said to go to Wanchai. They take all my documents, passport, ID, and all that, and then give me a letter that says to report to immigration in Kowloon Bay in two days."

The Kowloon Bay immigration office is where interviews or interrogations are conducted with people suspected of immigration wrongdoing. As Ayu said, "In Kowloon Bay, they do the interrogation. They show her the letter from Indonesian consulate, and they said it shows she is doing crime." Mina continues: "After the interrogation, the interview, they ask me to pay HK$1,000 bail. Then finally at seven p.m. the interrogation is finished. After that, every twenty-eight days I must report to immigration. In February, they take me to the fifth floor, and they read some charges." Ayu adds, "They read the charges and her rights, and they say she has broken the law." Mina goes on: "February is the first hearing in Shatin. Before I go, I asked the KJRI for advice, but they do not respond. I try to leave a message, but no response. I leave a WhatsApp and no response. I call many times. No response. I tell my employer and my employer tried to call many times and no response. After that I meet Sringatin [chairperson of IMWU and JBMI] before the hearing." Ayu continues:

> Sringatin gives Mina some advice. She always comes to her hearing and follows up with her. And then Sring also tried to call the Indonesian consul and then the consulate finally tried to help her. Well, the KJRI just came to the hearing [but gave] no advice. The consul staff says, "Tell the truth about what happened with the agency." But that made her situation, you know, much worse. It is better to say nothing. Advice from KJRI makes things

worse in this case. The [Hong Kong] lawyer helped her, but because of the letter from the KJRI and the advice from the KJRI, it's worse for her—so only fifty-fifty she can win.

Mina interjects, "Ninety-nine percent chance I will lose." She sighs and looks at Ayu.

I ask Mina whether she will plead guilty. Ayu replies for her. "Until now, 'not guilty.' Because the lawyer says [to her], 'Because of your government's letter your situation is worse. They didn't help you. So, you are the only one to help you. But we cannot give advice that can help you to win.'"

"So, you will know what happens on June X," I say. Mina replies, crying,

I have no choice. I have one daughter, five years old, and I am a single parent. I also take care of my mother and father because they are so old. My employer wants to write a letter and give it to immigration and wants to tell them I am working for them and I am very good for them and the family. Because they also know it is not me who did it. It is the agency. They know. And they need me. They also know nobody [at the KJRI] answered. Nobody gives us the information [I need]. The employer is good. The government is not good. . . . I worked for my employer for five and a half years.

Ayu adds, "Our government cannot help us survive, they cannot take care of us." Mina continues: "They make promises, but when we have problems they just don't care. We want to work here because we want to survive. But the government forces us to go back like that. I want to work here for my family, for my daughter, because I am single parent. My daughter does not have a father. I am working for them and so she can study— just [to make] enough money to study and to buy milk."

Like many others, Mina expressed a strong sense of betrayal, disappointment, and anger toward the Indonesian consulate and "our government." She stressed that they did not help her, did not respond or protect her, falsely reassured her, and made her situation worse. Like Dwi, she did not tell her family. "I don't tell them; I don't know how to tell them because my mother and father are too old. My father will get sick if he knows. They depend on me."

The *Jakarta Post* article (Salim 2016b), published shortly before Mina's June court hearing in which the final judgment and sentence were expected, quotes Mina as saying, "May God grant me a miracle" and "God willing, I will humbly endure [the consequences] because there is no other choice." At the hearing in Shatin that I attended, Mina was prepared to plead guilty (upon her lawyer's earlier advice) in the hope of reducing her sentence. Meanwhile, her employers had hired another worker and told Mina to leave, so she threw out or gave away most of her possessions and moved to a domestic workers' shelter. She carried two small bags with her to court, things she could take to prison. She was covered head to toe in a black hijab, teary-eyed but calm.

Mina's Hong Kong government–assigned duty lawyer told her supporters before the court session that he had received the "mitigation letter" from the consul general and that it could only hurt Mina's case since it presumed a guilty charge, so he would not use it. To Mina's surprise, he advised her to plead not guilty. During the morning court session, Mina's lawyer first argued that her statement from the earlier immigration interview should be tossed out because it was made under pressure from the translator, who had advised her to "admit everything" to get a lenient sentence. Also, the transcript of the caution statement (the notification of her right to remain silent) and interview was not properly endorsed, thus putting its validity into question. Second, he argued that Mina had, for a long time, accepted that her true year of birth must be 1978, but that when the consulate said it was fraudulent and that 1979 was the true date, she assumed they must be right and that she was mistaken. He presented additional evidence that she was born in 1978. To Mina and her supporters' surprise, he aimed to discredit her *new* passport.

That afternoon, more questions were raised about Mina's immigration interview transcript, and her lawyer argued that her earlier statements should be dismissed. He demonstrated that her 2010 passport listed her birth year as 1979 but contained a certified endorsement correcting it to 1978. Her 2015 passport, issued by the consulate, removed the endorsement and read 1979. He argued that from 2003 to 2015, Mina had believed that the correct year was 1978 until the consul said, in 2015, that it was 1979. Finally, the judge scheduled another hearing for August, two months later.

Mina's lawyer explained to us after the hearing that the "caution statement" provided as evidence by the prosecution was not properly certified, which raised procedural issues in addition to the substantive ones about the changes and endorsement of the two dates. He was more optimistic, but Mina was again in limbo. Not legally permitted to work, she could not support her family, and remained at the domestic worker shelter. In late August, to Mina's surprise and relief, her case was dismissed due to lack of proper certification of the caution statement (JBMI 2016c; Salim 2016b). She exclaimed, "Thank God. Finally, this long and tiring struggle yielded sweet results."

Mina's case is especially interesting, not only because of its ultimate dismissal, but because of what it says about how identities are produced by the legal process. Not only do government offices produce documents and identities, but the "truth" of an identity (even a "false" one) can be produced through legal processes. Legal rules and procedures create their own legitimacy, such that Mina's lawyer could establish the "truth" of her identity through the legal narrative he created about her justifiable confusion.

IKA AND ANTI

Ika and Anti faced similar passport issues but handled them differently. Ika refused to follow the Indonesian consulate's advice, successfully renewed her visa, and got a new Hong Kong identity card to match her new passport, after a ten-month ordeal. Anti followed the consulate's instructions to "tell the truth" in her Hong Kong immigration interview and ultimately received a six-month prison sentence. Their stories are based on personal interviews, supplemented by conversations with activists. I also heard Ika speak at a migrant worker information session in Victoria Park. Anti's story is based on conversations during and after our first meeting at Shatin court, where we both attended Mina's June 2016 hearing.

Ika was introduced to me as someone who had "survived" the "changes to her identity" in her passport. When I met her, she was still fuming from her ordeal and eager to talk about her experience. She felt she had beaten the system and was simultaneously relieved and furious at the consulate.

Ika had first gone to work in Singapore in 2002. "I was very young. My parents were poor farmers, so I didn't want to go to school and decided to go to work. [At that time] I only had one document, my birth certificate, and it said 1985. I had no other ones, so the PL made them for me." The Indonesian legal age was eighteen and Ika was seventeen, so the PL arranged to make her three years older, changing her year of birth to 1982 and also changing her birth month. When the legal age for Indonesian migrant domestic workers was raised to twenty-one in 2004, the agency renewed her passport in Singapore and left the data alone. After two more years, Ika returned to Indonesia, planning to again return to Singapore. "But the agency will not let me go back to Singapore with the aspal passport, so they change it to the real [data, 1985], and I go back [to Singapore] for two more years." The same year that Indonesia raised the age to twenty-one, Singapore raised it to twenty-three. According to an Indonesian labor attaché in Singapore, "it was clear to all that higher age limits simply resulted in greater demand for aspal documents in Indonesia" (Palmer 2016, 161).

In 2010, Ika decided to go to work in Hong Kong.

> The agency arranges it all and makes the fakes. They make a new birth certificate, family card, school certificate, so I go to Hong Kong this time with the fake passport [reading 1982] again. I am working in Hong Kong, then the passport expires again, and in 2015 I apply to renew it in the KJRI. They say 1985 is revealed [by SIMKIM] and I explain [to KJRI] that the agency did it [originally] because I was too young to go. I had a Hong Kong identity card that said 1982. I wanted to change it to 1985, so I showed them all the documents with 1985.
>
> It was September 2015 when I apply to KJRI for a new passport. They issue the new passport [reading 1985] but said that the change in the passport and the documents will mean problems with the Hong Kong government. They say, "I will give you a letter to take to apply for the new Hong Kong identity card." But Hong Kong immigration department won't accept it. "The documents are not right," they say. They send me from Wanchai to the Cheung Sha Wan Immigration Office near Kowloon City to apply for the identity card [before I can get the new visa]. I need my birth certificate, my family card, Indonesian identity card [KTP]—to all be translated into English—and a letter from the consulate to prove to them it is my identity.
>
> The whole thing took more than ten months. I have to explain to my employer why I have so many appointments and so much waiting. I say it is not my fault. They come with me to immigration and try to help. They are very good Chinese employers.

I was sent to Kowloon Bay for an interview, to see if I am guilty or not. I told the KJRI about it and I told them I will not go alone, that they need to go with me. I blame Consul P. I said to him [later], "Why change my passport?" I am very angry. "You didn't explain that I can go to prison!" One staff member from the consulate came with me. The consul said he would come, but he didn't. Another person came, but Hong Kong immigration won't let them in to the interview. I fight, argue, and they still won't let him in; he can only wait in the waiting room. I say, "You have to let him in, he is responsible for me!" I fight, fight, fight, but they won't let him in, only in the waiting room. When I finish, he is [already] gone. The KJRI staff doesn't even wait for me!

The interviewer says, "Why [did you] bring the Indonesian consul here?" "Because they changed my passport! It is not what I want! It's what—if you want to sue me, sue my country! I have no one to look out for me. I have to protect myself." I cannot just answer [their questions]. You can't say what you want when you want to! You can only answer their questions. Then they say [the caution statement], "You have the right not to answer," but then they ask my date of birth. I say, "I won't answer so don't ask me."

I don't answer their questions. They ask: "This is your identity?" "When do you know it is wrong?" "Yes, this is my identity." "Why didn't you report it?" "I don't know why I didn't report it. I don't know. I don't know what to do and I am all alone," I say. "I did not make the application, only the agency did. Indonesian immigration made the passport, not me." I tried to make [HK] immigration understand. "It is wrong because of the agency and the consulate. I can prove it with my documents." I say, "Ask the consulate, they make the changes." I want to use English and I ask them to use English, but they say I must use the Indonesian translator because I am Indonesian. The translator is worse. I can't understand what is said.

They wrote eight pages of [transcription] notes in four hours. It took a long time, but there was not much talk. They took my fingerprints and other things. In the end they make me pay HK$500 bail. They say to come back in two weeks. In two weeks, the case is closed.

Kowloon Bay is a problem. I tell people, "You must be careful there." The consulate is also a problem. I just said, "I don't know" when they asked me [questions]. I blame Consul P. "Why don't you have an agreement with the Hong Kong government?" I asked him.

In *Suara* [Indonesian newspaper in Hong Kong] they say everyone who has a corrected passport will have their bill paid by KJRI. But that isn't true! I sent the bill [for the bail and document translation] and they don't pay it! The documents had to be translated to English, and I paid the consulate to translate them, HK$250 per document—HK$1,000. They must endorse them. *Suara* does not say how the consulate made things much worse. My

friends did not have help and they give a little bit [of a] wrong answer, a little bit only. You tell the truth, and you will be arrested! So angry, laahh. The
consulate said they want to interview me [now]. KJRI does not do *their* job!

Ika was furious that the consulate did not help her but wanted *her* to
help *them.* I was impressed by her confidence and assertiveness. I asked
about her education and how she knew how to respond to immigration's
questions. She replied, to my surprise, that she only had a primary school
education.

I just always have [had] to protect myself. No one else will! Nobody teaches
me. I teach myself. If I need the consul now, I just go in! I wait, I try to go,
and then I just go in when I see him. Why wait until the TKI [domestic
worker] comes in? Why not contact her? You just wait for her to come and
you don't help?! You just wait for her to report! They talk about amnesty
[for people with false data] but we work honestly! But Dwi and people who
work here go to jail!

Now, I am very happy! I got my [HK] ID card last week. I went to
Cheung Sha Wan [immigration office] and got it. But I told you, I needed
my documents and to get them translated. My KTP expired and KJRI
rejected it because it had expired! They refused to translate the expired
KTP! So, I fight, fight, fight with them. They are not professional! I get in so
many fights with them. [I say], "You can translate it and say it is expired!"
They just need to say it is an Indonesian ID card! I need it! I must have it.

Before her passport ordeal, Ika had considered changing employers.
Afterward, because her employer was so supportive throughout her
ordeal, she changed her mind. In the several cases I followed, it was clear
that employers' involvement could make a difference. Once BMIs are
under investigation they are not permitted to work, so some employers
terminate their contracts. Most employers did not hire a lawyer, but those
who did, or who interceded with immigration early on, often saw results.
The consulate paid more attention to employers who advocated for the
BMI and appreciated their advocacy. Hong Kong immigration was more
receptive to the concerns of employers who accompanied a BMI to the
immigration office than to the BMI alone.

My boss did so much fighting with immigration to help me! Hong Kong
bosses will hire a lawyer to help if they like you. . . . I will work for the same

employer for a new contract. I might have looked for another job, but my boss is so good, I cannot look for another one. He did so many things to try to help. I am very thankful.

I will take a holiday after this contract ends, and . . . see my mother. I love my mother very much. I was so stressed for a long time. Very down. I told my mother—if I don't call you it is because I have to go overseas with my boss. I give them money [in advance] in case I cannot work and have to go to jail. I give them money.

I am not a criminal. I win the case and now can work peacefully. The consul sends me messages and wants to have me come and be interviewed by him. I am glad to explain to the girls [BMI] how [to fight], but I am too tired to talk to the consulate.

I will work maybe four more years, then will go home. I will already be thirty-five then. I am building my house. I'm starting a business with chickens. I'll take care of the chickens. I'll be with my parents. I'll get married. I'll have babies and look after the children. After I go back, I won't work abroad again.

Anti's passport story begins in 2003. Her father died and her family faced financial difficulties, so she wanted to work abroad to support her mother and siblings. She had a middle school certificate and a letter of permission. Both listed her year of birth as 1986, making her seventeen. She met with the PL, who arranged to get the other necessary documents and a passport from a local immigration office. Anti was unaware that her year of birth would be changed to 1984, making her nineteen, legally old enough to work abroad. Anti went to Hong Kong and was issued a corresponding identity card. Her employment contracts and documents all carried the same birth date for twelve years. Her passport was renewed in 2008, still listing her year of birth as 1984, but one of the pages had a handwritten endorsement and an Indonesian immigration office stamp that corrected the *day* of her birth, in which two digits were reversed, likely a typographical error. With the endorsement, it matched her earlier passports. Her next passport, issued in 2011, had the same data. Only after 2015 did she encounter problems.

Anti's passports had all listed 1984 as her birth year, but SIMKIM revealed a "duplicate identity" and flagged her case, either because her KTP listed her birth year as 1986 or because her earlier passport had been amended (with the birthday correction). When the consular official interviewed her, Anti said 1986 was her correct birth year. The official added an endorsement to her not-yet-expired passport, changing 1984 to 1986. Then, two days before her visa expired (but with one more year left on her employment contract), they issued her a new passport reading 1986. The consulate gave Anti a sealed envelope and said, "Give this to Hong Kong immigration and you will have no problems." She rushed to the eighth floor of the immigration office in Wanchai with her new passport. The staff sent her to the third floor, where they gave her an appointment in Kowloon Bay, telling her to be sure to bring her old and new passports and identity cards with her. Anti had no idea what was going on but trusted that the consulate's letter would help and that she would be fine.

Anti's December 2015 interview at the Kowloon Bay immigration office was very stressful and lasted from morning until night. In addition to the consulate's letter, the immigration officials had copies of her Hong Kong identity card from 2003 with the 1984 date, her 2008 and 2011 passports with the 1984 date, and the recent 2015 endorsement amending the date to 1986. They leveled six charges against her: three for using a "false travel document" upon her arrival in Hong Kong in 2008, 2011, and 2015, and another three for "making a false representation" to immigration in 2008, 2011, and 2015. Having been told by the consular staff to "just tell the truth and you will be fine," Anti admitted that she knew the date was incorrect and that she had not tried to change it. She tearfully admitted her guilt. Following her immigration interview (still thinking the truth would help), she wrote a heartfelt letter to the director of immigration to apologize. She wrote, "From X-X-2003 until X-X-2015 I know the birthday on the HKID card is not corrected. I am sorry I [was] still telling everyone my birthday is X-X-1984."

With her oral and written admissions of guilt, without proper legal guidance, without help from activists or an employer to advocate for her, and without Ika's disarming outrage or Mina's clever lawyer, Anti's case was hopeless. By the time she connected with the activists, all they could do was comfort her. In summer 2016, Anti received a six-month prison sentence. Had she said nothing, or had she understood that she could refuse to answer immigration's questions, charges would likely have been dismissed.

REAL AND FAKE DOCUMENTS

Few of the women I knew had birth certificates or identity cards when they planned to work abroad. Only a few married or divorced women had them, but many who did were given aspal passports anyway. Women usually relied on PLs to procure the required documents needed to get a passport, and to "escort and encapsulate" them through the process. If they later migrated to different locations, they might use a different agency, increasing the chances of inconsistent documents, since agencies often kept the original documents. Women needed their father's or husband's permission to work abroad. If they opposed it or she wanted to go without their knowledge, the PL could get papers from another region with a different identity. Riris ran away from her abusive husband and lived with a friend in Surabaya when she decided to go to Hong Kong: "They gave me new parents, new name, new birthday and a new place of origin." Gita, who left Sumatra because her fiancé was forced to marry another woman, had a similar story. Both left without their real father's or husband's signature.

Unlike Ari (chapter 1), who was aware of using her sister's name and birth date, most women were unaware of age requirements and often learned about their "new" names and/or birth dates after the passport was produced. Some learned of them at training camps in Java, while awaiting job placement. Agents and staff told them to memorize their information before leaving Indonesia. Some learned of new names or birth dates at the passport issuing office; like Ratna, many learned of them at the airport. Women who discovered the changes and complained were threatened (like Dwi and Mina) with further debt that was impossible to repay if they did not go abroad. Most Indonesian women go into significant debt to work abroad in any case, paying up to seven months' wages to cover recruitment "costs" including training, medical examinations, pocket-money advances, local transportation, and documents.

Several factors contribute to the likelihood of irregularities in passport data. Most women I knew had only an elementary or middle school "certificate," and if they were underage they could not use it to get other documents. Several women were fifteen or sixteen when they went to work in Singapore with aspal passports that made them older. Besides the lack of birth certificates, many Indonesians have only one name; those who went to work in the Middle East needed two, so their fathers' names were added (as in Mina's and Ratna's cases). This could create inconsistencies between their various identity documents (e.g., passport, identity card, family card). Since domestic workers previously received only three-year passports, changing agencies and employers for a second contract could lead to changes and typographical errors. Rural recruits often accepted such practices and changes, especially since PLs were often well-regarded community members, and agents had seeming power over them. Passports were usually held by the Indonesian agency, then the Hong Kong employer or agency, at least until their loans were paid off, so women often paid little attention to them.

Initially, before they realized the problems that could ensue, some women were relieved to travel with their "real data." Luckily, for most, due to decentralized passport issuing offices, inefficiency, and SIMKIM's incomplete database, many aspal passports were not flagged. Women who had worked in Hong Kong longer, had worked in another country first, were under twenty-one when the age limit was raised in 2004, or had e-KTPs (electronic national identity cards) were most likely to have problems. Younger women and new arrivals were likely safe if they had only ever held one passport identity (whether aspal or not). Surveys mentioned earlier estimated that 30 percent or more of BMIs' passports had non-original names and/or birth dates. My qualitative data since the 1990s suggests that over a third of Indonesian FDWs, and close to half of the migrant mothers I interviewed, had names and/or birth dates altered.

It makes sense that teenagers like Anti were made older to meet the legal age, but why were women who were of age made older or younger (Constable 2007; Yu 2017)? Ratna speculated that PLs and agents need to recruit women quickly or they risk losing them to other agencies. They also face monetary losses if a worker changes her mind or decides to use a different agency or PL (Lindquist 2012). This is tied to women's "encapsulation" throughout the process. They are not permitted to leave training centers and are required to have birth control injections to protect the agency's investment (Killias 2018; Lindquist 2012). A pregnant or runaway recruit represents a serious financial loss for the agency. Given the competition between agencies (and between PLs) for recruits, they sometimes use passports that are already available (even if they do not match the recruit's documents) or that can be most quickly produced. It can be to agencies' advantage to "change" aspects of a woman's data, as it increases her dependency on them. Such changes ultimately require more aspal documents and those, in turn, mean more money for those who produce them, including the brokers and the corrupt immigration staff.

Nur had not yet obtained a passport when the recruitment agent said that she was "very lucky" because another young woman whose passport was ready, and whose job had been arranged in Hong Kong, had a sudden change of plans. The agency told Nur she could either leave immediately for Hong Kong with the woman's passport and documents or wait several months for her passport and the required training. The agent told Nur she looked "enough like" the woman to pass for her and said, "Don't worry, this happens all the time." Afraid to make the agent angry and fearful of having to pay more if she delayed, Nur reluctantly agreed to travel with a different name, birth date, and photo.

Throughout 2015 and 2016, Indonesian workers learned about the new passport renewal process in Hong Kong through personal networks and BMI activist groups. Dwi's and Mina's cases were cautionary tales. Hundreds or thousands of women faced similar problems. At first, if their passports were flagged and the women could produce identity papers to confirm their identities, a new passport was issued with their "true identity." If they could not provide documentation, they were pressured to go home with their still valid passport, or they received a one-way travel document. Leaving without finishing the contract created problems for women with families to support and debts to pay, and for employers who relied on their labor.

In the past, aspal documents and passports could be cheaper than "extortion passports" (*paspor pungli; pungli* is short for *pungutan liar*, illegal fees) or those obtained through official channels that demanded bribes of up to three times the official cost (Hamim 2003, 145). By 2017, the Indonesian consul general in Hong Kong, Tri Tharyat, voiced a hard-line stance, saying there would be "more crackdowns on agencies in Indonesia" that "change the passports of prospective workers" (Yu 2017), and indeed, 190 Jakarta agencies were suspended for using "illegal procedures" in 2017. He also said KJRI was monitoring the forty-one cases of

BMIs suspected of using "forged passports" (Yu 2017). Yet the Hong Kong government showed no concern about the Indonesian context in which aspal passports were produced, or about the PLs, the agencies that procured the passports, or the immigration officials who produced them. From the Hong Kong government's perspective, the passport holders had broken Hong Kong law by "knowingly" committing immigration fraud.

PASSPORT STORIES

The passport stories recounted above took place while BMIs were facing passport problems in Hong Kong, often many years after they first obtained aspal documents. Their stories reflect their growing awareness of their aspal documents being (re)defined as criminal and that they — and not the agencies, recruiters, and immigration staff who produced the documents—would be blamed. BMIs sometimes claimed not to know about their aspal passports. Their stories must be understood within a context where the rug was pulled out from under them. They had long been told, by respected people who literally "authorized" their passports, that they had nothing to worry about. But now they could face prison. Their anger, frustration, and sense of betrayal were directed mainly at the consulate (or "our government") for failing to protect them, but they also blamed the agencies and, to a lesser degree, the recruiters.

The era of SIMKIM and of aspal passports represents a clash between two entangled and coexisting processes. One involves licit and widely accepted aspal documents that utilize extralegal (but accessible) means of obtaining documents for would-be migrant workers in impoverished rural and marginal regions with few other options. The other involves the push for supposedly reliable biometric passports and echoes global standards and measures of modernity and anticorruption. While Indonesian consular officials sought to produce a *transparan, akuntabel, dan responsif* (transparent, accountable, and responsive) system, it came at the expense of the well-being of BMIs with recognizably aspal passports. Such concerns about reliable passports and "good governance" are tied to the entanglements of state and society discussed in the next chapter.

5 State and Society

States may portray themselves as generic and immensely powerful in their own right, but in reality they are intimately embedded in their societies in historically contingent ways.

Gerry van Klinken and Joshua Barker (2009, 1–2)

The more I work on the state, the more skeptical I become of the theories of "the state" seen as some kind of singular and unified entity. Problems of coordination, scale, and representation make it hard for me to imagine what "the state" is and what "it" can do and why "it" appears so unproblematic to so many people including to officials.

Akhil Gupta et al. (2015, 588)

Anthropologists often define the *state* as a complex society with centralized authority that controls many facets of people's lives and is associated with a specific territory and identity. Max Weber's famous definition is often cited: "A state is a human community that (successfully) claims a monopoly of the legitimate use of physical force within a given territory" (1958, 78). *Societies*, for anthropologists, refers to various types and scales of interdependent communities and their political and social structures and relations. States are relatively large-scale, complex, and hierarchical societies that are associated with a territory and borders, an identity as a nation or nation-state, and a form of rule and governance that can be more or less democratic or authoritarian.

From an anthropological perspective, and that of some other social scientists, a state-society (or state–civil society) binary overlooks significant "blurred boundaries" or entanglements and reflects notions "that were forged on the anvil of European history" (Gupta 1995, 393). Despite scholarly criticism, this binary persists in the popular imagination, in official state discourses, and in scholarship that aims to analytically separate the "state" (and politics) from other sectors or aspects of society. It perpetuates the *idea* of a separation between the state as a political institution and the wider society that includes its members, citizens, the public, and non-governmental groups. The state is considered autonomous, dominant, separate from (and above) the society that "it" seeks to control. This image of the state as separate from society evokes older binaries of ruler and ruled, powerful and powerless, and of the state as a homogeneous and autonomous institution. Critics of the state-society binary point to the inability of an "autonomous state" to effectively account for conflict, change, the processes of rule, and differences between particular "states" (Gupta 1995; Migdal 2001; Wang 2021).

As noted in this chapter's first epigraph, the Indonesian state is socially and historically embedded in society, not separate from it (Klinken and Barker 2009, 1–2).[1] Klinken and Barker pay attention to "the processes of interaction and the techniques of rule," criticize the idea that the Indonesian state is homogeneous or a "coherent entity with a will of its own," and approach it instead as a "site of struggle among many competing groups" (2009, 2). Criticizing depictions of the Indonesian New Order state as an "authoritarian state," or as a "failed state," and building on the work of Joel Migdal, they argue for a "state-in-society" approach in which Indonesia, like all states, is embedded in society in "historically contingent ways" (2009, 4–5; Migdal 2001). Barker's own research shows how roles and relations of security, crime, policing, protection, and governance reach the smallest social units (including slum neighborhoods) and echo colonial patterns that blur boundaries between state and society (Barker 1999).

John Torpey's book on passports also examines the state-society relationship. He criticizes "the traditional (and unmistakably sexual) imagery of societies being 'penetrated' by the state" and takes the approach to task

1. For a study of the divisions and conflicts among Indonesian state institutions (e.g., Ministry of Manpower and BNP2TKI), their varied influence on the governance and implementation of international labor migration in migrant-sending regions of Indonesia, and their conflicting views on trafficking, see Palmer (2012, 2016).

for insufficiently addressing *how* states establish and maintain relationships "between themselves and their subjects" (2000, 10). He proposes instead the idea of the state's "embrace" of society, since "states *must* embrace society *in order to* penetrate them effectively" (linking *embrace* linguistically to the German term for "registration"), which better evokes forms of governmentality (2000, 11). Torpey argues that the passport, as a form of registration, illustrates the state's embrace of society. I agree that passports are forms of registration and governmentality, but I think that both *penetration* and *embrace* have drawbacks connected with the presumption of a state-society separation that maintains the binary. Metaphors of penetration and embrace reveal a construction of the state as separate from society, not embedded in or entangled with it. Both metaphors evoke an image of the state as an autonomous (masculine or patriarchal) agent that seeks to dominate a (feminized) society that can merely receive (or resist) the embrace (or penetration).

Despite my criticism, I agree that passports are a means of asserting the state's monopoly of legitimate control over the right and privilege of travel in and out of the country; and passports can provide the holder with an offer of aid and succor (Torpey 2000, 159–60). The laissez-passer statement inside many passports reflects their "partial origins in diplomatic practice" (2000, 160). The Indonesian passport, beginning in 2014, reads in Indonesian and in English, "The Government of the Republic of Indonesia requests to all whom it may concern to allow the bearer to pass freely without . . . hindrance and afford him/her such assistance and protection." Through the passport, as an instrument of the state, Torpey argues that the traveler receives the state's embrace and thus becomes a "quasi-diplomatic"—a "citizen-member" of the nation-state (2000, 160).

Indonesian passports, like other passports, document the state's citizen subjects and offer care and protection. They also create, assert, represent, and produce an image of the state and its authority. But rather than reading passports as indicative of the state's embrace of its citizens, I ask how—*on the ground*—such documentary practices take place and illustrate *both* government processes *and* the limits and contestations of the state's power to control mobility. The limits and contestations of state power are illustrated in Matthew Hull's study of paper files and documents in Pakistan. Hull challenges the Pakistani state-society divide by arguing that state governance is a "material practice" and that colonial and bureaucratic writing practices that were designed to *separate* government from society became, in practice, a means for people to participate in government by producing written forms, petitions, letters, and other written materials that brought together both government and nongovernment actors (Hull 2012). Akhil Gupta has argued, in his work on corruption in India, that "the state" is an ideological field that is discursively constructed in "multiple mediated contexts" by differently positioned people and bureaucrats (who make it difficult to distinguish between state and civil society) and by the press and in public culture (1995, 377, 393). Notably, he argues that discourses on corruption in India are mechanisms through which the Indian state is produced. These authors, moreover, point to the importance of the historical and cultural specificity of the state in relation to everyday practices.

Building on such work, this chapter examines the "image" (Migdal 2001) or the "symbolic representation" (Gupta 1995) of the Indonesian state in official state documents, especially the passport. "Official" government-produced images of the Indonesian state stress its autonomy, unity, and dominance, but this "image" is but a part of a wider, shifting entanglement of contradictory and competing discourses. Passport- and migration-related practices and processes of rule also show how the state (as an institution of governance) is deeply entangled in—and limited by—both governmental and other organizations and agencies with different and competing interests. Coalitions of competing interests in the migration industry, among various government offices and actors, migration and recruitment or placement agencies, and migrant workers and their communities respond, participate in, resist, and struggle to shape state actions and governance. Contemporary passports (aspal or not) reveal the knotted entanglements of the competing interests of migrant labor, capital, and governance in Indonesia. Ideas about "the state"—in relation to migration—are entangled with older, pre-independence patterns of escort and encapsulation, labor mobility, and social divisions and hierarchies of governance and indirect rule.

A history of Indonesian passports, travel documents, mobility, and migration has yet to be written. However, this chapter examines the Indonesian government's *self-representation* of the state-society relationship through the passport as a state symbol and technique of rule. I focus on Imigrasi (the Directorate General of Immigration) because of its unique role in relation to the passport project, but it is important to recognize that it is but one of several government agencies or ministries that deals with migration.[2] Below, I seek to complicate Imigrasi's and consular officials' version of the state-society dynamic in relation to migration and the passport. The chapter's overarching goal is to criticize the state-society binary and to show how the state is entangled with society, an argument that continues in the next chapter. The passport—in its modern and its earlier forms—is not *only* a tool used by modern states to rule or to make its citizens legible (Scott 1998; Scott, Tehranian, and Mathias 2002). It is a tool that also produces "imagined" nation-states (and relations among them) and depicts them *as though* they are separate from society (Anderson 1983). Yet, in practice, they are not.

The second goal is to point to some connections between post-independence passports, Imigrasi and Indonesian labor migration, and earlier historical patterns. The few sources on Indonesian passport and Imigrasi history point to official and unofficial entanglements of government actors with capital, specifically the migration industry. The third goal is to show how Indonesian passports, as independence-era material symbols of national identity, equality, and unity, simultaneously (re)produce and facilitate patterns of inequality and difference among the country's citizens. The introduction of biometric technologies and new passports, despite official rhetoric, illustrates the persistence of inequalities on both the individual and national levels, within a contemporary global arena where nation-states compete for status through passport rankings and ratings. The final, related goal is to indicate how passports and older documents of mobility are entangled not only with gender, regional, and class inequalities, but with both current and historical humanist debates regarding free and unfree labor. The existence of "modern passports" in

---

2. For other government offices and divisions involved in migration, see Ananta (2009) and Palmer (2012, 2016). The Foreign Ministry (which controls embassies and consulates), the Ministry of Manpower (involved with labor and worker issues), and the BNP2TKI and its successor, established to oversee the "Placement and Protection of Indonesian Overseas Migrant Workers," are most relevant.

the post–World War II era is *not* indicative of a linear historical progression from unfree to free mobility, or from slavery to free labor.

Today's Indonesian migrant labor—from plantation workers in Malaysia to domestic workers in Hong Kong—raises questions about "forced" labor and the limits of freedom and consent. The concerns of labor migrant activists and their allies today about coercion and consent are remarkably similar to those of both nineteenth-century abolitionists and advocates for free trade (including free labor). The debt bondage of domestic workers described in previous chapters bears a resemblance to early forms of forced labor, bonded servitude, and indenture. So does the labor recruitment industry, which still has strong support from (and influence over) government actors and recruiters, and brokers or smugglers and traffickers, who promote labor migration and profit from it. The passport is thus a tool not simply for "protecting" passport holders, as the cases of "passport victims" illustrate, but for protecting the industry.

Below, I first return to a conversation with Mr. P in 2016, then take a close look at the Indonesian passport itself, before turning to Imigrasi's official history and the views of one patriotic critic. Despite the state-society divide expressed in Imigrasi's own mini-historical account, M. Alvi Syahrin's blog, and Hong Kong consular officials' comments, government (or state) actors are clearly part of and entangled with society. Passports are tools of surveillance and governmentality that produce and promote the image of a unified nation-state; simultaneously, they produce *unequal* citizenship that echoes earlier patterns of migration. The government perspectives expressed below could be read as illustrating the state-society divide, but a closer look reveals embeddedness and entanglements. The later parts of the chapter turn to Indonesian labor mobility in relation to wider passport histories, the Dutch East India Company, and the Dutch East Indies colonial period.

PASSPORT PROTECTION AND BIOMETRICS

Consular officials I spoke with associated the passport project and SIMKIM with Indonesia's rising global status as a modern nation-state. They claimed that biometric technology would strengthen Indonesia's passports and its global standing, and they were committed to making the immigration system transparent, accountable, and responsive (*transparan, akuntabel, dan responsif*; Republika 2013). They talked about the consulate's and Imigrasi's duty to "protect" its citizens and defend the nation-state's borders. SIMKIM would help detect and correct passport "irregularities." Accurate passports, Mr. P explained, are essential for security, including the fights against terrorism and trafficking, as both trafficking victims and terrorists are known to use falsified documents. His goals echoed the language of development and Western ideas about good and bad states. Good ones—in the 1990s language of the World Bank and the International Monetary Fund (IMF)—promote transparency, accountability, and anticorruption, whereas bad ones are undemocratic and corrupt (Tidey 2018, 672). Fighting corruption, collusion, and cronyism was a central goal of the post–Suharto Era Reformasi (Reform Era). Reliable passports are part of becoming a good, modern state.

Because passports and passport identities should be reliable and accurate, they (and their predecessors) have historically been subject to evernewer technologies designed to thwart forgery or falsification (Cole 2002; Feldman 2012). Indonesian consular and immigration officials used the words *protect* and *protection* (a masculine form of care) in relation to the new passports, but not *control* or *surveillance*. The government was responsible for protection, so it was necessary for migrant workers to be properly identified. Mr. P spoke of "keeping track of" and "protecting" Indonesian workers but did not specify how "registration" can otherwise facilitate individuals' access to benefits (Breckenridge and Szreter 2012). Given Indonesian consulates' small staffs and tight budgets, much of the responsibility for the care of migrant workers who faced problems with their employers was shifted to employment agencies. As workers rightfully complained, agencies did not care about BMIs, but only about employers (the customers) and about their profits.

The new e-passports with data embedded in microchips were usually too expensive for BMIs, who normally opted for the cheapest option, the twenty-four-page regular passport. The new regular Indonesian passports issued to BMIs in Hong Kong nonetheless recorded their biometric data and entered it into the SIMKIM database. Consular officials asserted that this would create a more reliable system for documenting identities and mobility and supporting national and international security goals. When I asked how these new, more expensive passports would benefit BMIs, I was told that they were good for five years—rather than the older TKI passports' three—and thus required less time and expense for renewal.[3] Mr. P responded by asking if I had heard the recent tragic stories about BMIs who died while working abroad. In one case, a worker taken illegally to Shenzhen (the Chinese mainland city adjoining Hong Kong) for work had died after falling from a high-rise building under suspicious circumstances. Another woman's body had recently been recovered from the Hong Kong harbor. Stories spread of seriously injured or dead workers— like that of severely abused BMI Erwiana Sulistyaningsih in 2013, which was broadcast globally—and the Indonesian government was criticized for its inability to protect its citizens abroad. Members of the Indonesian public expressed outrage, demanding better care of women migrants. Some questioned whether women should work abroad at all. Societal pressure to "protect" young women was a primary factor in the increase, in 2004, of the minimum age for BMIs who work for "individual employers" (i.e., as domestic workers in private homes), from eighteen to twenty-one (Law no. 39/2004). This form of protection of young women evokes the Indonesian "family principle" (*azas kekeluargaan*)—that social and professional superiors (*Bapak* and *Ibu*; literally, "father" and "mother") should "look after" citizens and those of lower status and rank, or *anak* (literally, "children") (Tidey 2018, 669, 674).

Biometric data, including ten fingerprints, facial measurements, and iris scans, were required from everyone who applied for new Indonesian passports in Hong Kong, beginning in 2015. Mr. P said this would help identify women's bodies so that family members could be notified of the deaths of daughters, sisters, or wives. If the passport has inaccurate information—a false name, place of origin, or birth date—"how can we notify their families of their death?" This disturbed me, given his comments about migrant "protection." Identifying a corpse is not about protecting living persons, but about the circulation of and accounting for

3. TKI passports were free the first time, but subsequently required payment. Some workers acquired the more convenient regular five-year passports long before the three-year passports were phased out.

bodies—part of the wider process of "escort" of workers' bodies back home to their families.

Mr. P cited the fourth objective of the Global Compact on Migration, to "ensure that all migrants have proof of legal identity and adequate documentation," and echoed views of global authorities such as the International Organization for Migration (IOM 2005) and the United Nations' Global Compact for Safe, Orderly and Regular Migration (UN 2018). Indonesia was adopting global standards in which accurate passports play a key role in promoting safe migration and combating trafficking and terrorism.[4]

Public statements about Imigrasi and the Ministry of Law and Human Rights echoed similar points: SIMKIM would produce an efficient and transparent system for Indonesian emigration and immigration, increase care and safety (because it can track people's movements in and out of the country), protect citizens (including BMIs) from trafficking, and help fight terrorism. It would place Indonesia alongside its more advanced modern neighbors, Malaysia and Singapore—countries that have long issued electronic biometric passports and already had national e-identity systems (Malaysia was the very first country to adopt biometric passports, in 1998).

In 2019, Indonesia indeed rose in various rankings and was honored to receive the Public Key Directory (PKD) certification from the International Civil Aviation Organization (ICAO) for its biometric passports (Pascu 2019). The PKD is an ICAO database that allows for easy information exchange and passport authentication at borders of the sixty-nine certified countries (out of over 150 countries with biometric passports). Additionally, Indonesia planned to increase the number of offices issuing biometric passports and was piloting the use of polycarbonate instead of laminated paper, a security innovation designed to make passports difficult to forge or counterfeit.[5]

---

4. However, even biometric passport security is not failproof (see Nash 2021).

5. Other ways to securitize passports include encoded data on security threads that require special machine readers, chemical sensitizers that react to tampering, tactile features and fluorescent fibers in the paper and the bindings that reveal tampering, holograms, UV dull paper, watermarks, optically variable and unique inks, anti-scan and Guilloche patterns, special type fonts, and encoded data that is invisible to the naked eye or visible only in UV light. These security features make passports extremely difficult to reproduce, scan, or copy. See Passport Index n.d.

SIMKIM and the biometric passport project were thus held in high regard by officials. These innovations addressed long-standing problems within Imigrasi that had been criticized by the Indonesian public, including the inefficiency, inaccuracy, and corruption associated with obtaining passports. In 2015 and 2016, Mr. P did not say explicitly (perhaps he assumed I knew, or didn't want to air dirty laundry) that it was also intended to help eradicate passport KKN (*korupsi, kolusi, nepotisme:* corruption, collusion, and nepotism), in which immigration staff in Indonesia, as well as PLs and others in the recruitment industry, were implicated. I listened intently to Mr. P's and others' optimism about the new passports and migrant worker protection. Meanwhile, the downside of the passport project was becoming increasingly evident to migrant workers.

At the consulate, I saw the small room with the equipment for biometric photographs, measurements, iris scans, and fingerprints (from all ten fingers); another where interviews were conducted; and the office of Mr. P's colleague where the SIMKIM data system computer was housed, and where piles of passports and papers were stacked everywhere. They pointed to images on the computer screen and on detailed printouts that illustrated the inconsistencies between women's current and previous passports, especially errors in their names and birth dates, and sometimes marital status and places of origin or residence, all of which were referred to in English as "false" or "fake" (*palsu*) data. The printouts showed the two passport photos and the associated data, line by line below them. One case revealed two different people's photographs side by side with the same data. Another case showed two photographs of the same person (at different ages) with a different name, birth date, and place of origin. Handwritten amendments (or corrections) were often suspect. Some were manually and improperly entered and pasted into the passport. Amendments should carry a "stamp" of authenticity from local government offices, but stamps could be manufactured or obtained by corrupt Indonesian recruitment agents. Some amendments were likely legitimate efforts to update the marital status or to correct errors (as in Anti's case in chapter 4). Before 2015, and later in more remote regions, BMIs' passports were renewed at regional passport issuing offices that lacked connections to the national or SIMKIM database. The database had many omissions, and it no doubt contained some errors and irregularities, especially names, birth dates, or places of origin. Yet the goal was ostensibly to produce transparency and accountability, to care for and protect workers, and to be a good and modern state.

PASSPORT MATERIALITY

On the surface, passports can be read as telling a simple story of the state-society divide. They are official tools of governance and symbols of an independent and unified nation-state. Below, I tell the Indonesian passport version of that story and then question it, showing how state and society—and passports—are entangled with one another and non-government actors, within society as well as with wider international contexts. Examined closely, passports figuratively, literally, and historically reflect, create, and (re)produce social divisions, inequalities, and exclusions both within and between nation-states (Keshavarz 2019; McKeown 2008; Mongia 1999).

Modern passports (those of the postwar period) have been described as a "palpable manifestation of an idealized global order" and a "tangible link between the two main sources of modern identity: the individual and the state" (McKeown 2008, 1). It is no coincidence that modern passports all resemble each other on the surface, as they comply with international standards recommended by the ICAO (Keshavarz 2019, 28–29; Walters and Vanderlip 2015, 7–8).[6] Passport sizes, dimensions, contents, and their ever-changing technologies are similar, which reflects the relationship of nation-states to a larger global system. Yet within a common template, the colors, languages, and insignia differ. A nation-state's passports reflect its unique history, symbols, and national identities.

The soon-to-be-expired Indonesian passports, stacked in tall piles at the consulate in 2015, were the standard size, with dark green covers and gold emblems on the front cover. Without looking closely, I couldn't tell which were the older *Paspor TKI*, specifically for migrant workers, valid for only three years and now being phased out. The new regular passports are the same size and shape, but their covers are more of a turquoise green

---

6. For illustrations of the similarities, visit Passport Index n.d.

Figure 4 (left). Standard Indonesian passport, 2018. Photo credit: N. Constable.

Figure 5 (right). The Garuda Pancasila, Indonesia's national emblem. Photo credit: Flickr, public domain.

or teal and they are valid for five years. Green and turquoise green, colors commonly displayed on Indonesian mosques, carry a cultural resonance associated with Islam, Indonesia's dominant religion. The new regular passports, like the old ones, identify migrant workers by their destinations, by stickers naming the recruitment agency, and by their visas.

The visual elements of the old and new passports' front covers are mostly the same. At the top, large gold letters read "REPUBLIK INDONESIA."[7] Near the bottom, in a smaller typeface, is "PASPOR" in Indonesian (and below it, in smaller letters, "PASSPORT" in English). Like most passports, the national emblem is at the center of the front cover. Adopted in the 1950s, the Garuda Pancasila is a mythical bird resembling an eagle that embodies the nation-state's ideals (see figures 4 and 5).[8] Evoking Indonesia's diverse religious and multicultural history in Javanese and Balinese mythology, and in ancient Indonesian Buddhist

7. The previous version also said "Republic of Indonesia" in English below.
8. The new passport's Garuda is slightly larger than the old one's. *Garuda* is also the name of Indonesia's national airline.

and Hindu temple sculptures (predating European contact by centuries), the Garuda is the vehicle of the Hindu god Vishnu. The Garuda carries a shield at its chest and a banner in its talons. On the shield are Indonesia's five national principles, or Pancasila (literally, *panca*, "five," *sila*, "principles"). The banner displays the national motto, "Bhinneka Tunggal Ika" (unity in diversity), which refers to the cultural, linguistic, and religious diversity of the widely spread population of the thousands of islands that Indonesia has comprised since its independence in 1945.[9] This diversity and idealized national history is symbolized by the elements of the shield.

The Garuda Pancasila on the passport is gold, but printed representations often depict the shield's upper left and lower right quarters in red, and the upper right and the lower left quarters in white, the colors of the Indonesian flag. Black at the center of the shield signifies nature, and the black line across the middle represents the equator crossing the Indonesian archipelago's regions of Sumatra, Kalimantan, Sulawesi, and Halmahera (in North Maluku). The golden star in the center of the shield symbolizes the first principle of the Pancasila, the *belief in one supreme God*, and the star's five points represent the nation's five official religions: Islam, Christianity, Hinduism, Confucianism, and Buddhism.

Each quarter of the shield contains an image. The lower right depicts a chain with round and square links signifying women (round) and men (square); it also represents an unbroken generational chain, and the second principle, *justice and humanity*. The upper right depicts the *beringin* (banyan tree, *Ficus benjamina*) and represents the third principle, *unity;* the outreaching tree roots signify the far-flung connectedness of the many cultures of the Republic. The upper left depicts the head of a *banteng* (wild bull) and represents the fourth principle, *democracy* and leadership by representation. The lower left depicts *padi dan kapas*, rice and cotton: the lower stem, holding seventeen grains of rice, and the branch above it, holding five cotton balls, together symbolize the human need for sustenance and livelihood, representing the fifth principle, *social justice*. Every detail is significant: seventeen feathers on each of the Garuda's wings,

9. Indonesia has the world's fourth largest population (260 million). The geographically dispersed lands of linguistically, religiously, and culturally diverse groups were claimed as Dutch East Indies territories, which later became Indonesia.

seventeen grains of the rice *padi*, eight tail feathers below the banner, nineteen tail feathers below the shield, and forty-five neck feathers. Together they represent the date of Indonesia's proclaimed national independence: the seventeenth day of the eighth month, August 17, 1945.[10] The passport thus documents the birth of the Indonesian nation-state (from the former Dutch East Indies).

The new, turquoise green, regular passports are but one of several types of official Indonesian passports. In addition to the phased-out Paspor TKI, there were special passports issued to people going on the hajj pilgrimage to Mecca, until 2009, when they were disallowed by the Saudi government. The price of regular passports depends on whether they have twenty-four or forty-eight pages and whether they are e-passports. There are also *Paspor Diplomatik* (Diplomatic Passports) with black covers, and *Paspor Dinas* (Service Passports) with blue covers, which distinguish people who are traveling for diplomatic or other government purposes. Another type of passport (or travel document) is the *Surat Perjalanan Laksana Paspor* (SPLP), or "Travel Document in Lieu of Passport" (literally, "travel letter like a passport"), used by people without passports (or with lost, stolen, or expired passports) to travel to or from Indonesia. BMIs in Hong Kong who were not permitted to renew their passports were given an SPLP to return home. Another type of one-way travel document, *Paspor Orang Asing*, is given to stateless people or foreigners without passports. And *Surat Perjalanan Linas Batas* (Cross-Border Travel Passes) are issued to Indonesians who live in border regions for crossing into bordering countries. Such passports produce and reflect social differences, distinguishing important officials and civil servants from "regular" travelers, migrant workers, hajj travelers, and local border residents.

Modern official passports explicitly express both state identity (citizenship) *and* individual identity and thus contrast with early travel documents and forms of identification (McKeown 2008; Torpey 2000). In his historical study of Asian migration and borders, Adam McKeown argues that after the abolition of slavery and the prohibition of indenture, identities and forms of identification that were "produced by evasive and potentially exploitative social networks [were] inherently unreliable" because

10. The Dutch officially gave up sovereignty in 1949.

they could be indicative of "unfree" labor or false identities. "A new identity had to be generated. . . . The very construction of the 'free' migrants was the act of ripping them out of the previous social networks and reinserting them into the new matrices" of bureaucratic state power (McKeown 2008, 12). While the methods and technologies of identification have developed and shifted over the centuries, the modern passport, McKeown argues, repositions the individual in relation to the nation-state and is intended to be more reliable. The assumption was that *state bureaucracies* would produce reliable identification and not exploit migrants like the exploitative and profit-driven "previous social networks."

Indonesian aspal passports in the late twentieth and twenty-first centuries show that former social networks and older patterns of "encapsulation and escort" (described in the previous chapter) are still highly relevant in Indonesia. BMIs' stories show how personal networks and connections, coercion and questionable consent, and forms of corruption, collusion, and nepotism exist at various levels of the recruitment process. The production of passports (aspal or not) is often profit-driven, but can also be justified as helping the "little people," which entangles ideas about "the ethical [helping 'family'] and the right thing [opposing corruption]" (Tidey 2016, 2018). When it comes to the regulation of migrant workers, officially, "legitimate migration" should be "uncoerced, voluntary, undertaken as a result of individual decisions and for the sake of a better life," and "transportation agents, brokers, and recruiters of all kinds were potential abusers and rightful targets of suppression unless they collaborated with government regulation" (McKeown 2008, 10). McKeown writes about the nineteenth and early twentieth centuries, but the concerns he described resemble the contemporary entangled interests of government actors and economic agents in the labor migration industry. Government regulation claims to regulate and protect "free migration," but in practice such "freedom" is not so easily assured.

The Indonesian passport proclaims the unity of the state and the central role of government officials (as state representatives) in issuing and verifying passports; it defines the individual as a member of (or belonging to) the nation-state. Yet the nation-state's role—read through the passport—is far from autonomous or independent. It adheres to *global* standards that serve as measures of good and modern states. Indonesian passports (like others) contradict the idea of equality and unity, as they simultaneously produce and reflect historically and culturally shaped inequalities and differences. The passport reveals the state's deep entanglement with the economy (specifically the migration industry), and with society.

IMIGRASI AND PASSPORTS

Today's Directorate General of Immigration (Imigrasi) is under the Ministry of Law and Human Rights, which is under the Coordinating Ministry for Political, Legal, and Security Affairs, one of four coordinating ministries in the executive branch of the government,[11] under which is also the Ministry of Foreign Affairs, responsible for diplomacy, including consulates and embassies. Imigrasi's own account of its history, posted on its website, is the only history of Imigrasi and passports that I could find. Imigrasi's main role is expressed in "Mars Imigrasi Indonesia," an anthem that proclaims the patriotic duty of immigration officials to protect and safeguard the nation.[12]

We are Indonesian Immigration,
Ready to carry out our duty,
To safeguard the country,
With law enforcement,
Dedicated to the community.

Authoritative and friendly,
In carrying out our obligations,
Maintaining the country's gateways,
To achieve justice and prosperity.

Bhumi Pura Wira Wibawa,
Indonesian Immigration Service,

11. The other three are the Coordinating Ministry for Economic Affairs, the Coordinating Ministry for Human Development and Cultural Affairs, and the Coordinating Ministry for Maritime Affairs. The Ministry of Manpower is under the Ministry of Economic Affairs.

12. Unless otherwise indicated, this section refers to information available on the Imigrasi website (Imigrasi 2012, n.d.a). The longer version of Imigrasi history referenced in this chapter (Imigrasi 2012) was replaced by a shorter version (Imigrasi n.d.a) sometime between 2018 and 2021.

Based on the National
Principles of Pancasila
And the Constitution of '45.

Face the challenges and temptations
That inhibit development,
Serve with sincerity and purity,
For the sake of Indonesia's glory.[13]

Imigrasi's official purpose is to protect the country; maintain its ports and borders; support development, justice, and prosperity; and reject temptations (corruption), for the sake of the glory of the nation-state, and in keeping with the 1945 Constitution of the Republic of Indonesia. The phrase *Bhumi Pura Wira Wibawa* sums up the idea, referring to Imigrasi as "guardian of the gateway" (Syahrin 2013, 2018). The Five Principles of Pancasila (discussed above) were announced by Sukarno, Indonesia's nationalist leader, before independence and were incorporated into the constitution.

The region known today as Indonesia, it should be clear, was not "discovered" by European travelers or explorers, nor are global mobilities and labor migrations in the region new or unique to the current period of globalization. Rather, the region experienced many waves of migration and mobility for centuries before Portuguese and other Europeans were attracted by the mineral and spice trade in the sixteenth century. Centuries of precolonial travelers and settlers brought Buddhist, Hindu, and later Muslim influences with them to the region.

In 1602, the multinational Dutch East India Company or VOC (Dutch: Vereenigde Oostindische Compagnie) was set up in Batavia (now Jakarta) to control the spice trade. Indigenous forms of slavery and bonded servitude existed there already, but by the seventeenth century the VOC was the largest slave-owner in the region (Reid 1993, 72). By 1800, the VOC was awash in debt and corruption, so the Dutch government nationalized the company's possessions and expanded the territory to include much of the region within Indonesia's contemporary borders (Missbach and Palmer 2018; Ward 2009).

---

13. See Imigrasi (n.d.b) for lyrics of Mars Imigrasi Indonesia. The musical version is also available on YouTube (2017, 2016).

The development of Imigrasi—and the Indonesian travel documents for which it was responsible—marked a shift away from some Dutch colonial policies and the maintenance of many bureaucratic structures and functions. The Dutch established the Immigration Commission in 1913, later changed to the Immigration Agency (Immigratie Dients) in 1921. All but a few staff were Dutch, and all the key positions in immigration services were held by Dutch officials from the Netherlands. The Dutch promoted an "open-door policy" (*opendeur politiek*) aimed at "attracting foreigners to enter, stay and become citizens of the Dutch East Indies." Dutch policy was intended to attract "foreign allies and investors" to develop plantations and exports in the Dutch East Indies. Collectively, they "exploited and suppressed the native people of the region." The Dutch East Indies immigration agency was small, with three sections managing arrivals and departures; they dealt with entry permits and permits of stay, foreign residency, and citizenship (see also Stoler 1985).[14]

The Japanese entered Indonesia in 1942, marking the end of Dutch rule. They took over Imigrasi's top posts but instituted few changes. At the end of World War II, with Japan's surrender, Indonesia proclaimed independence on August 17, 1945. The Netherlands fought to reclaim the region, lost the Indonesian War of Independence, and finally recognized the Republic of Indonesia on December 27, 1949.

At that time, Indonesian independence fighters traveled freely to Malaya and Singapore without passports, but the Asian Relations Conference in New Delhi in 1947 marked the need for travel documents, so the Indonesian Ministry of Foreign Affairs issued its first Indonesian interstate travel document (the SPLP mentioned above) to members of the Indonesian government. This was followed shortly after by the Paspor Diplomatik. In the spirit of independence, Dutch immigration laws requiring entry and exit permits were (eventually) revoked.[15]

The Provisional Constitution of 1950 stipulated that all persons within the territory of the new republic are entitled to equal protection of person

14. The three sections were Admission Decision (Toelatings Besluit) 1916; Admission Order (Toelatings Ordonnantie) 1917; and Passport Scheme (Paspor Regelings) 1918 (Imigrasi 2012).

15. For more on this history, see Imigrasi (2012, n.d.a) under Independence and Revolution Era.

and property (Article 8); that all persons have the right of freedom of movement and residence within the borders of the state; and that all have the right to leave the country and—being citizen or resident—to return thereto (Article 9).[16] After 1949, three hundred thousand Dutch and Indo-Dutch families were repatriated to the Netherlands, while the few remaining Eurasians (or "Indos") "took up Indonesian citizenship, and over the following decade virtually the entire Dutch population left." In the 1950s, another fifty thousand Dutch citizens were expelled and over a hundred thousand Chinese Indonesians left for China, their property and businesses confiscated (Missbach and Palmer 2018, 2).

In 1950, H. J. Adiwinata was the first native Indonesian to become the head of Imigrasi, but few indigenous officers fully understood the duties and functions of immigration, so Imigrasi hired Dutch employees during a transitional period. Of its 459 employees, 160 were Dutch, and the "basic law and regulations were still inherited from the Dutch East Indies."[17] By the end of 1952, the Dutch immigration employees' contracts ended and they were repatriated. In the same decade, new immigration offices and landing ports were opened. By 1960, the main immigration office was established in the capital city of Jakarta, and twenty-six regional and three branch offices, an immigration inspection office, and seven immigration posts were established abroad. Employees grew to 1,256 (all Indonesian). The former Dutch open-door policy shifted from protecting Dutch interests and security to protecting Indonesian interests. They instituted inspections of ships' migration documents for passengers and crew, and new laws pertaining to the control, surveillance, and registration of foreigners—especially of Chinese, who were treated with suspicion—and to citizenship and immigration-related crimes.

In the early period of the new state, new types of visas and travel documents were developed, replacing the Dutch Passport Scheme of 1918 with the 1959 Travel Documents Act (Regulation no. 14/1959, which replaced the 1950 Republic of Indonesia Emergency Law no. 40). The

16. Such rights marked a significant legal change, but it was difficult to put into practice.

17. Namely, the Indies State Regulations (Indische Staatsregeling), Entry Decisions (Toelatings Besluit), and Entry Ordinance (Toelatings Ordonnantie). See Imigrasi (2012, n.d.a) under United Republic of Indonesia.

Travel Documents Act included the SPLP and five other types of travel documents (Imigrasi 2010).

The New Order regime (1966–98) followed a coup to oust President Sukarno and marked the ascendance of President Suharto, who was later toppled during the Asian Financial Crisis in 1998, marking the start of Era Reformasi. Although both free and unfree labor migration had existed for centuries within and beyond Indonesia (Breman 2020; Rossum 2018; Stoler 1985; Ward 2009), the Reformasi marked a phenomenal increase in the scale of women's labor migration to the Middle East and the Persian Gulf and into the Asia-Pacific, especially Hong Kong, Taiwan, and Singapore.

During the New Order period, Imigrasi grew and aimed to "professionalize" its service. In 1966 the Directorate of Immigration was elevated to the Directorate General of Immigration, one of the main directorates under the Ministry of Law and Human Rights.[18] Its physical infrastructure was expanded, including new offices, official residences, and detention centers. Immigration officials' posts rotated every few years, as they still do, allowing for career development and the influx of new (and younger) officials (like Mr. P). In 1979, the Director General established a new computerized immigration data system to streamline services and create new "immigration regulation products." These included regulations and services (e.g., landing documents for hajj pilgrims; airline onboard document checks; better print quality of passports; and regulations concerning border crossing, immigration facilities, and illegal Indonesian workers in border zones). New visa regulations and rules regarding "illegal immigrants" were established; exit permits previously required for *all* Indonesian citizens were abolished.[19]

The Reformasi was marked by public aspirations for and commitment to law and justice; human rights; fighting corruption, collusion, and nepotism (KKN); and greater democratization, government transparency, accountability, and regional autonomy, all of which correspond with World Bank, IMF, and World Trade Organization (WTO) ideas about "good governance." According to Imigrasi, globalization, by way of the WTO, aimed to link the world into a global free market, requiring greater

18. The Directorate General of Immigration is under the Ministry of Law and Human Rights, not the Ministry of Foreign Affairs. Both are under the Coordinating Ministry for Political, Legal, and Security Affairs.

19. See Imigrasi (2012, n.d.a) on the New Era.

attention to human rights and democratization. Globalization would create increasingly "borderless countries" and increased mobility, resulting in challenges for many countries, including Indonesia and its Imigrasi. Regional economic cooperation increased the number of Indonesians and foreigners entering and exiting the country, requiring more reliable and accurate field management and services. Imigrasi sought to be more responsive to mobility and, as noted above, "the growing problem of terrorism." Older regulations (e.g., Regulation no. 9/1992) emphasized service and efficiency in support of the global free market but were less focused on law enforcement and security. Reform-era policies sought to strike a better balance between free-market interests and security.[20] Imigrasi was thus concerned with good governance and modern statehood.

Post-1997 Imigrasi projects associated with reform included new training for immigration officers and staff to become "better qualified and professional, have a better work ethic, higher dedication and better morals," in order to establish better relations and trust with the public, echoing many workers' and activists' complaints during my research. The Immigration Academy opened in 2000, offering immigration-related technical education, training, and master's and doctoral programs at the University of Indonesia and Padjajaran University. Other universities and programs expanded their capacity, with short courses offered in Australia, Taiwan, Japan, and South Korea. Mr. P's generation of immigration officials were the product of this educational and professional shift.

Imigrasi grew, with new regional immigration offices, detention centers, border checkpoints, and visa arrival facilities at international airports. A new program called Intelligent Character Recognition (ICR) was introduced at checkpoints, and new electronic filing systems were utilized. SIMKIM, forensic laboratories, and procurement of EDISON equipment were used to meet international passport-security specifications. New devices were utilized to detect false documents, and Imigrasi worked with the Australian Department of Immigration and Multi-cultural and Indigenous Affairs, and the International Organization for Migration, to

---

20. Missbach and Palmer (2018) observe that Indonesia has focused more on policies and protections for migrants from Indonesia than on immigrants, asylum seekers, and others coming to Indonesia.

devise better border-management information and alert systems. By 2003, Imigrasi focused on arrival and departure processing of Indonesian citizens and foreigners, who were recorded at checkpoints via the ICR system and whose data was recorded and electronically filed. "Stickier" visas that could not easily be removed were adopted to prevent falsification. TKI passports were a matter of concern, especially in relation to Indonesian workers in Malaysia. Government agencies collaborated to address national security and immigration matters.[21]

By 2012, still facing criticism, Imigrasi made infrastructural plans to increase its reach domestically and internationally; numbers of regional offices grew and more immigration attachés were placed in consulates and embassies, such as in the consulate office in Guangzhou, China. New and amended laws and regulations were proposed to fight international crime, coordinate international reciprocal visa agreements, impose higher penalties for smuggling, expand migration crimes to include sponsors and corporations (not only individuals), and impose higher sanctions to deter violations of immigration laws. Utilizing modern information and communication technologies to manage and verify international travel documents is highly relevant to the passport project.

M. ALVI SYAHRIN'S BLOG

M. Alvi Syahrin—an Indonesian immigration officer, a department head at the Immigration Polytechnic in 2021, and an expert in Indonesian immigration law—was an avid blogger on *Petak Norma: Bunga Rampai Tulisan Seputar (Isu) Hukum, Sosial, Politik, dan Humaniora* (Norms: An Anthology of Articles on Legal, Social, Political, and Humanities [Issues]; www.petaknorma.com). His blog posts in 2013 and 2014 included critical insights about Imigrasi and its policies and into the motivations behind SIMKIM, the passport project, and the wider national anticorruption campaign in relation to Imigrasi. Although he was more critical of Imigrasi than Mr. P, he was similarly deeply committed to reform and "good governance."

---

21. Much of the information on the reform period from Imigrasi (2012) no longer appears in the new Imigrasi history section (n.d.a).

In a November 2013 blog, while Imigrasi was facing public criticism and SIMKIM was in the works, Syahrin wrote that public antipathy toward Imigrasi is unsurprising, given that corruption is rampant and the directorate is losing its "national authority" (*wibaya bangsa*) by not dealing with internal problems. Most Indonesians, he wrote, know little about Imigrasi, and even some of its staff don't understand its history, including its important roles in the establishment of the Republic of Indonesia and in maintaining the border. Imigrasi has been "lulled by the so-called glory of its past" but is at an all-time low, "rooted in practices of KKN," including the rampant illegal practice of demanding additional money to issue passports. It is common knowledge, he writes, that immigration service activities are "wetlands" (*menjadi lahan basah,* metaphorical "fertile grounds") for immigration corruption. Corruption and lack of transparency in issuing passports indicate Imigrasi's failure in its duties, and its having become "prostituted from within" (*Imigrasi seolah dilacurkan oleh internalnya sendiri*).[22]

As Bhumi Pura Wira Wibawa, or guardian of the gates, Imigrasi has the authority to determine whether a person can enter or leave the territory and whether foreign nationals are deported (Syahrin 2013). Alongside the military, it "safeguards the country." Imigrasi should be on the front line in maintaining Indonesia's sovereignty, but Imigrasi is not consulted or taken seriously regarding national security. It should not blame others but must clean up its reputation. Immigration staff bring it down. Syahrin argues that "changes in mindset" are necessary for Imigrasi to regain public respect, as is the case, he claims, in Western countries.

In an era when development demands bureaucratic reform on all fronts, Syahrin urged Imigrasi to reform the passport-issuing system. He noted three new policies that would increase speed and efficiency, cut down on corruption, and help restore public confidence: (1) issuing passports without requiring the issuing official's signature; (2) adding new services in Central and West Jakarta with one-day passport replacements and online applications; and (3) facilitating direct payments to Imigrasi through the Indonesian National Bank. In 2013, direct payment was possible at only a few immigration offices. Most such changes took place in

22. My translations.

Jakarta, where businesspeople and wealthier citizens had ready access. People from more remote regions (including Central and East Java, where most Hong Kong–bound domestic workers originate) lacked such safeguards against KKN practices. As Syahrin writes, eliminating required signatures of immigration officers (*petugas imigrasi*) on every passport would help eliminate officers' power to delay or withhold passports and to demand bribes to issue them. Notably, new biometric passports no longer have signatures *on* the passport, but they are held in the biometric record.

Having acknowledged many of the problems, and the necessary improvements that the Directorate General of Immigration must make to regain its dignity and authority, Syahrin ended his blog on an optimistic note: Despite public mistrust and criticism, Imigrasi "has not remained silent." Imigrasi must be recognized as a partner in the nation's development and in safeguarding state sovereignty. It "reflects the dignity of a nation," and "community participation is necessary" to improve it. He writes of Imigrasi's "proud but tainted history" and notes the central importance of passports as key documents in relation to the state and its borders, security and sovereignty, and national dignity. Without reliable passports—which rely on the effectiveness of Imigrasi—Indonesia lets down its citizens, he writes, and cannot join the modern nations of the world.

PASSPORT HISTORIES

During this research, I hoped (to no avail) to find a detailed historical analysis of the Dutch East Indies and Indonesian travel documents, contemporary passports, identity documents, and apparatus, similar to the writings of Radhika Mongia (1999, 2018), Radhika Singha (2013), and Adam McKeown (2008) about passports and migration of South Asians and Chinese, in and beyond Asia. A rich scholarly literature illustrates historical entanglements of passports with forms of governance, labor, and capital in other regions and historical accounts of passports and travel documents in Europe and the United States (e.g., Torpey 2000; Robertson 2010; Caplan and Torpey 2001).

There exist meticulous historical and social science studies of files and filing (Vismann 2008; Hull 2012), fingerprints and criminal identification (Cole 2002), and registration, documentation, and security (Feldman 2012; Breckenridge and Szreter 2012). There are far fewer studies of passports and identity documents in Asia, with some exceptions, including studies of Indian passports and electronic identity documents (Cohen 2019; Mongia 1999, 2018; Rao and Nair 2019; Singha 2000, 2013; see also Yamamoto 2017, on Japanese passports); on "blurred citizenship" among "illegal citizens" in Malaysia, India, and Pakistan (Sadiq 2009); and on birth certificates and other identity documents in Indonesia (Butt and Ball 2017, 2018; Ball, Butt, and Beazley 2017). There are also noteworthy historical and anthropological studies of documentation and classification in Asia (e.g., Friedman 2015; Hull 2012; Sadiq 2009; Stoler 1985, 2002, 2009; Strassler 2010). But besides Imigrasi's history, and Indonesian historical sources that briefly mention labor and travel documents, a detailed history of passports and other labor and travel documents in the Dutch East Indies and Indonesia remains to be written.

Passports are at the knotty center of this study, but what are the relevant historical connections to the contemporary passport project? Ann Stoler argues that the present is hardly "postcolonial," as "colonial inequities endure" in "temporal and affective spaces" (2016, ix). It is important to see colonial or postcolonial periods, not as fixed or distinct points in time and space or as past and present, but as temporal entanglements that continue to shape inequalities. In Imigrasi's history, the very idea of Indonesian passports—as opposed to Dutch colonial passports and Dutch East Indies travel documents—marks Indonesia's relatively recent, post–World War II, independence and nation-state-building project. However, Indonesian passports were not simply born at that point.

Citizenship and the "documentary apparatus of identification," including passports, are said to have "*driven* the history of categories and collectivities" (Caplan and Torpey 2001, 3; McKeown 2008). Long before passports took their current form (little booklets with the holder's photograph, biometrics, name, date of birth, place of birth, and nationality), other types of travel passes and documents were used to permit or restrict the travel of particular persons or categories of persons, but they did not necessarily have much to do with nation-states. International or "external" passports likely developed out of "internal passports" or passes (Torpey 2000, 158). Historical studies point to "letters of introduction" as precursors that were written by an authoritative person to identify or vouch for the traveler and request that *he* be permitted to enter another region (Cole 2002, 8).[23] In medieval and early modern Europe, national borders were far less significant, but social rank was important, and journeymen received passes from the guilds to which they belonged, or travelers used "specialized knowledge which proved their initiation . . . or demonstrated their membership in a community" (Fahrmeir 2001, 218). Codes, passwords, objects, and tattoos could also indicate membership and facilitate mobility. For hundreds of years, travel documents had no photographs but used other means of identifying or describing the holder (e.g., signatures, stamps, seals; descriptors or anthropometric measurements such as the famous Bertillon method). In more recent times, travel documents have incorporated fingerprints, photographs, and biometric measurements (Cole 2002; Lyon 2001; Sengoopta 2003). From the start, there were concerns about forgeries and fakes (see Cole 2002; Noiriel 2001; Sadiq 2009; Ford and Lyons 2011).

Scholars often trace the origin of passports to revolutionary France, ideas about state control of borders, and distinctions between citizens and noncitizens in Europe and the West (Torpey 2000). By the late eighteenth century in Europe, passports were already "intimately connected to the concept of distinct nation-states inhabited by subjects or citizens equal before the law and distinguished only by wealth, not rank" (Fahrmeir 2001, 219). The passport's link to citizenship is a product of the 1789 French Revolution that led to the establishment of the Republic in 1792, "where the first modern passport regulations, which obliged all travelers to carry state-issued official identity documents with them at all times, were introduced" (2001, 219). This was motivated by efforts to prevent the entry of hostile foreigners, bandits, criminals, and vagrants. Borders and identification gained importance. A key difference of the new identity documents was that they espoused the ideal of "equality" among citizens, rather than older, highly ranked, often inherited social inequalities. "The fact that passports are issued by governments, not least in order to document the bearers' nationality, indicates the immense importance of citizenship in a world of nation-states" (Fahrmeir 2001, 218; see also Noiriel 2001).

---

23. The male pronouns in these studies are noteworthy; travelers were often men or assumed to be men.

The use of passports *to control migration* at borders, according to McKeown, developed later than many assume, during the late nineteenth and early twentieth centuries. He argues that "most of the basic principles of border control on techniques for identifying personal status were developed from the 1880s to the 1910s through the exclusion of Asians from white settler nations" (2008, 2). Modern passports and border control can be traced, in other words, not to the rights of privileged whites and Europeans to travel per se, but to *preventing* unwanted Asians, Africans, and formerly unfree indentured people from doing so (McKeown 2008; Mongia 2018, 1999).

Radhika Mongia forcefully argues that modern passports are not simply a product of the development of nation-states that spread from Europe to other parts of the world after the world wars. Rather, they reveal varied and specific genealogies of empire-states, their techniques and technologies for managing migration, and their transformations into nation-states (Mongia 2018, 2–4). She examines the process through which British passports during the colonial period served to distinguish their subjects by race. This was shaped by the Canadian (British) white settler colony's desire to exclude or limit the permanent settlement of South Asian men who sought entry as free laborers in the early twentieth century, in the wake of the abolition of slavery and the later abolition of indentured labor in the West Indies (Mongia 1999, 2018). Passports did not simply grow out of modern ideals of equal rights of individuals and nations-states. The right to global exploration and mobility was asserted and assumed to exist among privileged whites and Europeans in various contexts in the sixteenth and seventeenth centuries.

The late nineteenth-century and early twentieth-century colonial passport history of exclusion is echoed, today, in the more recent feminized labor migrations from Indonesia and the Philippines to East Asia and the Middle East and Gulf States. Indonesian or Filipino migrant workers' passports allow them to enter Hong Kong as temporary labor migrants, with FDH (foreign domestic helper) two-year visas and employment contracts. Short of marrying a local, they cannot apply for permanent residence, live apart from their employers, establish a home there, or bring family members with them. Their labor is wanted and needed, but they must leave when their contracts end, echoing patterns described by

Mongia and McKeown. Their passports mark them racially as non-Chinese "other Asians," who are often looked down on in Hong Kong.

Modern passports developed hand in hand with the goal of controlling the mobility of Asians, Africans, and poor whites (McKeown 2008; Mongia 2018). During much of the colonial period, privileged white settlers assumed the right to travel freely. "Unfree" people were documented, like commodities, by shipping companies, brokers, and "owners" or investors, but further research is needed to compare such historical documents with the passports of today. Inventory lists of human cargo were likely used to facilitate the recruiters' and owners' records, as well as to calculate shipping costs and taxation. Such documents were not likely conceived of as "passports" that track the departure and entry of presumably "free" individual citizens and noncitizens.

By the mid-twentieth century, in Indonesia and elsewhere in Asia, passports were "no longer just travel documents, but also documents of citizenship: a tool through which states sifted citizens from aliens. In the unsettled and uncertain conditions of Asia's decolonization in the 1940s, passports came into use on a scale never seen before" (Amrith 2011, 120–21). Passports were also a way for imperialist governments to restrict the entry of their former colonial subjects, as in the aforementioned Chinese Exclusion Acts in the United States and restrictions on South Asians in Canada. Although Asian and African labor was sought by many settler-colonies after the abolition of slavery and indenture, new restrictions were imposed to permit the free flow of labor, justified by liberal abolitionists who defended "free labor" and the advocates for "free trade" who wanted *cheap* labor (McKeown 2008, 66–89).

While Indonesian passports today are shaped, literally and figuratively, by contemporary global standards, they are also entangled with earlier regional histories. Indonesia's definition of the "citizen," of who belongs to the Indonesian collectivity and who is entitled to an Indonesian passport (or similar documents), is shaped by and in response to former Dutch colonial rule. Indonesia's national borders, its constitution, and the workings of its immigration apparatus in relation to labor migration and capital are also historically shaped. In other words, the passport may be "new," but it entangles rather than separates past and present, colonial and postcolonial, global and local, free and unfree mobility.

(IM)MOBILITY IN THE DUTCH COLONIAL PERIOD

Entanglements of government actors with profit-driven labor migration industries, and with forced and coerced labor, have deep historical roots in the colonial era. The colonial era left a pattern of local rural poverty in many of the regions from which Indonesians today migrate abroad for work. When the Dutch government replaced the VOC in 1800, they desperately needed more labor to rebuild. Penal, bonded, and corvée labor were arguably cheaper than keeping slaves (Reid 1993, 70).[24] Forms of indentured or bonded labor (labor owed to the patron without direct recompence) and corvée labor (labor owned as tax) were practiced from the mid-nineteenth to the early twentieth century (Reid 1993). From 1830 to 1860, during the Cultuurstelsel (Cultivation System) period, Javanese peasants—among those most impacted by poverty and overpopulation—were forced to contribute the equivalent of three months' labor annually to the Dutch as a form of taxation. When the Cultivation System was dismantled in the 1860s, impoverished Javanese landless peasants were desperate for work (1993, 73). A new system of labor contracts, modeled on British indenture (referred to as "the new system of slavery") was adopted, whereby Javanese and Chinese "coolies" were sent to rubber and tobacco plantations in East Sumatra and elsewhere on three-year contracts, working in what were essentially "outdoor prisons" (1993, 77).

Forced convict labor during the VOC period was expanded under Dutch rule. Aside from the death penalty for the most serious crimes, other punishments were replaced by forced penal labor. The Dutch colonial penal labor system has been described as an early and advanced carceral state (Rossum 2018; Breman 2020). Slaves, convict laborers, and indentured workers were forced to work far from home and faced worse treatment if they tried to escape. The opening of the Suez Canal in 1869 attracted more migrants—including traders, merchants, Islamic teachers and preachers, and, especially, Chinese "coolies"—from Singapore and elsewhere to the Dutch East Indies.

24. The Dutch banned slavery in 1818 but did not prohibit (preexisting) ownership of slaves until 1860, long after the French and the British (Reid 1993, 77).

Dutch colonial rule in the nineteenth and early twentieth centuries reflected regional, racial, and class divides. The East Indies were officially stratified into a tripartite system of rule with the Dutch (and other Europeans) on top; "foreign Asians" in the middle (including Chinese and those of Chinese descent, Indians, and "Arab" entrepreneurs and traders); and "native" (*pribumi*) Indonesians, including residents of thousands of islands with cultural and linguistic differences, at the bottom (Vandenbosch 1942, 189).[25] There were "mixed" populations and differently ranked categories within each stratum (Stoler 1989, 1992).[26] The Dutch assigned local high-ranking rulers (*priyayi*)—in Java, the hereditary princes and their officials, for example—and a range of lower-ranked local leaders to convey and enforce the Dutch requirements for labor, land, and produce or taxes from local native villagers and farmers (Sutherland 1979). This diffusion of governance, which echoes the infrastructural pattern of migrant recruitment, points to the embeddedness of rule within communities (Barker 1999).

One's status as "Asian," or as "native" (indigenous), shaped internal travel and travel regulations since at least 1816, when the Dutch pass system (*passen stelsel*) was designed to keep the local labor force in place and required "Asians" and "natives" to carry travel documents presented at each *onderdistrict* (subdistrict) office when traveling (Cribb and Kahin 2004, 438; Vandenbosch 1942, 189). Both groups were subject to pass laws from 1816 to 1863, and to residential regulations (*wikjen stensel*) that separated them. Most small urban entrepreneurs were Chinese, but thousands of Chinese were brought in as coolies and indentured servants, whose mobility was closely controlled. Chinese were required to live in "Chinatowns" (Chinese districts) from 1835 to 1919 and could not travel freely. "For every trip the Chinese merchant made he had to obtain a pass from Government officials." The Dutch East Indies government "held that segregation was necessary to control and protect both Chinese and natives" (Vandenbosch 1942, 357).

25. After 1899, for official and legal purposes Japanese were included in the "European" category. "Foreign Asians" did not include Japanese, Filipinos, Turks, and Christians (Vandenbosch 1942, 189).

26. Children of mixed couples fell under the father's category, if he recognized them. If not, they were under the mother's category.

During the Cultivation System, as planned, the Dutch "amassed a fortune" as a result of forced labor that was facilitated by "forbidding peasants from leaving their villages without a permit (the pass system)" (Aidit
1958, 31). The internal pass system was largely abolished in 1863, and
travel and residence regulations gradually became more lenient until they
were "virtually unrestricted" by 1914 in Java and by 1918 in the outer
islands (Cribb and Kahin 2004, 438). Until the second decade of the
twentieth century, travel and residential restrictions "reduced the mobility
and inconvenienced the Indonesian and 'Foreign Asian' members of the
populations, but not the Europeans" (Milone 1966, 28).[27]

Some Dutch-era policies and patterns of mobility continued into
the period of Indonesian independence. The transmigration policy
(*transmigrasi*), which officially began in 1905 as part of the Dutch "Ethical
Policy" after a Calvinist-Catholic Coalition came to power in the
Netherlands, is one such example (Rigg 1991, 83–86; Tirtosudarmo
2018, 50; see also Hardjono 1977; MacAndrews 1978). The program
echoed patterns of labor mobility that began in the 1880s, of Javanese and
Sundanese indentured laborers brought to work in Sumatra (Barter and
Côté 2015, 65; Hardjono 1977; Stoler 1985). The post-independence
transmigrasi continued the policy with Javanese (from Central and East
Java) and Sundanese (from West Java) migrating to Sumatra, and with
later migrants from Bali and Madura to other destinations such as Borneo,
Papua, and West Papua. The Dutch government justified the *kolonisasi*
(colonial) transmigration program as a means to improve Javanese wel-
fare, a cheap way to establish plantations, and a way to suppress unrest
(Rigg 1991, 85; Tirtosudarmo 2018, 50).

The new Indonesian government proclaimed similar goals in its post-
independence five-year plan for 1956–60: to reduce population pressure
in Java, provide labor in sparsely populated provinces, support military
strategy, and accelerate the process of assimilation (Tirtosudarmo 2018,
51). The Dutch colonial government "implicitly used its migration policy
as an instrument of demographic engineering for security purposes, [but]

27. Anti-Chinese regulations were abolished by 1919 when they became subject to the
European Civil Code, but they were subject to the same criminal laws as local Indonesians
(Vandenbosch 1942, 25).

the government of the Republic of Indonesia explicitly relocated people to fulfill political and strategic goals" (2018, 52). Under the Indonesian New Order (beginning in 1966 with President Suharto), "transmigration reached its zenith, becoming 'a social engineering project of monumental proportions'" (Barter and Côté 2015, 65, citing Arndt 1983, 54). Critics of Indonesia's transmigration policy blame it for fueling Muslim-Christian conflicts and violence in West Papua and among Dayaks and migrant Madurese in Borneo, spreading dominant Javanese and Islamic political and cultural influence, and causing environmental destruction (e.g., Arnt 1983; Fearon and Laitin 2011; O'Connor 2004; Rigg 1991, 98–105; Tirtosudarmo 2018).[28]

Some internal and external travel restrictions continued after independence. A "fiscal fee" was levied in 1982 "to discourage Indonesians from traveling overseas"; and in 1989, as overseas jobs gained popularity among Indonesians, the government abolished the required "exit permit." Indonesians no longer needed a *surat jalan* (literally, "letter of the road") for inter-provincial travel (Cribb and Kahin 2004, 438).

Connections between labor and forced mobility were apparent in the VOC period and the subsequent Dutch colonial era, as natives of Java were forced, lured, or pressured to move to regions where their labor was needed. By 1860, slavery was officially abolished in the East Indies but indenture continued (Stoler 1985, 28). Plantation estates were established on Sumatra's East Coast, especially the region of Deli that Stoler studied, and "initially Chinese and later Javanese workers were imported by the hundreds of thousands . . . bound by indentured status" (1985, 2). As late as 1930, Javanese plantation coolies were nearly 50 percent of the native population (1985, 4). In 1911 alone, "more than 50,000 contract coolies were imported from central Java to fill the urgent labor demand [of] . . . rubber estates" (1985, 30).

By the start of the twentieth century, recruitment agencies "mushroomed" in large coastal cities and on Java, and "fly-by-night 'immigration agencies' reportedly took on the air of wholesale markets dedicated to *the sale, not recruitment,* of labor. In the contemporary Dutch press, sandwiched

---

28. Barter and Côté (2015) argue that the role of transmigration in interethnic conflicts and violence is exaggerated.

between news of animal auctions, public notices advertised the guaranteed delivery of 'strapping healthy young men and women' at the 'modest' cost of 60 guilder per head" (Stoler 1985, 30, citing Brand 1904, 41; my italics). It is no coincidence that Central Java, East Java, and parts of Sumatra—where overpopulation, inequality, and poverty are deep legacies of the colonial era—are still major suppliers of global migrant labor. Between 1890 and 1939, the Dutch Ministry of Labor (the precursor to Indonesia's Ministry of Manpower) sent almost thirty-three thousand Indonesians from Java, and also Madura, Sunda, and Batak (including some women and children) to labor on plantations in the Dutch colony of Suriname, replacing African slaves. The "sale, not recruitment" of Javanese workers in the early twentieth century, and the "fly-by-night immigration agencies" described by Stoler, still resonate with the patterns of migration today.

ENTANGLEMENTS OF STATE AND SOCIETY

Were we to look only at the modern Indonesian passport, the history of Imigrasi, and the views of Mr. P, we might be convinced that a clear state-society divide exists, and that passports are "modern" tools that allow states to "embrace" citizens. Yet a closer look shows that state control is never complete because it is entangled within and produced by society. The state is not a "coherent entity with a will of its own" but is a site of contestation and "struggle among many competing groups" (Klinken and Barker 2009, 2). Contestation is evident in public responses and criticisms of the Indonesian government and its inability to protect (let alone embrace) migrant workers who are injured. Contestation is evident when Syahrin challenges Imigrasi to address corruption, collusion, and nepotism within its ranks.

The entanglement of government and economy within society is evident when we look at the collusion and complicity of government actors, recruiters, and agencies in relation to the production of aspal documents to facilitate migration. The government's monopoly on passports and mobility, as this study shows, is incomplete and still challenged. Indonesian migration infrastructures echo patterns of indirect rule, utilizing respected locals to connect villages and small towns to urban recruitment centers.

The modern Indonesian nation-state may be *imagined* as equal and unified, offering care and protection, but governance *in practice* belies such ideals. Passports may symbolize national identity, equality, and unity, but they (re)produce and facilitate inequality and difference. Inequalities might not seem so obvious now that BMIs use regular passports and regular airport terminals, but they are still identifiable. Their data is electronically accessible, and the different types, lengths, and costs of e-passports and regular passports point to socioeconomic divides. Biometrics produce inequalities within and between nation-states within a wider global arena, as they compete for passport rankings and ratings.

Passports today and travel documents of the past—like shipping inventories of slaves or coolies as cargo (not individuals), for "sale" not for hire, and travel permits and indenture contracts—create unequal categories of people and mobility restrictions that are largely motivated by economic considerations. Passports with accurate and reliable *individual* identities are intended to distinguish free and unfree labor mobility and to identify terrorists and trafficking victims. Yet, despite attention to accuracy, ever-more-advanced technology, and lofty ideals of freedom, equality, and security, Indonesian passports are not indicative of a clear or linear historical progression from unfree to free mobility—or from slavery, to indentured or bonded labor, to free labor.

Indonesian BMIs' passports are often tied to informal and personal networks, to corrupt entanglements of labor recruiters and labor brokers with government officials, and to the coercion and exploitation of workers. The hugely profitable labor migration industry of today—which, like that of the past, entangles economic and government interests—echoes older questions and debates about "modern slaves" and "passport victims," and about choice and consent. State and society, free and unfree, care and control are entangled.

Passport stories, histories, and relations show *how* state and society are entangled through "everyday face-to-face exchanges between individuals, in the formal and informal settings where state power is exercised, discussed, and contested" (Klinken and Barker 2009, 5; Migdal 2001). The heterogeneity of state actors (including corrupt officials) and an array of actors with economic interests in the labor migration industry illustrate entanglements of state and society (Palmer 2016). The history of passports and travel documents illustrate entanglements of state and capital in society and the (re)production of unequal forms of mobility, labor, and types of documentation. The passport renewal project and its implementation reveal the "discretion" of Indonesian consular officials to decide which passports are corrected and which are not. The next chapter shows how BMIs, BMI activists, and their networks and allies mobilized to contest government actions and state power to create change.

6 Migrant and Citizen

We—from an organization of migrant workers, former migrant workers and migrant families called KABAR BUMI (Keluarga Besar Buruh Migran Indonesia) [who] work with Hong Kong migrant workers in Macau, Taiwan who are members of JBMI (Indonesian Migrant Workers Network)—are sending this open petition to Bapak [Joko Widodo], as the President of the Republic of Indonesia, asking for protection for Indonesian Migrant Workers who are threatened with criminalization due to the forced changes of identities in their passports.

JBMI and KABAR BUMI (2016)

We learned to bring the passport victim, the family, and the supporters together. We learned to be careful with new regulations. The government is not transparent about laws. We need to listen to everything and study carefully. We ask more and consult more, with everyone, elsewhere too. We must ask who is impacted and where. The victim's situation needs attention, and the regulations need to change.

Sringatin, chairperson of JBMI (interview with author, 2017)

This chapter focuses on migrant-citizen entanglements, specifically Indonesians in Hong Kong who make their activist claims as *both* migrant workers *and* citizens. It responds to the calls of Bridget Anderson (2013) and Janine Dahinden (2016) to "de-migrantize" our work and to dismantle the separate conceptual "containers" of citizen versus migrant that often shape our studies and underlie many anti-migrant policies. The citizen-migrant binary, like the state-society binary, creates and essential- izes an artificial sense of two separate and homogeneous groups, "us" and "them," often imagined from the perspective of the "receiving" state. As we see below, both the Indonesian and the Hong Kong "state" containers are insufficient. The citizen-migrant binary implies that people are one or the other and that migrants (as outsiders) and citizens (as insiders) have opposed interests, which is not necessarily the case in Hong Kong. Yet the presumed binary naturalizes and hardens "sides" in relation to assumed conflicting interests, thus obstructing any understanding of their overlap- ping interests and entanglements.

The substantial economic and social contributions of migrant domestic workers in Hong Kong and the economic class spectrum among their employers were discussed in chapter 3. Employers of FDWs may be wealthy or solidly middle class; some live below the poverty line yet embrace middle-class aspirations, while struggling to obtain decent hous- ing and to provide for their children's education. Locals' concerns about decent and affordable housing, medical care, and education are shared by migrant workers and asylum seekers. Citizenship, or "right of abode" in the context of Hong Kong, asserts the rights and superiority of locals and "permanent residents" versus the relative lack of rights of migrant work- ers, refugees, and asylum seekers. Foreign domestic workers are welcome in Hong Kong, but only as workers (Constable 2014).

Most of Hong Kong's Chinese residents, moreover, are also immigrants or refugees from mainland China or are descended from them. They or their families arrived during China's civil unrest during and after the establishment of the People's Republic. Yet an imagined binary prevents the formation of alliances that might otherwise be mutually beneficial between permanent residents and temporary migrants. This benefits the state and the privileged, protecting the status quo. In Hong Kong and elsewhere, this binary helps justify the creation and maintenance of eco- nomic and social inequalities that are reinforced by gender, ethnicity/race, class, and nationality. It is important to stress, therefore, that migrant workers are also citizens (in the legal sense): they are Filipino, Indonesian, Thai, Bangladeshi, Indian, or Sri Lankan citizens. Like many Hong Kong permanent residents from European and Asian countries, they carry a range of different passports and nationalities, just as most Hong Kong Chinese are citizens of China and carry Hong Kong SAR passports, while others hold British National (Overseas) (BNO) passports or have multiple passports and "flexible citizenship" (Ong 1999).[1]

The passport project and the problems it caused help us see the simultaneous importance of both migrant *and* citizen status in BMIs' lives. By focusing on both at once, we see them as entangled, not binary. Indonesians who work in Hong Kong expect protection as Indonesian *citizens*. However, their rights, benefits, and protection as citizens *and* migrant workers depend on the ability and willingness of the Hong Kong and Indonesian governments to provide them. In the laissez-passer statement in their passports, the Indonesian government requests that the bearer be given safe passage and receive "assistance and protection" in the destination country. Although Hong Kong is widely reputed to be a "good place to work" because of the rule of law and the standard employment contract that ensures a minimum salary and a day off, such assurances are only as good as their enforcement (Constable 2016).[2] There are several reasons why Indonesian officials were unable or unwilling to protect Indonesian migrant workers from passport problems—including, it seems, seeing them as "migrant workers" rather than as equal "citizens." Yet migrant workers did not simply accept their fate as "passport victims." This chapter shows how they struggled for their rights in the face of passport problems by activating their widespread connections with non-migrant citizens and family members, governmental and non-governmental leaders and organizations (NGOs), and networks of former-migrant-worker activists in Indonesia. Their actions ultimately resulted in changes in the Indonesian consulate's passport policies, thus further complicating the state-society binary and showing how the state is a site of struggle.

1. BNO passports were first issued in Hong Kong in 1987 after the Hong Kong Act of 1985. Their numbers increased during the Occupy and Democracy Protests of 2014 and the protests in 2019.

2. The protests and police violence beginning in June 2019 and the COVID-19 outbreak months later created serious concerns among migrant workers who lost access to their regular Sunday meeting places, often lacked masks and other protection from the virus, and were often prohibited from going out at all. In February and March 2022, the situation was even worse as employers, in fear of COVID-19, forced domestic workers out of their homes and workplaces (Magramo 2022).

Below I argue that, based on both their citizenship claims and their migrant status, Indonesian domestic workers exerted tremendous and widespread efforts to mobilize against the passport project. They appealed to their government and activist support networks in Hong Kong and in Indonesia. This ultimately led to changes in the process of passport renewal. Relatedly, their ongoing campaign against Indonesian Law no. 39/2004 on the placement and protection of migrant workers was also partly successful and yielded some improvements in its replacement, Law no. 18/2017. The voices of Indonesian citizen migrant workers carried significant weight in Indonesia, especially when echoed by local voices that criticized the Indonesian government, especially the consulate, for failing to protect (*perlindungan*) its citizens and migrant workers abroad. The passport project revealed some of the wider problems faced by BMIs and how they fought to resolve the problem in Hong Kong.

The Indonesian government has long been criticized for insufficiently protecting vulnerable migrant women (Blackburn 2004; Rudnyckyj 2004; Silvey 2004, 2007).[3] The ability of foreign officials to protect citizen-migrant workers abroad depends in part on their authority within the "host" country and their relationships with local government officials. One problem in Hong Kong was that Indonesian consular officials lacked the respect, power, and authority that was necessary to protect migrant worker citizens. Consular officials, as described below, could not work effectively with their local government immigration counterparts. Another factor was that the consulate and related government labor and immigration departments are often hesitant to criticize private and registered recruitment agencies (PPTKIS) and their agents, including their role in producing aspal passports in the first place, most likely because of their own entanglements with government actors and migration industry interests. Indonesian recruitment agencies (and their partner agencies

---

3. In the past, such criticism led to new laws and organizational changes, including wider coordination of the government agencies that are responsible for the protection of migrant workers. Examples include Law no. 39/2004, followed by Law no. 18/2017; and the BNP2TKI [National Agency for the Placement and Protection of Indonesian Migrant Workers] and subsequent BP2MI [National Agency for the Protection of Indonesian Migrant Workers], established in 2017 (see Indonesian Government n.d.).

abroad) wield significant power and provide economic benefits for Indonesian government officials and ministers and their family members, some of whom are deeply invested in the migration industry, as I was told by officials, scholars, and migrant workers (Palmer 2013, 2016; Silvey 2004).

The passport project had, in the first place, created tension between agencies and consular officials. As a consular official explained, Hong Kong agents have long been involved with *paspor pungli*—extorting many times the actual cost of the passport from migrant workers for renewal. Agents have benefited from maintaining the status quo to prevent the loss of revenue. While migrant workers often direct blame at the agencies, consular officials were much more cautious about pointing the finger at them. Despite their individual understandings of the agencies as "much too greedy," as one consular official put it, the new law on the placement and protection of migrant workers (Law no. 18/2017) increased the agencies' responsibility for the care and protection of migrant workers and maintained the requirement that migrant workers must use such agencies, thus strengthening their hold on workers, to the disappointment of many BMI activists. From the activists' perspective, agencies are at the root of many BMI problems.[4] Migrant workers rely on agencies for placement and protection, but the same agencies often force them into debt, overcharge and extort them, encourage them to tolerate bad employers, and reap profits along with government offices and agencies that are part of the endemic corruption and aspal process. "Central government authorities are well aware of the involvement of local government authorities on the *aspal* route. . . . These ongoing efforts have had little success in stemming the practice of issuing 'real but fake' documents" (Ford and Lyons 2011, 112–13).

---

4. A short story by and about a BMI beautifully illustrates how trust and respect for the consulate turns into disappointment. The main character is abused by her employer, and the agency makes the situation worse, so she phones the "lucky number" of the consulate, trusting that "all her problems would quickly be sorted out." Instead, the consular staff replies, "You should be grateful that you are working in Hong Kong. If you were in Indonesia . . . your earnings would be lower. So why are you complaining? . . . Our business hours have ended and we're about to close for the day." "*Click.* The line had been cut" (Khaerudina 2019, 37–38).

Despite the Indonesian government's stated good intentions, the passport project failed to anticipate the problems it would create for migrant workers. Consular officials failed in their diplomatic efforts because they naively assumed that Hong Kong immigration officials would simply accept their passport data changes as "correction of clerical errors." The consular officials must have known of the massive scale of passport irregularities, so BMIs concluded that the consulate simply did not care about them. Migrant activists managed to cast a national spotlight on the problem in Hong Kong, while arguing that the passport project's failings are tied to deeper socioeconomic and political issues at the root of many of the problems faced by migrant worker citizens, not only those regarding passport renewal.

G2G DISCUSSIONS

When I talked to Mr. P in February 2016, he knew of two Indonesian women who were in prison and had recently learned about two more women from JBMI (Indonesian Migrant Workers' Network). I asked him whether he had anticipated that women would be arrested and investigated by Hong Kong immigration and end up in jail because of the changes that the consulate had made to their passports. He confidently replied that he had not. He knew that SIMKIM would reveal some women's "true identities," but before the project began in January 2015, he and his colleagues met with their Hong Kong government counterparts. As he explained, "in January 2015, when there is a change [in the passport renewal process], we held some informal talks with our colleagues in Hong Kong immigration. We asked, 'What about if I find these kinds of cases? What are your reactions to this?' And they said to me that 'as long as you have provided a letter from your good office, then we will appreciate such a letter, and consider no further action.'" Despite having no formal MOU (memorandum of understanding) or other written agreement, based on those "informal talks with several immigration officers," Mr. P said, "we produced a letter to be addressed to immigration officers in Hong Kong which tells them the reason why we amend the passport" (see box 1).

Konsulat Jenderal Republik Indonesia
Hong Kong

Hong Kong
DATE, 2015

To: Immigration Department of HKSAR
Our reference: NUMBERXXXXX-Date

Dear Officer,

First of all, the Indonesian Consulate General in Hong Kong presents its compliments to the Immigration Department of Hong Kong Special Administrative Region of the People's Republic of China.

Secondly, we have an honor to notify your good office that since January 2015, the Indonesian Consulate General in Hong Kong has been operating "the Online Passport Issuance System" connected directly real live with the Central Immigration Database and Adjudication Office in Jakarta. The system is an advanced technology that requires [the] applicant to take biometric components such as facial recognition and fingerprints directly at our office. Applicants also must follow verification and adjudication process endorsed by the Central Office.

Departing from above information, we have examined the Indonesia passport renewal application from an applicant with details as follows:

Name:	ANDRIYA XXXXX
Place of Birth:	SRAGEN
Date of Birth:	30-02-1985
Passport number:	AP XXXXXX

To further follow up the application, we would like to inform your good office that a series of examination process, including verification to our immigration database in Indonesia and also adjudication process to confirm the personal identity of the applicant had been carefully conducted.

The basis of this examination derived from the passport system:

a. Applicant's biometric data (status verified/ok) ANNEX A.
b. Applicant's formal educational certificate as the data basis for name, place and date of birth (status: verified/ok) ANNEX B.
c. Applicant's Indonesian National Resident Card as the data basis for residential address in Indonesia (status: verified/ok) ANNEX C.
d. Applicant's birth certificate as the data basis for name, place and date of birth (status verified/ok) ANNEX D.

Based on our examination, verification and also approval from our Central Office's adjudicator, I would like to confirm that the applicant's personal identity SHOULD be READ as follow[s]:

Name:	ANDRIYA XXXXX
Place of Birth:	SRAGEN
Date of Birth:	30-02-1990
Passport Number:	B 3333XXX

We believe that based on our investigation, there was such a mistaken data entry procedure of her date of birth procedure caused by our internal business process at the issuing office and already confirmed. We apologize for any inconvenient [sic] occurred at your end.

In addition, the correction of Ms. ANDRIYA XXXXX data is fully a deliberate action taken by our office's judgement to protect the passport and also the bearer's integrity and therefore we will fully bear such responsibility thereof.

Allow me to also assure your good office that for future interest, the said data correction has been locked at our central immigration database and thus any further correction will not be allowed.

Furthermore, any further investigation upon such data correction shall ONLY be directed to our office by contacting me through my mobile number +852 9XXXXXXX or email to XXXX@cgrihk.com.

Finally, the Consulate General of the Republic of Indonesia avails itself to the Immigration Department of Hong Kong Special Administrative Region of the People's Republic of China assurances of its highest consideration.

Thank you,

Sincerely Yours,
[Signature and consulate stamp]
[Name and title]

Mr. P described the process of evaluating the cases identified by SIMKIM and the letter the consulate wrote to immigration:

> We talked about the investigations that we have done, and [whether] . . . the data should be read as the true or original one. And in the [letter's] last paragraph, *I also mentioned that these mistakes were mainly caused by our internal business process.* So, I explained [to the HK officials] why the state makes all those mistakes, and *I apologize for that*—that we made such mistakes and we promised them that no further [passport] changes would be allowed.

Mr. P and his colleagues fully expected that the Indonesian consulate's letter of explanation would do the trick. It was given to women, like Anti and others (who shared it with me), to hand deliver to the Hong Kong immigration staff when they applied for a new visa and identity card after their passports were "corrected." The letter, written in English and addressed to the Immigration Department, said that the passport changes were administrative "corrections" and that the "mistaken data procedure" was caused by their "internal business process." The letters provided the name(s), dates, and identification details of the original passport, a list of the documentation the woman provided (points A–D in the letter; this varied from letter to letter—some included only A and B, for example), and the dates and identification details of the new passport.[5] In the 2016

5. This generic letter is constructed from six similar letters that I was shown by individuals, activists, and the consulate. Names, dates, and passport numbers are fictitious; any resemblance to real ones is coincidental.

version of the letter, the two short paragraphs (italicized in box 1) that follow the "new" passport data are changed to

> We believe that there was such a mistaken data entry procedure caused by human error and we apologize for any inconvenient [*sic*] occurred at your end.
>
> And also may I take this opportunity to confirm that based on our investigation, there was no such "mens rea" (criminal intention) from Ms. XXXXX to alter her personal identity.

As Mr. P explained in February 2016, out of the many thousands of new passports issued by the consulate so far, they had changed the data in only twenty-five. Eleven of those twenty-five had been granted new visas without a problem, but another twelve were facing investigation. The consulate could not explain why some of these women had no problems renewing their visas and identity cards, while others were denied renewal and investigated. Two women had been investigated very quickly, convicted in court of "false representation," and put in jail. After that, BMI activists and affiliated NGOs quickly became aware of the problem. They approached the consulate and spoke to officials there, including the consul general. Then, as Mr. P explained to me:

> They asked to have a hearing with our DG [director general] of immigration in Jakarta—without my knowledge. *Without my knowledge!* And then the central office asked me to write a report on what happened. So, I wrote a report telling the whole story of what I've done. The meeting took place between the [activist] NGOs and the DG in Jakarta in January 2016. DG will of course support our position. He said that when immigration officers find inconsistencies, the officer in charge has to conduct interviews to find out why such irregularities happen and must correct the data if it is supported by the documents. *And the NGO* was blaming [us], "Why do we have to do this? Why the amendment?" And the DG referred again to why we set up the new system. "It's because we want to protect our DH [domestic helpers] overseas and we want to know their *real identity.*"

At that meeting, according to Mr. P, the DG explained that a migrant worker's "true identity" is important to protect them from "accidents and incidents like civil rights claims." The DG also expressed "his hope to work closely with the NGOs" who could help them "combat illegal activities" that are tied to "data games" like those played by the "bad PPTKIS" or even "some bad officers" in the field.

"So, it was *not* a good start for 2016!" said Mr. P with a big sigh. The activists had also written a letter to the Indonesian Ministry of Foreign Affairs and the Ministry of Labor. A friend of Mr. P's in the Ministry of Foreign Affairs asked him what was going on, and other colleagues urged him to get in touch with his local counterparts in Hong Kong immigration and find solutions. They suggested that he consider suspending the policy of changing the data until everything is resolved "on the G2G level, between consulate and HK government." Yet Mr. P was hesitant to stop, and instead strongly urged women with inconsistencies to "just go home," which further infuriated BMIs because it showed a lack of understanding of their economic precarity and the reasons they worked abroad to begin with.

During the first few months of 2016, while BMI activists were meeting with various government ministers in Jakarta, Mr. P and his immigration colleagues set up a meeting with Hong Kong's director of immigration. Consular officials had already met with the Hong Kong deputy director who oversees enforcement, and they had agreed to enhance communication between the consulate and immigration enforcement. "They promise[d] us that they will *not* look at prosecution, but they will look at evidence," Mr. P said. He laughed sardonically, "I'm still wondering about my letter. My letter is already strong evidence that they are *not guilty* on this! So, this is a bit confusing. So, we are trying to sort that out."

"Surprisingly," Mr. P said, "after the meeting we heard from our colleagues and from [JBMI coordinator] Sringatin that there are two other Indonesians who will be heard in Shatin Magistrate Court." Those additional cases meant that the meetings with Hong Kong immigration were ineffective. "So, after that we decided to see any kind of legal advisors," not only the consulate's lawyer. On the recommendation of Sringatin of JBMI, and Cynthia Abdon-Tellez from the Mission for Migrant Workers (MFMW), Mr. P consulted in February with Melville Boase, a lawyer and longtime migrant worker advocate (see chapter 4). Mr. Boase recommended that the consulate engage with the Hong Kong government and, most importantly, that they change the letter they sent to Hong Kong immigration because it served as evidence of guilt, contrary to Mr. P's assertions to the contrary.

Given what Mr. P described as the "lack of any positive results from our [seemingly] positive bilateral with Hong Kong immigration," with two more women facing court hearings, they decided to write a letter to Hong Kong's chief executive. Mr. P recounted:

> On the eighteenth of February, we sent a letter from the consul general to the chief executive *to ask for his attention, and also his wisdom.* We ask for his wisdom to see this matter from a bigger perspective. Such as, how come Indonesia has a common language [i.e., a common goal] with Hong Kong of protecting Indonesian migrant workers—or even all migrant workers in Hong Kong? And it [that language] came from the CE [chief executive] when he met with President Joko Widodo in December 2015. So, we would like to recall his promise to us on how we are going to protect domestic helpers. And we also recall the contribution of the domestic helpers to Hong Kong's economy and, also, we recall the meeting between ourselves and the immigration department about the promise to open [up] more communication with the consulate. So, based on those communications we end our letter and say we would like to kindly seek his wisdom on that. . . . And we also mention these two girls already sent to jail and two others under hearing in Shatin. And this is already [February] twenty-fifth—it is already a week ago and we are still waiting for a response from the chief executive.

Yet, despite the problems encountered by domestic workers so far, and the lack of response from the chief executive, Mr. P maintained confidence in the passport project and SIMKIM. He told me proudly: "My good friend in Hong Kong [government] says, 'You are the first officer who does this!' I don't know if the Hong Kong government is surprised or not, but I think sooner or later we have to do this. We have to amend the data as long as we find strong evidence of that. Because . . . this is the state's action *to protect their citizens* and their true identity, and then of course it is human rights. Identity is human rights."

By the time I spoke to Mr. P in summer 2017, after dozens of women had been investigated and a dozen or more had been imprisoned, his perspective was largely the same. He explained that at the time (2015), an MOU had not seemed necessary, because their counterparts in the Hong Kong immigration department appeared to be supportive and understanding. "The Hong Kong immigration officials appeared [then] to understand and appeared to agree that this would be understood as a project to *correct errors*, but not to correct criminal offenses." He explained:

When we speak about data, we cannot reveal someone's identity if we have false identity on the girls. Right? So eventually what we propose [to the Hong Kong officials] is that, "If I rectify the data you should cooperate with me rather than bringing the girl to jail." Why? Because this is part of our strategy to unveil their—*their true identity.* And I can assure them [the Hong Kong government] that the rectification of the identity will only be done once and will be locked! You know. So, "We are putting back their original identity into their original position, but *please don't put them into the jail*" because this is part of the strategy to unveil the identity.

This resembled what he had said one year and two years earlier. However, he described a "new strategy" the Indonesian government was using in their "G2G" with the Hong Kong government, which was to tie the passport project more explicitly to their wider shared international concerns, including Indonesian initiatives regarding security and counterterrorism, and to new special training programs that Indonesia could offer in Indonesia to Hong Kong immigration officials.[6]

When we talk about terrorism and we talk about counterterrorism we talk about someone's identity. That's why the branch of this cooperation is on intelligence information sharing. But we are getting there. And we want to share data information with them. We want to share suspects of potential danger that will harm our community together. We can prevent someone from entering our jurisdiction by having this mutual information sharing, at first and before their appearance at our borders. So, this is kind of, progress to move forward without [explicitly] saying that we are objecting to their policy on the data rectification. *So, I think this is a strategy. This is a reroute of the first agenda to protect our citizens who have been rectifying their data by having this new route which finally we are going to reach our same goal as the first one.*

In summer 2017, Mr. P sounded tired. He said he had lost weight, that it had been "a long journey," and that the past two and a half years had taught him a lot. First, "applying technology to society has to be followed by education and also communication with the society themselves, to transform themselves into the new system." Second, he said, "I want to be

---

6. It was interesting that he did not mention anti-trafficking in this context (as discussed in chapter 7). Trafficking would have pointed the finger at the agencies, which was not their plan or their strategy.

blunt with you. Beforehand, before the new system there were a lot of middlemen [agents] arranging passport renewal, Nicole. With high prices." He described a case in which a Hong Kong agency had charged domestic workers HK$1,800 for a new passport when the actual price was only HK$280, a classic case of passport extortion (*paspor pungli*).

> So, I am just guessing that there are a lot of people [agents] who are just not happy when we started this new system. Because everybody has to come in and everybody has to have the biometrics taken. It cut the agents' profits [since they had previously renewed clients' passports] and the agent-and-client transactional relationship. That is another consequence. Lastly, of course, I want to share with you that building relationships with all components in the community is important. I agree that we have to engage closely with NGOs [activists] and the wider community in Hong Kong to resolve any problems that relate to domestic helpers because a lot of domestic helpers tell their stories not to us but to them. So maybe they will be more blunt and more honest if they see more people from their side. And maybe NGOs can tell us, "Sir, this is wrong, this is how they really feel. You have to fix this; you have to fix that." Then okay. If that makes sense and it is not against our law, then we can consider it.

Mr. P's description of the consulate's meetings with their Hong Kong government counterparts illustrates the unequal relationships not only between BMIs and Indonesian officials, but also between Indonesian and Hong Kong officials. Indonesian immigration officials had mistakenly assumed they were being taken seriously and had been *heard* as equals by their Hong Kong counterparts, and that if they submitted a letter documenting the passport changes, everything would be fine. But that was not the case, partly because of Indonesia's political capital. Indonesia is one of the most populous countries in the world, and its citizens provide essential low-cost labor to Hong Kong, but such human capital does not translate into political capital. In contrast to Asia's more powerful "economic tigers" (Japan, South Korea, Taiwan, and Singapore), other regions of South and Southeast Asia are often looked down on for having weak economies and weak and corrupt governments. Echoing historical patterns of China's relationship with Southeast Asian tributary states, Indonesia (like the Philippines) is regarded as a poor country that supplies Hong Kong with so-called unskilled women workers.

Indonesian consular officials' diplomatic credibility with their Hong Kong counterparts was not what they hoped for or expected. They underestimated Hong Kong immigration's legal considerations, despite the fact that Hong Kong's immigration department had been openly reporting on passport fraud, including the numbers of "fraudulent" Indonesian passports, for several years. Although the actual numbers were small, Indonesians were the third most represented nationality in passport fraud in Hong Kong in 2013 and 2014 (with twenty and sixteen cases, respectively) and the fourth in 2015, 2016, and 2017 (with sixteen, seventeen, and seven).[7] The Indonesian consular communications, moreover, were tinged with formal and submissive language, appealing, for example, to the chief executive's "greater wisdom" and sending compliments to Hong Kong immigration. But while appealing to the superior wisdom of the Hong Kong government, they made no mention of the role of recruitment agencies or brokers who most likely procured the aspal documents (and in some cases clearly coerced the women into using them). The Indonesian officials' own sense of superiority over "TKWs" or "helpers" is also clear.

Indonesian citizens in Hong Kong are clearly not immune to the social hierarchies of gender, class, education, and urban-rural divides that exist at home and are reflected in the attitudes of Indonesian officials and consular staff toward domestic workers abroad. Some migrant workers willingly situate themselves as "below" the consular officials in social standing. Activist migrant workers, however, are critical of being treated as subordinates or unequal citizens. In recent decades, migrant workers rejected the label *TKW* (*Tenaga Kerja Wanita,* woman migrant worker) because it signified an undervalued feminine labor regime. *TKI* (*Tenaga Kerja Indonesia,* Indonesian migrant worker) was considered preferable to *TKW* and was widely used by activist domestic workers and by the Indonesian government until around 2017. However, *TKI* was subsequently criticized by activists because it still served to distinguish between "formal" and "informal" labor sectors, thus maintaining the stereotypical

---

7. HK Immigration reports from 2013 to 2017 list total numbers of "fraudulent" passports and Chinese travel documents. Indonesian passports accounted for 2.6 percent ($n = 20$) in 2013; 3.1 percent in 2014 ($n = 16$); 3.1 percent in 2015 ($n = 16$); 3.7 percent in 2016 ($n = 17$); and 1.4 percent in 2017 ($n = 7$) (Hong Kong Immigration Department 2013, 2014, 2015, 2016, 2017).

derogatory implications of less valued women's labor.[8] By the time of this research, many Indonesian domestic worker activists in Hong Kong embraced *BMI (Buruh Migran Indonesia)* as a more empowering term that was more in keeping with the vocabulary of migrant labor used by the United Nations.[9]

The consulate's sentencing appeal letter (see chapter 4), intended to provide support for migrant workers whose passport identities were changed, echoed the condescending view of migrant workers as poor, rural, and too naive or "simpleminded" to have willfully misrepresented themselves. Along the same lines, Mr. P was appalled that BMI organizations would go over his head and approach his superior, the director general of immigration in Jakarta, especially without his knowledge. That they also wrote to the president and met with officials from all the relevant top ministries—including the Ministry of Foreign Affairs, which oversees consulates and embassies; the Ministry of Manpower, under the Coordinating Ministry for Economic Affairs; and BNP2TKI, an agency established in 2004 to protect migrant workers in Jakarta—was not the expected, "appropriate" behavior of rural "girls." This might also explain why Mr. P often referred to the main critics of the passport project as "NGOs" or "their NGO friends" (instead of activist BMIs). He seemed to refer to the international organizations that helped migrant workers, rather than the activist organizations of migrant workers themselves, as the objectors. Mr. P reserved the term *activist* for specific individual women domestic workers, like Sringatin, Eni Lestari, and others. His expectation that BMIs and "their NGOs" would come to him and say "Sir, we have a problem" reflects an assumed gender and class hierarchy that echoes in the migrant worker–employer dynamic as well.

Yet BMIs' actions (described below) asserted their place both as migrants and as citizens who demand better care and a response from their government. From the perspective of the top Indonesian government

8. One activist said that *TKI* was associated with Terminal 3 (in Suharto airport in Jakarta), where returning migrant workers were targeted, extorted, and forced to pay for services they did not need (Silvey 2007).

9. Law no. 18/2017 on the Placement and Protection of Migrant Workers refers to the migrant worker as *PMI* instead of *TKI* as in the earlier Law no. 39/2004. Both terms, and *BMI*, are often translated in English as "Indonesian migrant worker" but carry different connotations.

ministers who traveled to Hong Kong in a diplomatic effort to address their complaints (described below), BMIs may be unequal citizens in relation to their class and migratory status, but they had become a political force to be reckoned with as many Indonesian citizens (and prospective voters) rallied to their cause.

ACTIVISM AND ACTIVIST PERSPECTIVES

Indonesian migrant activist groups such as JBMI and its affiliated organizations—PILAR (United Indonesians Against Overcharging), ATKI (Association of Indonesian Migrant Workers), IMWU (Indonesian Migrant Workers' Union), and many others—were alarmed by the problems that arose from the passport renewal project. By the second half of 2015 and early 2016, they had held rallies and issued a call for action (see figure 6). They had long worked with local Hong Kong organizations and activists, including the MFMW, Bethune House, the Asia-Pacific Mission for Migrants, and others that had initially, in the 1980s, supported Filipino migrant workers and, by the late 1990s, expanded to include Indonesians and all nationalities of migrant workers as their numbers grew. They also worked closely with KABAR BUMI, an Indonesia-based organization that was established by local Indonesian activists, former migrant workers, family members of migrant workers, and members of JBMI affiliate groups. Together, they advocated for migrant workers in Hong Kong, Macau, and Taiwan and for returned migrant workers and their families (Fatharini 2018; Hsia 2009).

The passport problems in Hong Kong were but one part of the activists' larger, longer-term struggle to repeal or amend Law no. 39/2004 on Placement and Protection for Indonesian Overseas Workers (i.e., TKIs). Hong Kong migrant worker activists and members of JBMI had long been working with KABAR BUMI and associated lawyers and legislators in Indonesia to criticize Law no. 39/2004. When the passport renewal problems arose, JBMI and KABAR BUMI contacted their Indonesian networks of lawyers and politicians and pressured government officials for change through meetings, petitions, and protest actions.

Almost every summer, I met with domestic worker activists I had known for many years. These included Sringatin, chairperson of JBMI

Figure 6. Passport protest, May Day, 2016. Photo credit: JBMI Media Team.

and IMWU, who coordinated most of their local outreach efforts for the passport project; and Eni Lestari, founder of ATKI, founder and chairperson of the International Migrants Alliance (IMA), who was deeply involved with outreach in Indonesia and on wider issues. Eni Lestari, Sringatin, and several others had carefully studied the passport situation. In June 2016, they voiced the organizations' growing concerns. They were especially angry at the consulate, and the Indonesian government more broadly, for their lack of consultation and communication about the passport project before it started, for the problems that it caused, and for their responses to the problems. As Eni said,

> We were so mad at the [Indonesian] government because they didn't inform anyone about these things! They just did it. And then we find another [passport] victim and another one and another one. Why are more people falling down?
>
> And then they [consular and government officials] say, "Don't worry, don't worry, they [BMIs] will be fine! We already talked to Immigration. They will be fine. Just tell them the truth." But we cannot accept any more of

this when people came to us in December [2015], and we say, "This is not alright!" If you [the consulate] talk like this to Hong Kong immigration, it will not be effective! People went to prison!

Not receiving satisfactory responses in Hong Kong, JBMI representatives traveled to Indonesia to meet with members of KABAR BUMI and many top-level government ministries. Eni Lestari recalled:

We went to Indonesia a lot—because there is no point—this is a small [consular] office [in Hong Kong]. If you want to complain to their boss, you have to go to Indonesia. We went to Indonesia and talked to several ministries, including the Ministry of Foreign Affairs, the Ministry of Manpower, The Ministry of Placement and Protection of Migrant Workers (BNP2TKI), and others . . . and then finally the [Indonesian] government ministers came here two weeks ago, and we told them, "You are going to put everyone in prison!" They [the government] says, "This is not our intention, this is *unintended consequences*. We don't have any [such] intent."

The consulate reinforced the idea of BMIs as flexible labor. Mr. P had told me not to worry about women having to leave, because others would come to take their place. Several BMI activists referred to the passport project as a "soft deportation policy," an indication that the government simply wanted migrant workers to return home or didn't care if they left. Eni continued: "When you make this change you need to plan, in advance, and you need to tell your people overseas. You *have to* tell them! Don't keep it silent and under the table. People come out and then go to prison. So, we are putting the consulate in the public hot spot. We are organizing actually and reaching out to workers. It is supposed to be *their* work [the consulate's]!" When the activist workers proposed that the consulate hold a large meeting with BMIs, of the sort that the migrant workers organized at the University of Hong Kong (see chapter 2) and at Hong Kong Polytechnic University, the consulate replied, "We don't have a budget to have this [sort of] big meeting." The activists responded, "Well you have all the power to get Victoria Park or any park, to talk to your people! I'm sure the Hong Kong government will understand [and let you use the park]. You don't need to pay either because it is a diplomatic request." But, Eni continued, "instead of initiating such meeting and forums, KJRI [consulate] officials willingly attended the forums organized by migrant workers." As BMIs chanted at the 2016 forum described in chapter 2, "Meet us in Victoria Park!"

Migrant worker activists in Hong Kong, like Sringatin and Eni Lestari, consulted with Hong Kong NGO leaders Cynthia Abdon-Tellez of the MFMW and Edwina Antonio-Santoyo of Bethune House migrant shelter and with lawyers, including Melville Boase. They networked with JBMI's member groups' leaders and representatives and instructed them to reach out to their members and urge them to contact all their migrant worker friends and relatives to let them know about the potential pitfalls of passport renewal. They referred them to the main team of domestic workers who studied different courses of action. They provided mobile phone hotline numbers where activist BMIs responded night or day to provide guidance and collect data on the problems that workers encountered. They worked not only on their Sundays off, but whenever their employers allowed, or when they had time after or between work duties, sending text and WhatsApp messages. JBMI had teams of volunteers who, along with Sringatin, accompanied women like Mina and Anti to Shatin court.

Activist volunteers offered women advice based on the data they had collected about passport problems. Their strategies shifted through time, responding to subtly changing conditions and new outcomes of specific cases. Table 1 represents some of the options, and the pros and cons of each, as they were understood in June 2016. A version of it was presented at the JBMI worker forum in July 2016. Another option, considered later, was to legally change their names in Hong Kong or in Indonesia to the name in the passport. Options that were not recommended by the activists were (a) overstaying the passport and visa or (b) filing a refugee claim under Hong Kong's USM (Unified Screening Mechanism), neither of which would allow them to continue to work legally, and overstaying would likely eventually result in criminal charges.

Meanwhile, members of KABAR BUMI in Indonesia and JBMI in Hong Kong met with government officials and ministries. In May 2016, they sent a letter that was circulated as a petition to President Joko Widodo. It was signed by Iwenk Karsiwen, chairperson of KABAR BUMI, a former Hong Kong domestic worker, and an early member of ATKI; and by Sringatin, chairperson of JBMI and IMWU. Both of them had worked with Eni Lestari to build a broader coalition of ATKI, IMWU, and other

Table 1   Passport Options, June 2016

Option	Pros/benefits	Cons/risks
1. Go home before passport expires	• Won't be arrested/ investigated etc.	• Probably can't come back to Hong Kong (but see options 5 and 6 below) • Loss of income • Might not be able to finish contract • Inconvenience for worker and employer
2. Get SPLP* to finish work contract within a year, then go home.	• Allowed to finish contract within a year. • Less risky than changing to revised passport	• Greater risk trying to get revised passport in Indonesia and then returning to Hong Kong (see options 5 and 6 below); likely can't come back with revised passport
3. Get SPLP* to finish contract and meanwhile try to process new Hong Kong identity card in Hong Kong.	• Allowed to finish contract within a year. • Can apply for a new Hong Kong identity card and then change to new passport and visa. • If successful, can continue to work in Hong Kong. • Useful to press the legal/political issues in a collective way if a large number of people do so	• Might be investigated/ interrogated by HKID • Can go to jail if found guilty of immigration fraud • After jail, likely can't come back to Hong Kong
4. Get new passport printed by KJRI-HK (Indonesian consulate in Hong Kong).	• Might work out okay and can continue to work in Hong Kong (14/36 so far).	• Might be investigated/ interrogated by HKID • Can go to jail if found guilty of immigration fraud • After jail, likely can't come back to Hong Kong
5. Leave Hong Kong and get new passport with same identity issued in Indonesia.	• Can come back to Hong Kong with less risk.	• Can cost a lot of money to get documents • Risky if Indonesian immigration is aware of identity differences in SIMKIM
6. Leave Hong Kong and get new passport with "revised" identity in Indonesia.	• Easier than facing immediate risk of investigation in Hong Kong. • More convenient to get documents if not accessible in Hong Kong.	• With new passport with revised identity, can have trouble re-entering Hong Kong or can be investigated upon return to Hong Kong • Can go to jail

* Travel Document in Lieu of Passport (see chapter 5)

Indonesian migrant worker organizations in Hong Kong (and in Macao and Taiwan). The petition expressed their demands and appealed to the government to act to protect its citizen workers from becoming passport victims (see box 2).

A key strategy of the petition was to remind President Widodo of the promises he had made to migrant workers and other citizens when he campaigned for president in 2014. The petition publicized their concerns—including major problems with agencies guilty of overcharging and falsifying identities—and the various government ministries they had communicated with. No doubt, groups like JBMI and KABAR BUMI also had an impact in their efforts to alert the Indonesian public—especially the family members of migrant workers—to the issues faced by migrant workers abroad and the overall problem of the recruitment agencies. The month after the petition was sent, as the situation continued to escalate and more Indonesian news media covered the passport problems, two top-ranking Indonesian officials—the minister of foreign affairs and the minister of law and human rights—traveled to Hong Kong to meet with Hong Kong government officials and with representatives from migrant worker organizations.

INDONESIAN MINISTERIAL VISIT, JUNE 2016

Throughout the spring and summer of 2016, news in the Indonesian-language press in Hong Kong and in Indonesia drew attention to the correction of passport data (*koreksidata paspor*) or to fraudulent passport data (*palsukan data paspor*) in relation to the Hong Kong Consulate (KJRI-HK) (*Suara* 2016a, 2016b; Tempo 2016; Voice of Migrants 2015, 2016; Yosephine 2016a, 2016b). As a result of concern over the growing numbers of BMIs who were being investigated by Hong Kong immigration, had gone to court, and were going to prison, Indonesian government ministers began paying close attention and started communicating with the consulate, while activists continued to pressure them and offered support to passport victims.

Activists were cautiously optimistic when, on June 16, 2016, another "G2G" meeting was held in Hong Kong with top Indonesian ministers and

Box 2. PETITION TO THE PRESIDENT FROM JBMI AND
KABAR BUMI, MAY 2016

May 20, 2016

#Sampai_Kapan_BMI_Terikat_PT_dan_Agen
#Jokowi_Lindung_BMI_Hukum_PJTKI
#Selabungan_Korban_Koreksi_Data
Cabut_UU_39_2004

We—from an organization of migrant workers, former migrant workers
and migrant families called KABAR BUMI (Keluarga Besar Buruh
Migran Indonesia) work with Hong Kong migrant workers in Macau,
Taiwan who are members of JBMI (Indonesian Migrant Workers'
Network)—are sending this open petition to Bapak [honorific for man;
Joko Widodo], as the President of the Republic of Indonesia, asking for
protection for Indonesian Migrant Workers who are threatened with
criminalization due to the forced changes of identities in their passports.

Since January 2015, the Consulate General of the Republic of Indonesia
in Hong Kong (KJRI-HK) has implemented a new biometric passport
renewal system, Immigration Information Management System
(SIMKIM) for Indonesian citizens abroad to renew their passports.
We appreciate the government's intention to improve the data of
Indonesian citizens that has been in disarray, including that of
BMI[s]. But unfortunately, the KJRI-HK has unilaterally changed
the existing passport identities of the BMI[s].

When data in the passport, specifically the name and place of birth date,
does not match the government database, the KJRI-HK changes the
identity according to the identity stated on the birth certificate, family
card and diploma. The government does not consider the risks that will
befall Indonesian migrant workers when their identities are corrected,
given their vulnerability and low bargaining power in the eyes of the
Hong Kong government.

The government has turned a blind eye to the fact that for decades the
PPTKIS [agencies] have falsified the identity of BMI[s] in collaboration

with corrupt individuals in the ranks of the government from the village level to the immigration office itself. The Hong Kong regulation states that anyone who enters/lives/works in Hong Kong with an identity that does not belong to them is considered [to have committed] a criminal offense and [is] threatened with imprisonment.

Since the distribution of identity reform policies in Hong Kong there have [so far] been 6 people in JBMI's records who were sentenced to 14–18 months in prison in Hong Kong courts, 4 people [currently] in court proceedings, dozens of others who were arrested and interrogated by Hong Kong immigration, dozens of others [who] were denied work visas, and many more who were pressured or forced to return to Indonesia before their passport expiration out of fear of the threat of imprisonment. All those convicted and put in prison, are then deported and barred from working again in Hong Kong.

A brief study conducted by JBMI in January–March 2016 related to falsifying data on 497 BMI[s] in Hong Kong found that 231 BMI[s] had data that was falsified, and in 91.7% of cases, PPTKIS were careless about the migrant workers' passport data. Worse yet, the KJRI-HK does not provide lawyers to assist BMI[s] who are facing arrest and imprisonment.

Meanwhile, the service quota which is limited to a maximum of 120 people/day (100 via WhatsApp and 20 urgent cases) is inadequate. Whereas before, the queue for passport production reached 150 people/day. If calculated from the number of BMI[s] of 153,000, then the KJRI-HK should be able to serve 250 people/day. As a result, BMI[s] are required to wait 6–7 months starting from the date of booking via WhatsApp to renew their passports. Frequently changing WhatsApp numbers also adds to the anxiety.

Coupled with that, the lack of widespread and comprehensive communication and outreach about the biometric passport-making system at the locations where BMI[s] gather on their holidays, has raised confusion. The KJRI-HK did not give an official announcement or an open warning about changing the identity for [a] BMI whose identity was falsified. As a result, BMI[s] did not know that their identity would be changed and only found out when they renewed their passports. We regret this forced policy of identity reform.

In the midst of the state's inability to create decent jobs and alleviate people from poverty in the country, the government should not create policies that plunge BMI[s] into the position of criminalization outside the country, depriving them of their source of livelihood. Who will provide for the family's livelihood if the BMI is convicted and imprisoned abroad?

We become BMI[s] abroad not from choice but from compulsion. Our identity is falsified not because of our wishes, but due to the crimes of PPTKIS. BMI[s], the majority of whom are female domestic workers, are the biggest contributors to foreign exchange, but until now there has been no recognition or protection.

The view of us as weak and ignorant and required to use [i.e., affiliate with] PPTKIS is completely wrong. Thus far, it is not the PPTKIS and agents who protect our rights and dignity, but we ourselves through the organizations that we have formed.

We work together, study and continue to fight for what we think is right and fair. It is still fresh in our memories when you met with RUMAH RAKYAT and BARA JP to directly convey the view that pressing issues and urgent problems that BMI[s] face must be resolved.

What Mr. Jokowi [i.e., Joko Widodo] promised then, if he became President, was the following:

- Build a government that provides comprehensive protection to Indonesian migrant workers
- Build a protection system to guarantee the rights of migrant workers and eliminate the migrant trade mafia
- Stop any form of discrimination against Indonesian migrant workers

In addition to this petition, we have also conducted hearings with various related institutions including:

- January 5 hearings with the Directorate General of Immigration
- January 7 hearings with BNP2TKI [National Agency for the Placement and Protection of Migrant Workers]
- April 12 and 20 hearings with the Ministry of Foreign Affairs
- April 27 hearings with the Ministry of Manpower
- April 21 KABAR BUMI together with KOMNAS PEREMPUAN [National Commission on Violence Against Women] held a forum with 4 government agencies:
  1. Directorate General of Immigration
  2. Ministry of Foreign Affairs
  3. Director General of the Ministry of Home Affairs
  4. Ministry of Manpower

We believe any regulations introduced by the government must protect victims and punish perpetrators, not criminalize victims.

With this, we urge Mr. President Jokowi and all his staff:

1. Stop changing the identity of Indonesian citizens abroad before there is a Memorandum of Agreement between the governments of Indonesia and Hong Kong or other countries where the policy will be implemented.
2. The MoU must ensure that there is no criminalization of Indonesian citizens, including BMI[s] whose identities are addressed, and guarantee the right of BMI[s] to continue working in the country, and free migrant workers who have been arrested or imprisoned.
3. Provide competent lawyers who are ready to assist Indonesian migrant workers who are arrested and imprisoned in Hong Kong.
4. Provide a complaint mechanism and legal representation for Indonesian migrant workers who want to suc the PPTKIS [agencies] for falsifying BMI identity.
5. Criminalize overcharging and create a complaint mechanism and compensation for BMI victims of overcharging and other violations committed by PPTKIS.
6. Clear the PPTKIS control of BMI[s] by removing the "Placement Agreement" rules, prohibiting the transfer of PPTKIS and imposing an independent contract.

7. Revoke Law No. 39/2004 and Create true protection laws that adopt the 1990 UN convention and C 189 for Indonesian migrant workers and their families.

We regret the revisions planned for the law replacing law UUPPTKILN No. 39/2004 because almost nothing has changed, essentially because it still forces BMI[s] to be tied to PPTKIS. The new law must adhere to the principle of the 1990 Convention concerning the Protection of Migrant Workers and Their Families which the government ratified in 2012.

Your involvement to ensure the safety of Indonesian migrant workers abroad, especially those victims of false identity abroad who are threatened with criminalization, is very urgent and hoped for. Moreover, we also hope that you will immediately realize our demands above. For the sake of upholding justice for the foreign exchange heroes BMI[s].

Best regards,
Chair of KABAR BUMI, Iwenk Karsiwen   *Chair of JBMI, Sringatin*

top Hong Kong officials in response to the passport problems that had been brought to their attention. Ms. Retno Marsudi, Indonesian minister of foreign affairs (to whom the consul general reports), and Mr. Yasonna Laoly, minister of law and human rights (Menkumham, for short, under which is the Directorate General of Immigration, or Imigrasi), came to Hong Kong and met with Hong Kong's acting chief executive, John Tsang, and its secretary for security, Lai Tung-kwok. The ministers had expected to meet with Hong Kong's top official, Chief Executive Leung Chun-ying, but when they arrived they were told he was "unavailable." One consular official I spoke with took this as an intentional slight.

In the meeting with Hong Kong officials, Foreign Minister Marsudi was quoted as saying that "cooperation in the fields of manpower and immigration in Indonesia and Hong Kong is an important part of relations between the two parties," and according to the Indonesian press, the Hong Kong government officially welcomed Marsudi's proposal to build closer cooperation in the field of immigration through the establishment of an MOU between relevant agencies. A report on an Indonesian government website described the meeting:

> During the friendly meeting, the Indonesian Foreign Minister described several legal cases involving Indonesian citizens and related to the implementation of the Immigration Management Information System (SIMKIM). Responding to this, the Hong Kong Secretary of Security said that the strong bilateral relations between Indonesia and Hong Kong are an important basis upon which to discuss this issue further in order to find the best solution for both parties. At the meeting they agreed to intensify cooperation between the Indonesian Consulate General in Hong Kong and the Hong Kong Immigration Office through the establishment of a working group to overcome various problems faced by Indonesian citizens in Hong Kong.

The foreign minister and the minister of law and human rights also attended a meeting hosted by the Indonesian Consulate General in Hong Kong and chaired by Mr. Chalief Akbar, Indonesian consul general at the time, with "Indonesian citizens"—around fifty representatives of Indonesian migrant worker groups. During that meeting, Minister Marsudi reiterated the commitment of President Widodo's government to protect Indonesian citizens abroad, including migrant workers. "The government, together with BMIs' friends, are all there to protect you. If friends cry, we also cry. Problems always exist, but the government is committed to helping find solutions." The ministers said that many of the complaints that had been conveyed to them by BMIs in Hong Kong had to do with the implementation of SIMKIM, explained by Minister Laoly as "a government effort to make the passport more secure and to improve the process so that Indonesian passports meet international standards." Minister Marsudo said, "The president [Joko Widodo] asked me and Menkumham to immediately take strategic steps to overcome the side effects of implementing SIMKIM."

After the meeting, the website of the Ministry of Law and Human Rights reported on both meetings and quoted Sringatin as saying, "We are very pleased, because this is the Foreign Minister's first direct meeting with BMI[s] in Hong Kong for at least the last 13 years" (Indonesian Consulate General 2016; Salim 2016a). JBMI also issued a press release on the meetings (JBMI 2016b), reiterating the demands it had made earlier in the JBMI/KABAR BUMI petition to President Widodo. JBMI applauded the arrival of the ministers to address migrant workers' concerns, especially that of preventing them from becoming victims of passport data corrections. Sringatin spelled out what the ministers seemed careful to sidestep about the role of agencies (PPTKIS). "The main problem that BMIs face," she said, "is that the falsification of BMI documents is carried out by PPTKIS" and that the PPTKIS, in turn, are empowered by Law no. 39/2004. "PPTKIS are required to take care of all departure requirements for BMIs including passports" and "PPTKIS falsify passport data for prospective BMIs to speed up the bureaucratic process of acquiring documents so that workers can quickly travel." This, in turn, maximizes the number of workers they can send abroad, and thus increases their profits. Sringatin also mentioned JBMI's survey finding that at least "31 percent of migrant workers in Hong Kong (accounting for around 47,000 data changes) had their data changed and faced potential correction by the consulate and the potential threat of criminalization in Hong Kong." In the first four months of 2016, JBMI had "received 1,430 migrant worker passport-related complaints, including problems with passport booking, incorrect passport data, forced overstaying because the passport was not ready on time, and salary deductions because of repeated visits to the consulate."

Sringatin voiced JBMI's demands, including a call for the government to "increase its diplomatic efforts and establish an MOA [memorandum of agreement] to ensure that *no Indonesian citizen, including [any] BMI* is criminalized, deported or prohibited from working because of data correction" and that the consulate provides "competent lawyers to assist migrant workers who are victims of data forgery and criminalized by the Hong Kong government, and [likewise] in other countries where data correction is enforced." She reiterated the demand that the consul general "distribute informational pamphlets to all BMIs in Hong Kong, the New Territories and Kowloon, including information about: a) the booking procedure for getting a new passport; b) conditions for renewing a passport; c) requirements for BMI whose passports have an endorsement or whose passport data is incorrect." JBMI urged the consulate to facilitate passport booking by telephone for BMIs who do not have smartphones. This would allow them to obtain a passport booking number or change passport appointments by phone, which would reduce congestion and confusion at the consulate. They called for more staff and better dissemination of information to "Indonesian *migrant workers and citizens* in Hong Kong." Sringatin reiterated the demand that consular officials meet with Indonesian migrant workers who have been identified by JBMI as having falsified data, and that they exert greater diplomatic efforts to release the imprisoned victims and revoke the charges against those who are in court.

As described in news reports and press releases, in the meeting with BMIs, Minister Marsudi said that she and Minister Laoly were taking "four strategic steps" in response to the problems and complaints arising from the implementation of SIMKIM in Hong Kong. The first step was meeting with the acting chief executive of Hong Kong to develop a G2G understanding and an MOU regarding the passport changes. The ministers explained to the Hong Kong officials the purpose of SIMKIM and the passport correction policy. They asked the Hong Kong government not to criminalize BMIs on the basis of passport changes.

The ministers responded to the problem at hand, not the wider underlying ones. In response to complaints about long lines, delays, and other difficulties in renewing passports at the consulate, Marsudi acknowledged that there was a serious gap between supply and demand for passports. The consulate currently had enough staff and equipment to serve 120 passport applicants a day, but the demand was 300 a day. The second step was thus to accelerate the process of obtaining new passports by sending additional staff and technical assistance from the Ministry of Foreign Affairs and from Imigrasi to the consulate to help. The ministers agreed to send six additional temporary staff members from Jakarta to speed up the process, with a goal of reducing the seven- to twelve-day passport renewal time to five days. The third step was to simplify the process of obtaining the new passport, so that Indonesian citizens had to go to the consulate just once. As BMIs later learned, the consulate had no budget to mail the passports, so the cost was passed on to BMIs, who had to provide a prepaid registered envelope for the service. The fourth step was to send additional specialized and secure computer equipment and software with access to the SIMKIM database to speed up the review and processing of renewal applications.

The 2016 meeting was tremendously important. It would not have occurred without JBMI's efforts. The meeting might seem like a victory for migrant workers, and it was in some ways, but the agreements described above did not take place overnight, nor did the situation improve right away, and demands to address wider issues and underlying causes of aspal passports were not mentioned in that context. As Sringatin explained to me in 2017, activists learned many things from the passport project ordeal, including the value of connections between migrant workers and their non-migrant-worker supporters, especially family members.

> The government will implement changes secretly without consulting, without transparency and honest open discussion with those whom the policies will impact. We learned from the past, from the Erwiana [Sulistyaningsih] case, that we will win from providing services for migrant workers who need assistance and are harmed. We need to work with the person and the person's family.
>
> The family often assumes the migrant worker is just not sending money; they mistrust her, as opposed to understanding the situation. In one case we mediated, for example, the husband said his wife must have consented to sex with the employer, but it was rape. For those migrant workers who need assistance, it helps to contact the family and have them on board, like in Erwiana's case. After Erwiana, the family is key. So, we learned to bring the passport victim, the family, and the supporters together.
>
> We learned to be careful with new regulations. The government is not transparent about laws. We need to listen to everything and study carefully. We ask more and consult more with everyone, elsewhere too. We must ask who is impacted and where. The victim's situation needs attention, and the regulation needs to change. There are three main activities we work on: (1) provide services, (2) prevent the next victim, and (3) collect facts and analysis to give the government. *We consider carefully how the government and the grass roots can work together.*

Not only did JBMI and KABAR BUMI recognize the importance of drawing in family members as supporters of BMI issues, but in so doing, they also broke down the citizen-migrant binary and produced cross-cutting alliances.

Over the years, Sringatin had organized and run many workshops for migrant workers. She described the barriers they face, including especially "family, poverty, education," and the self-defeating view that "they are *just* migrant workers." Moreover, "their attitude is mainly that they are too poor, that their families need them to just buck up and work, and that they are uneducated." Indonesian social expectations, she said, are the biggest problem. BMIs "think they have no need or no right to complain or criticize. They have been threatened on social media for being too demanding. They are told they should be happy and grateful to have a job." Sringatin and other BMI activists teach women not to underestimate themselves or their rights. "The only limitations are that they are shy and afraid. They don't feel they have the right or ability to stand up for themselves, but they do. They want to be more educated and learn about the wider situation. They get together and share experiences." The Indonesian government wants to help them access education while they are in Hong Kong, but the problem is that they have very little time and are often exhausted on the day off. "Why not give them education in Indonesia?" Sringatin asked rhetorically.

CITIZEN *AND* MIGRANT

This chapter has questioned the migrant-citizen dichotomy and has described a momentous meeting of Indonesian ministers with Hong Kong's second in command, a meeting that occurred largely in response to the problems experienced and the demands made by activist migrant workers. As illustrated above, consular officials likely underestimated Indonesian migrant workers, seeing them as rural "girls," "helpers," and TKWs more than as "citizens" who could raise their voices and make demands of their government. BMIs participated as citizens *and* migrant workers, demonstrating to non-migrant-worker citizens—including their family members and others, by extension—their shared interests and why citizens should support workers. Top-ranking officials responded to migrant workers, as citizens, by meeting in Hong Kong with key local officials. In their "demands" to the ministers at a meeting hosted by the consul general, as in their communication with President Widodo, JBMI was neither subtle nor meek and submissive. They did not adhere to an expected subordinate posture (or appeal to the officials' greater "wisdom"). They did not follow what some would consider proper feminine etiquette for domestic "helpers," or village "girls" without higher education, in relation to national government officials. Instead, they made their demands *as* workers and citizens and *for* workers and citizens.

Some migrant workers and officials criticized BMI activists for not behaving properly and respecting the government, but many members of the Indonesian and activist communities came to their defense. As more BMIs encountered problems with their own passports, they came to view the activists with deep respect. The ministerial event would not have occurred were it not for migrant worker activism and networking in and beyond Hong Kong. The ministerial meeting and the changes to the passport project that followed (see chapter 7) were the result of efforts to publicize criticism of the project, consulate, and government, and of the consulate's need for reinforcement from higher officials to reach Hong Kong government leaders.

It is important to note that BMI activists explicitly said that they were not "for or against" the government, the president, or the consular officials. They networked and utilized a range of alliances with governmental and non-governmental actors. At election time, they worked hard not to support specific political candidates but rather specific issues and proposed policies. They opposed policies that negatively impact migrant workers. They criticized laws and policies that harm or endanger them. Largely, they criticized the laws that continue to require migrant workers to utilize employment agencies (PPTKIS), which they consider deeply entangled with their deeper problems, and increasingly empowered by the government rather than controlled by them. They criticized the "business" of recruitment in which migrant workers are "sold" or traded for low wages accompanied by increasing government fees and migration costs, and the lack of "real protections" from the government against corrupt agencies.

Although the consulate had slowly and selectively cracked down on some Hong Kong agencies over the past several years—not renewing their licenses and setting new sanctions and requirements—activist workers insisted that it was not enough. They observed that government leaders and bureaucrats have, at best, mixed feelings about the agencies, which they depend on and often profit from. Government officials, likewise, expressed frustration that agencies they had shut down in Hong Kong often reappeared with different names. Similar anticorruption and anti-agency crackdowns in Indonesia appear futile to many observers. The government "cracks down" on agencies but simultaneously empowers them and gives them more responsibilities for the protection of migrant workers. Meanwhile, the activists have, over the past two decades, gradually shifted their language from that of "labor rights" to that of "human trafficking" and "debt bondage," the latter of which deeply resonates with Indonesian labor history.

7 Temporalities and Scales

> The sites, spaces, and scales through which domestic
> workers are controlled and empowered are not fixed, nor
> are they shaped solely by the disciplinary power of the
> state. Rather, this very geography is an arena that is
> struggled over, entered into by activists, and affected by
> the political agency of domestic workers and non-state
> actors.
>
> Rachel Silvey (2004, 248)

> Understanding travel and mobility as rooted in antar-
> jemput [escort] complicates liberal dichotomies of state
> power versus individual freedom, and introduces a complex
> continuum between control, exploitation, comfort, desire,
> trust, and care in the context of migration. . . . This leads
> back to the indirect rule of the Dutch colonial state, which
> relied on a wide range of intermediaries to mediate
> between villages and urban centers of power.
>
> Johan Lindquist (2018a, 94)

It might seem as though the "passport project" of the Indonesian consular immigration officials *took place* in Hong Kong—at the Indonesian consulate, in Victoria Park, at the Hong Kong immigration offices, in Shatin court and Lo Wu women's prison—from 2015 to 2017, and that it caused problems for a relatively small number of Indonesian migrant workers. Reaching temporally and spatially beyond a narrow situational analysis of the passport project in Hong Kong, however, reveals larger lessons. I have argued that it is important to question popular binaries and to look instead at entanglements. Following passports—not only people—across different times and places, following their social and historical threads, their connections and entanglements with those who issue and procure passports, carry them, confiscate them, alter them and renew them, and with the people and institutions that benefit or profit from them, reveals insights about the inequalities of the migrant labor industry and the entanglements of state and non-state forms of governance.

Unlike the previous chapters' binaries, *temporalities* and *scales* are not assumed to be oppositional or dichotomous. Both terms evoke binaries (e.g., past and present, now and then, here and there, local and global), but such pairs all conjure a continuum or a span between time periods or distances, not just oppositions. Temporalities remind us of multiple time frames and senses of time, not simply the past and present, and that an "era" does not simply end when another is said to begin. Scales are envisioned as zooming in and out to focus on microscopic or wider geographic spaces, instead of a fixed scale or region on a map.

Recent shifts in anthropological and historical studies, often building on geographers' insights, show the value of following and examining threads, connections, and movements through time and space, rather than delineating a single point and place in time. The limitations—literal and figurative—of conventional scalar units and conventional time periods are well illustrated. Historians of Asia have moved beyond the study of conventional bounded regions and periods—the seemingly discrete epochs, dynasties, and colonial or postcolonial periods. They no longer focus only on a nation-state or a narrow geographic region, but increasingly attend to mobilities and connections between them. Inter-Asian connections (like Atlantic or world history) reflect critiques of older analytic boundaries and the Western versus non-Western binary. Asian history is depicted as flows of time, in "circular histories" that connect regions through oceanic currents (Duara 2013, 2019) or trace centuries of Asian connections in relation to mobilities that extend beyond conventionally defined regions (Amrith 2011, 2013, 2018; Ho 2006). Rather than focus on "China" or "Southeast Asia," new histories explore entangled temporalities and scales pertaining to migrations, mobilities, and power (e.g., Ghosh 2008, 2011, 2015; McKeown 2008; Mongia 2018).

Older anthropological studies of discrete social groups and regions, once written in the "ethnographic present," have long been criticized for creating a timeless other (Fabian 1983), "people without history" (Wolf 1982), and treating "a culture" or "a society" as bounded wholes "discovered" by westerners. Such studies often ignored social connections, mobilities, and entanglements between social groups, and downplayed the roles of missionaries, colonial powers, and the wider political economies with which they were entangled.[1] Evolutionary studies that reflected deeply rooted Euro- or Western-centric, racist views of so-called primitive versus civilized people—utilizing simplistic and misleading binary assumptions such as "tradition" and "modernity"—have also been repudiated (Marcus and Fischer 1986; Fabian 1983). World systems approaches responded to such criticisms, examining connections between center and periphery, local and global, but still echoed overly binary views of the world.[2] Anthropologists interested in connections, movements, and mobilities have long criticized binaries of global and local (Appadurai 1996; Gupta and Ferguson 1992).[3]

A global-local approach risks ignoring all the connections and entanglements that exist between—and *in between*—the "global" and the "local" of labor recruitment. Passports force us to consider distant and recent pasts that connect (however vaguely) Dutch labor mobility regimes and *passen stelsel* (pass system) to now defunct three-year TKI passports and biometric passports that adhere to current global standards. Passports point to minuscule, seemingly irrelevant, but historically rich microdetails, such as the feathers of the Garuda, that are tied to Hindu travelers in Java centuries ago (predating European exploration) and to Indonesian

---

1. For related criticisms, see Abu-Lughod (1996); Clifford and Marcus (1986); Marcus and Cushman (1982); Marcus and Fischer (1986); Rosaldo (1986).

2. "Local and global"—and related spatiotemporal locations such as "global north" and "global south," "developed world" and "developing world," or "first world" and "third world"—are often used, but they are problematic because they refer to separations, rather than to past and present entanglements (Mohanty, Russo, and Torres 1991, ix–x).

3. This includes studies of "transnationalism" that criticized assimilationist, unidirectional ideas about migration and looked at circulation/movement of people, goods, ideas, and capital in multiple locations, scales, or periods (Appadurai 1996; Kearney 1995; Vertovec 1999; Basch, Glick Schiller, and Szanton Blanc 1994). Multi-sited research also drew attention to global connections and assemblages (Ong and Collier 2005).

independence and nationalism—and to current global concerns about securitization, terrorism, and human trafficking.

As we have seen, passports—like patterns of encapsulation and escort—are literally and figuratively entangled in multiple temporalities and scales. The passport problems and the "passport victims" described in this book are connected by a migration infrastructure that connects—or entangles—villages and small towns in relatively poor regions of Central and East Java (and elsewhere) in a web of government agencies and ministries at the national, provincial, and regional levels. As Lindquist notes in this chapter's second epigraph, the Dutch system of indirect rule relied on a range of intermediaries that connected villages and small towns to larger regions and urban centers of power. The letter from JBMI and KABAR BUMI to President Widodo (chapter 6) echoes the same pattern, noting that for decades the government has ignored that PPTKIS (agencies) "have falsified the identity of BMIs in collaboration with corrupt individuals in the ranks of the government from the village level to the immigration office itself." The production of passports both echoes and troubles the same arrangement: PLs, sub-PLs, and local immigration officers and staff serve as intermediaries, connecting would-be migrants from villages and small towns to urban centers and agencies that—in alliance with the government—determine their ability to work overseas.

Prospective migrant workers rely on PLs or regional sub-PLs, who facilitate migration and help them acquire the necessary documents and permissions to obtain passports. PLs introduce prospective migrants to recruitment agencies in smaller cities that are linked to recruitment agencies in Jakarta or Surabaya and other larger Indonesian cities, which in turn are tied to counterpart placement agencies in Hong Kong, Singapore, Taiwan, Malaysia, the Middle East, and elsewhere. Government institutions have a similar structure. Agencies, PLs, and other brokers wield significant power over migrant workers and their communities. They are thus entangled with them and with different levels of government in Indonesia, Hong Kong, and other BMI destination countries that also profit from the migration industry. This blurs the assumed divides between citizen and migrant, and between state and society. It entangles care and control—giving and receiving, protection and surveillance, corruption and care—in various spaces across time.

The connecting threads between 2015 and the colonial era are not obvious; they are frayed and weak at times, but some threads persist, such that the present is never entirely "postcolonial" (Stoler 2016; Lindquist 2018a).[4] Like systemic racism, the threads and filaments that produce inequality can endure in ideologies, discourses, structures, and institutions.

In relation to scales "through which domestic workers are controlled or empowered," in Rachel Silvey's words from this chapter's first epigraph, the ethnographer can *focus in* on individuals and their passports—on Mina's and Ratna's fingerprints, irises, birth dates, and names—or take a wider look at their villages and provinces, and follow their travels to Singapore and Hong Kong, or to Victoria Park on a Sunday. Silvey evokes the different "sites, spaces, and scales" that are not fixed or controlled solely by the state but are struggled over by migration-related actors, including non-state actors, domestic workers, and activists. As we have seen, the Indonesian passport project in Hong Kong, and Indonesia's laws on placement and protection, are shaped by international security recommendations and technologies and by migrant worker and activist struggles. BMI activists ultimately demanded improvements in the process of scheduling appointments and obtaining passports. Most important, the consulate shelved (at least temporarily) the "bleaching" or correcting of passports in Hong Kong, and BMIs could finish their contracts. Passports thus reveal not only shifting security technologies but also shifting policies, practices, and politics.

Historical anthropologist Ann Stoler has insightfully questioned colonial and postcolonial temporality. She writes that in practice, "the term 'postcolonial' often refers to a critical perspective on a past colonial situation . . . or on those who bear the costs of living in a space that was once colonial and is no more." She argues that attention should be paid to "the temporal and affective space in which colonial inequities endure," and her interest is in "the forms in which they do so" (2016, ix). Stoler's view is highly relevant to Indonesian passports that contain and reveal enduring temporal and affective entanglements of labor mobility and exploitation,

---

4. Ethnographers have attended to migratory time and temporalities. For example, *Follow the Maid* (Killias 2018) focuses on the temporality of migration from a north-central Javanese village to Malaysia and back. See also Liebelt (2008).

driven by interests of the state and the labor industry, and tied to questions of individual freedom and choice.

Ties to the Dutch East India Company and the Dutch colonial period exist in the poverty and overpopulation of specific regions that propel residents to seek work abroad. Moreover, Indonesia, Singapore, and Malaysia, all independent nation-states today, were part of the "Malay world," where movement was relatively free until it was carved up by the British and Dutch in colonial times in ways that have shaped the current borders of nation-states. Hong Kong was a British colony for over a century before it became a Special Administrative Region of China in 1997. The colonial government shaped Hong Kong's legal and legislative structures and its immigration laws and policies. Yet Hong Kong and Indonesia are hardly postcolonial, as the "postcolonial," like the "global" and the "local," is neither fixed nor a distinct point in time and space. Passports and passport stories illustrate the multiple temporal and scalar entanglements that continue to shape migratory inequalities.

INTERWEAVING LOOSE ENDS

Today, both the older hajj passports and the TKI passports that identified individuals by type of travel have gone by the wayside. Yet the feminized Indonesian labor migration that rapidly expanded into parts of East Asia by the late 1990s—during the Asian financial downturn and the demise of Suharto and the New Order government—is still tied to earlier histories and structures of hajj pilgrimages to Mecca. Such pilgrimages fueled the market for Indonesian "maids" in Saudi Arabia decades earlier (Kloppenburg 2013, 140; Rudnyckyj 2004; Spaan 1994). One earlier pilgrimage travel agency in Jakarta that responded to the growing demand for domestic workers in the Middle East and Malaysia in the 1980s and 1990s was transformed into a more lucrative domestic worker recruitment agency (Rudnyckyj 2004). The former dormitory for hajj pilgrims was repurposed as a training center for the mandatory training of domestic workers who require certification to work abroad (Rudnyckyj 2004, 407; Killias 2018).

Historical ties to "escort and encapsulation" in the movement of both hajj pilgrims and various types of free or bonded laborers within and beyond the East Indies during the colonial period, and in relation to twentieth-century *tranmigrasi* of Javanese and others, also illustrate continuities. Historical threads connect the genealogies of passports, travel passes, and identity documents of Indonesian migrant workers in Java and Sumatra, overseas to Suriname during the Dutch colonial period, and in Hong Kong since the 1990s. In 2020, many Indonesian migrant workers are still from Central and Eastern Javanese towns and villages that were impoverished by the extraction of labor, land, and wealth a century or more ago; others are from Sumatra, where their Javanese parents took part in the Indonesian version of the Dutch *transmigrasi* in the 1960s and 1970s, laboring on jungle-clearing projects for plantations in harsh and often life-threatening conditions. Such patterns are not "survivals" from the Dutch period, but connections that inform and shape the recent past and the present.

Passports contain and continue to evoke moral discourses that justify control in the name of protection, as a paternalistic form of care, while simultaneously rendering workers vulnerable to exploitation and other abuses, as in the case of encapsulation in the infamous Terminal 3 exclusively for migrant workers, where they were easily targeted for extortion. A new Terminal 4 was opened in 2008, in response to the damning criticisms of Terminal 3, but returnees are still directed or forced to take official buses directly to their home villages, and are still pressured or forced to pay illegal fees along the way, despite the widely posted signs in the terminal announcing that tips and additional payments are illegal (Kloppenburg 2013, ch. 4; Silvey 2007).[5] Specific TKI passports were being phased out in 2015, and airport terminals are no longer exclusively for them, but migrant workers are still easily "classified, examined, and controlled" upon landing in Indonesia (Kloppenburg 2013, 112). Despite their regular passports and regular terminals (with special lines), workers are still identified and often extorted. With electronic data now linked to every new passport, border officials can easily identify migrant workers if it is not already obvious from their travel itineraries, visas, or appearance. In 2019, women still complained about being singled out when they

---

5. Kloppenburg (2013) describes ongoing patterns of escort and exploitation after Terminal 3 was closed. See Juwita (2019) for a short story that illustrates attempts to extort BMIs on their bus journey home.

landed in Indonesia and were "forced" to use the required transportation and were "escorted" home. If they had friends or family waiting at the airport, or did not want to return home directly, they were treated with suspicion and sometimes harassment.

Activist migrant workers commonly chant at Hong Kong protests, "We are workers, we are not slaves." The economic value of workers—to brokers, managers, and employers and to the government and the state economy—is another thread of continuity through time. The less workers are paid and the more they can be charged for services, the more others profit from them. In the worst cases, a BMI's economic precarity is a form of debt bondage that resembles older patterns of bonded labor. In the past and today, brokers and middlemen (or PLs) have been described by their clients more positively as "patrons" or "sponsors" or more negatively as *calos*, smugglers, or traffickers (Killias 2018; Lindquist 2015; Rudnyckyj 2004; Silvey 2004; Spaan 1994). In the past, such brokers facilitated passage (escort) from one location to another—whether for labor migration, forced or coerced labor, or other types of travel such as the hajj—and they assisted people in obtaining documents, passage, and shelter. By the late 1990s, as international demands for feminized labor grew, so did the moneymaking opportunities for labor brokers and the recruitment industry, including agencies, government offices, banks, insurance, and transportation—all of which were empowered to make money from BMIs.

Rudnyckyj argues that globalization utilizes and draws from older patterns, such as the moral economy of the patron-client relationship in Indonesian migration (2004, 413). McKeown suggests that what we consider "globalization" today is not new or unique to the postwar period but is clearly a continuation of earlier forms of migration and mobility (2008). Prospective workers who lack the networks, information, or capital must rely on brokers who "develop a loyal following" for their ability to facilitate employment abroad, including their ability to facilitate acquisition of the twenty documents that are needed for migration (Spaan 1994, 103). Contemporary BMI activists criticize the government "requirement" of using an agency. Given their experiences, their networks and connections, and the fact that they widely and increasingly consider such links exploitative and risky, they prefer a self-referral or "direct hire" option that allows them to circumvent exploitative agencies.

Documents are central to the process of international migration and to the mobility of workers. In the past and at present, brokers provide contacts and connections to Indonesian workers. They facilitate a transfer of the worker's patronage to the agency, which resembles an older "moral economy" between patrons and clients (Rudnyckyj 2004, 416; Spaan 1994). Similarly, despite widespread criticism of corruption among high-level officials in Indonesia, lower-level regional civil servants and officials who do favors for family and community members are seen more favorably, as helping the little people (Tidey 2016, 2018). Agencies and brokers are critically important actors in the bigger picture of Asian migration. They are also central to the passport project, passport problems, and the "passport victims" described in this book. Law no. 39/2004 required workers to use agencies, as did the subsequent Law no. 18/2017 (in most cases), despite activist workers' complaints and documentation of the problems that agencies caused, and that the government largely ignored. Passport problems and passport protests in front of the Indonesian consulate in 2016 were not simply about migrant workers versus government or consular officials, nor were they simply about the passport renewal policy, although they might appear to be so on the surface.

The letters from the Indonesian consulate to Hong Kong immigration officials claimed that passport data was being "corrected" because of earlier "clerical errors," and the Hong Kong courts claimed that the women passport holders were guilty of immigration fraud, punishable by law. But there was a large elephant in the room. Agencies and recruiters—and the corrupt government officials with whom they worked—were and are at the core of the problem. Agencies and brokers are deeply entangled in the process and also the problems of migration. Their role in relation to aspal documents may be blurred or hidden at times between layers of middlemen, including PLs and government officials. Yet agencies and recruiters are the ones who procure and facilitate access to documents, aspal or not. Some women were willing participants because they were underage and were reassured that changes in their names and ages were fine, common, or necessary.[6] In other cases, women resisted using aspal documents but

---

6. See Niok (2019) for a short story about a BMI whose altered date of birth brought her good fortune.

were pressured or coerced, threatened with enormous charges and impossible debts. Some felt they had no choice but to comply. Many women
discovered the changes after the fact, when it seemed too late; some tried
to "correct" them in Hong Kong and were told by agents and by consular
officials, before 2015, not to bother and not to worry.

Agencies and recruiters are an essential part of the criticism of the main
binaries discussed in this book. Migrant and citizen, state and society, and
care and control are not just about the consulate (or the government
and the variety of state ministries and organizations tied to migration) and
migrant workers as citizens. Recruitment agents, government actors, and
migrant workers represent a spectrum of Indonesian "citizens." Some PLs
were migrant workers themselves, or their relatives were. Officials and staff
at every level of state, provincial, and regional government, inside and outside of Indonesia, are also heterogeneous, and some have close familial economic ties to agencies. It is widely known that "some highly ranking civil
servants own and operate labor brokerage companies" (Silvey 2004, 252).
Some government officials would talk to me about agencies only off the
record, as the problems are deeply entangled with government actors.
Various state and non-state actors have allied interests when it comes to
profits to be made from them and the costs of caring for them. That is why,
for example, only certain taxis or vendors obtain permits to do business at
the airport (Silvey 2004). Fundamentally, government officials—especially
those involved with migration infrastructures, banking, new mandatory
insurance programs for migrant workers and their families, and transportation industries—share economic interests with recruitment and placement
agencies. The government continues to expand the roles and responsibilities of recruitment and placement agencies in "protecting" migrant workers.[7] Ford and Lyons write: "To fully comprehend the nature of 'state
corruption' in labour migration flows, . . . we must pay attention not only to
the ways in which individual claims to licitness intersect with state practices, but also with the *interstices* of such competing regimes. What this
points to is a need to invoke *the concept of scale* . . . in relation to the state
itself. In particular, we need to consider differences (and similarities) in the

7. One view is that the government lacks the funds to protect workers, so it shifts
responsibilities to agencies because they can afford it (Palmer 2016).

ways that local, provincial and national level governments and officials respond to labour migration flows" (2011, 117; my italics). Ford and Lyons raise excellent questions, many of which still require further research. Individual claims to the "licitness" of aspal passports at the regional or provincial level clearly conflict with state-level anticorruption proclamations and campaigns visible in government offices and posted at airports. Yet I would argue that the state (through the layers of government) in fact *reproduced* the very aspal passports that they claim they sought to eliminate, as discussed below.

SINGAPORE AND HONG KONG

Passports, as we have seen, are entangled with other types of required identity documents (so-called breeder documents). People from Java's rural villages and small towns do not usually have birth certificates or other documents; thus, they often rely on PLs to help obtain them from larger towns or cities. Yet different relationships exist between local and provincial governments and the wider national institutions, recruitment agencies, and processes that shape the regional migration infrastructure (Ford and Lyons 2011; Palmer 2016; Xiang and Lindquist 2014). Individual women's mobilities are shaped by shifting policies and patterns at the local, provincial, and national levels, related to the Ministry of Manpower, national BNP2TKI and BP2MI and regional BP3TKI offices (agencies for the placement and protection of migrant workers), and international agreements and guidelines (e.g., the International Civil Aviation Organization [ICAO] or the UN definitions of trafficking and child labor and the International Labour Organization [ILO] guidelines on safe migration; Palmer 2016). These mobilities are entangled with older histories and policies that have origins in Dutch colonial or pre-independence and early post-independence patterns of governmentality, including domestic and international labor migration regulations, restrictions, incentives, and safeguards. Importantly, Wayne Palmer shows how the interpretation and shaping of Indonesian migratory processes in overseas consulates and embassies can vary.

When I began this project, I wondered why "passport problems" seemed to occur only in Hong Kong. It's true that Hong Kong was among the first places to use SIMKIM, but apparently Saudi Arabia, Malaysia, Taiwan, and Singapore were early adopters too. When I asked why women in those regions were (presumably) not investigated and imprisoned for immigration fraud, Hong Kong's consul general and others said that it was because those countries' governments (unlike Hong Kong) had no problem with the changes or "corrections" to passports. However, activists, members of NGOs, and researchers suggest there is another answer: other Indonesian consulates and embassies chose not to make changes to passports that would potentially endanger or cause problems for their citizens abroad.

Palmer describes the situation in Singapore until 2010, before the introduction of SIMKIM and the passport project. The Indonesian labor attaché with whom Palmer spoke in Singapore described a very different approach to aspal documents than the one described by Hong Kong consular officials I talked to between 2015 and 2019. It is also important to note that Palmer spoke to the labor attaché in Singapore, whereas I spoke mostly with the immigration consular staff in Hong Kong in charge of the passport project, which the labor consul appeared to have little to do with. The Singapore attaché expressed greater concern over women who were underage (especially fourteen to sixteen years old) if they seemed to have been coerced by older family members to work abroad, but she took a much more cautious approach to presumed aspal passports of women who were over eighteen, even though the minimum age in Singapore after 2004 was twenty-three (Palmer 2016, 159–61).

As in Hong Kong, Indonesian workers in Singapore had to visit the embassy in person to renew their passports. Sometimes cases involving girls in their mid-teens were handled privately with a meeting of the Ministry of Manpower and the agency (Palmer 2016, 159–60), but on other occasions "the labor attaché chose not to respond to the inclusion of false data in migrant workers' travel documents at all." Most notably, "in instances where workers were found using forged or misappropriated passports, she mostly chose not to file reports with law enforcement" (2016, 160). Instead, she "coordinated with the immigration attaché, *who issued the migrant worker ... a limited validity travel document so they could legally return to Indonesia*" (160; my italics). The labor attaché's reasoning was—importantly—that reporting such "passports would only cause complications with Indonesian authorities but could also land immigrants in a Singaporean prison for ten years or result in a fine of up to SGD 10,000 (USD 7,900)" (2016, 160–61).[8] At first the labor attaché had reported recruitment agencies that recruited underage workers, but later made exceptions because "barriers to overseas employment were too high" and stories about "the lack of employment opportunities at home eventually tipped the scale in favour of ignoring such transgressions" (2016, 161). As Palmer explains, she thus "began to turn a blind eye to the overstating of migrants' ages when the passport bearer was over the age of 18 and appeared to have the level of maturity required to deal with the challenges of working in Singapore" (2016, 161).[9] Moreover, she "chose to ignore evidence that passports did not contain true names." After reporting some such cases, "she decided that efforts to identify and report false names in passports were an unwise use of her time" and that such "doctored identities" (aspal documents) were a "symptom of a systemic failure rather than individual deviance [which] disproportionately penalized Indonesian migrant workers themselves" (2016, 161–62). From Palmer's eye-opening study, we see that the Indonesian embassy in Singapore at that time dealt very carefully with cases of underage workers who might be coerced or trafficked. They did not want to risk sending Indonesian women to prison, so they let them finish their contracts and return home, or they simply left those cases alone. Why didn't the Hong Kong consulate follow suit?

STATE AUTHORIZATION OF ASPAL PASSPORTS

In 2015 and 2016, the Hong Kong consulate advised women with inconsistent passport data to "just go home." In at least some cases I knew of, they refused to give them papers or new passports that would allow them

8. Singapore's prison system and sentences are much harsher than Hong Kong's. Most women I knew ended up serving six months or less with good behavior and reduced sentences.

9. She also instituted "a 'two-strikes-and-you're-out' system for cases that involved women below the age of 18, giving labour recruitment companies a verbal warning for the first transgression and reporting them through formal channels for any subsequent violation" (Palmer 2016, 161).

to finish their contracts. Women felt they were being forced to return home mid-contract. Later, when the consulate faced major criticism and protest, and the top Indonesian ministers visited in June 2016 (see chapter 6), they still encouraged women to go home, but they agreed to give them one-way passes so they could finish their contracts. By 2017, I was told in a meeting with the consul general that women's passports were once again being renewed, much as in the past, until their contracts finished.

In 2016, Mr. P said, "I apologize for those who have been [criminally] charged. We didn't mean for that to happen. We just want a better system in Hong Kong. Before the system is completely ruined [because of aspal documents], we need to fix it. We need clean [bleached, corrected] data. We need Hong Kong as a model and as an example of how to do this. Immigration in Indonesia is angry at the Indonesian consulate in Malaysia for not doing this. They say, 'Hong Kong is doing it despite the blame and the protests.'" In other words, other consular offices did not change BMIs' documents while they were still working abroad. By 2017, Mr. P was resigned to the new reality and was no longer bleaching passports. He warned BMIs, however, that the penalties for false passport data are much harsher in Indonesia, and that there was only a "temporary moratorium" for women to correct their data. After that, he said, they would be imprisoned in Indonesia, where "the condition is much worse than in Hong Kong prisons." He was clearly upset that when SIMKIM revealed inconsistent passport data, the passport could no longer be corrected and reissued in Hong Kong. The data, Mr. P feared, "was not clean," and he was disappointed that he had not been able to correct the documents and improve the overall system.

One thing that kept nagging at me was that ultimately, fewer than fifty passports were "corrected" or "bleached" (*pemutihan*) in Hong Kong before the consulate reverted to renewing them and allowing workers to finish their contracts. These cases and the renewal process created serious tragedies for many of those passport holders (as described in chapter 4). However, compared to the 150,000 or more BMIs in Hong Kong, the number was too small. This points to the less told story of the nonevent of passport renewals. Ultimately, the consulate reissued as many as 150,000 passports, a third of which almost certainly contained names, birth dates, or other aspal data that was undetected by SIMKIM or consular staff. These cases slipped past them because the SIMKIM database was incomplete or because the person had only ever had one passport identity (albeit an aspal one). In the end, by renewing tens of thousands of aspal passports, the consulate essentially legitimized or bleached them, thereby authorizing them. Those passports then became the epitome of aspal documents: they are "real" (government issued and authorized documents) that contain "fake" (inauthentic) or altered identity data, but they have "passed" the test and literally carry the stamp of authority.

This is oddly similar to the case Palmer describes in Nunukan, East Kalimantan, Indonesia, where *pemutihan* was the term used to refer to new birth certificates, identity cards, and passports issued by the "authorities" and furnished to "intending migrant workers . . . [and] that hid the fact that they were from another jurisdiction, in some cases also changing their personal details" (Palmer 2016, 128). In other words, the Hong Kong consulate certainly knew that the number of "corrected" passports was but a drop in the bucket. What likely concerned them more was the *appearance* of massive irregularity in the data system. That helps explain their frustration with Dwi, whose passport record was consistent, but who simply "admitted" that her passport was wrong. The corrupt system that produced aspal documents was a nonissue unless it conflicted with the database. The database was what produced the truth.

That is not to say that ignoring aspal passports was a bad solution. In fact, ignoring them as a form of bleaching them is an ideal way of authorizing them (once and for all) and would have been far better for migrant workers than having tens of thousands of women risk investigation and imprisonment in Hong Kong. What it indicates is that despite the passport project, and despite the women with aspal documents who went to court and sometimes jail—or the thousands who left Hong Kong out of fear of what "might" happen, or those who paid to acquire aspal matching documents—aspal passports are truly both licit and legalized through the reproduction of passports in Hong Kong and elsewhere. Corrected passports created disastrous results for many of those passport holders, but they created the impression of a system that was "working." In fact, the system overlooked or validated most of the aspal passports, but at a very high cost to the passport victims.

It is also interesting that (unlike in Singapore) Hong Kong's labor consul seemed largely uninvolved in the passport project, as far as I could tell.

When I asked to meet with the labor consul, Mr. P relayed to me the message that he would not have anything to add to what Mr. P and others had told me about the passport project. I cannot help but wonder whether the labor consul might have preferred to follow the example of his colleague in Singapore. The immigration consul had approval, if not explicit directions from Jakarta, for the passport project. Yet the temporary crackdown on BMI passports in Hong Kong had reverberations in Indonesia, drawing greater attention to local immigration offices that produced aspal passports, the agencies that knowingly sent women overseas with them, and the PLs who were probably as surprised as the workers by the crackdown. Cracking down on relatively powerless workers in Hong Kong was much easier than cracking down on powerful and well-connected agencies from the government perspective, but perhaps the passport renewal project sent a message or a warning to agencies about the capabilities of Imigrasi's new surveillance and security technologies. Clearly, agencies and issuing regional immigration offices could be held accountable, should the government decide to do so. But given the entanglements of interests, that is easier said than done.

PASSPORT VICTIMS AND HUMAN TRAFFICKING

Protection of migrant workers in general, and the belief that women in particular should not travel alone or without male protection, is widespread in Indonesia and many parts of Southeast Asia (Killias 2018; Lindquist 2018a, 2018b; Silvey 2004; Spaan 1994). The officially state-sanctioned form of escort and encapsulation for protection of migrant workers is demanded of the government by the public, especially loudly after high-profile cases of abused workers and repatriated corpses of migrant workers (Blackburn 2004; Robinson 2000). Set against the public demand for protection against potential victimization is the idea of protection versus victimhood, not victimhood versus agency.

I was intrigued by the term *passport victims* used by migrant workers. Although BMIs were highly critical of the consulate, they were also vocal in their position that the agencies (PPTKIS) were at the heart of the problem. The consulate and the Indonesian government assigned much of the responsibility for safe migration to the agencies and expressed little criticism or blame toward them, except occasionally and privately. However, the workers who were investigated, lost their jobs, and/or went to prison were "victims" of the recruitment industry. The main criticism voiced by BMI activists was focused on the capitalist greed of the recruitment agencies (and their collusion with corrupt immigration offices), but the shape and tone of the criticism has shifted over the past twenty-five years.

The discourse of victimhood was especially striking to me because, during my research among FDWs in the 1990s and early 2000s, migrant workers' and migrant worker advocates' activism in Hong Kong was mainly voiced as a struggle for *labor rights and protections,* both in Hong Kong and in the migrants' home communities in Indonesia and the Philippines. Their concerns included exploitation and "victimization," including physical and emotional abuse, but they primarily took a labor rights approach. Gradually, activists and supportive NGOs expressed growing frustration over the unwillingness of the Hong Kong government to respond to their labor demands and to change laws and policies pertaining to migrant workers' rights. Issues like the two-week rule, the "live-in rule," low wage increases, high recruitment costs, and exploitation by recruitment agencies (including forced loans) were largely ignored.

Meanwhile, international attention to human trafficking grew. In my conversations with activists in the early 2000s, many insisted that they "chose" to work abroad and were not "trafficked" (even if they had initially been legally underage). They discussed being "forced" by economic circumstances to have to work abroad, but also stressed their individual decision to do so. They would have preferred good jobs at home, were they available, or pursuing further education, if it was affordable. They did not want to end migration per se but wanted to address wider conditions that caused them to migrate and to improve the conditions under which they did so.

In the 2000s, as the discourse on trafficking gained popularity, the U.S. consulate in Hong Kong invited migrant worker activists and NGO advocates to meet with them and to provide information for the annual Trafficking in Persons (TIP) Report. Each year, the mentions of foreign domestic workers grew—from no mentions in 2001, to twenty in 2003, to 190 in 2007, to over 1,300 in 2018 (Constable n.d.). The TIP Report raised global attention to the issues faced by migrant domestic workers, including their maltreatment and the risk of bonded labor (debt bondage) or trafficking. The UN, the ILO, and the U.S. anti-trafficking task force put pressure on countries with lower TIP ratings and urged the Philippines, Indonesia, and Hong Kong to increase the legal mechanisms available to "fight trafficking."

Hong Kong long maintained that it did not need specific anti-trafficking laws because its existing criminal laws sufficed. FDWs and their advocates, however, worked with sympathetic Hong Kong lawmakers who argued for the value of such legislation, especially for the victims of trafficking who would otherwise be criminalized. Meanwhile, Indonesia and the Philippines had already passed such laws (see Palmer 2012, 2016, 2020b). Today, migrant worker activists have taken a sophisticated strategic approach to increase global attention to the problems they face as precarious workers. The key factors that underlie their vulnerability are the rural poverty of most migrant workers and their families and the exorbitant costs of recruitment that create enormous debts for them and profits for others, while rendering them vulnerable to abuse.

Eni Lestari, Sringatin, and other activists and NGO advocates were careful to say that not all migrant workers are "trafficked" but that the coercion involved in forcing women to accept aspal documents, compounded by their debts and the Indonesian agencies often holding on to their identity documents, meant they were the ones who were vulnerable or penalized if their documents were "corrected," not the agencies or brokers who essentially "trafficked" them. Some scholars and activists justifiably describe the situation of migrant workers as "debt bondage" (Killias 2018).

Aspal passports are but one important symbol and symptom of the systemic exploitation and potential victimhood of migrant workers. Anti-trafficking experts argue that having legitimate and reliable travel documents is a key step in preventing human trafficking. Yet traveling under a false name criminalizes the migrant worker, not those who produce or procure her documents, who told her it was fine, or who pressured or forced her to use them. Given the lack of specific anti-trafficking laws in Hong Kong, the idea that the woman was trafficked or coerced to migrate with false documents was not a successful legal defense.

In addition to agents and recruiters, consular officials and Indonesian officials were deeply implicated in this process as well. The accusation from activist workers was that the government benefits most from assigning the responsibility for the well-being of BMIs largely to the recruitment agencies. Law no. 18/2017 makes an exception for workers who renew their contracts with the same employers, allowing them to sidestep the agency, but most workers still must use an agency. The consulate had neither the "manpower" nor the willpower to disassemble a system from which they, and those they know, likely benefit. The trafficking discourse allows migrant worker activists and their supporters in Indonesia to demand greater protection, while the response has been mixed at best. Agencies and PLs still have much control over workers, and aspal documents are reportedly much more expensive and less easily obtainable since 2015; presumably, they will be even more difficult to get once Indonesian e-KTP (electronic identity cards) become widespread.[10]

Another point to stress is that Indonesian migrant worker activists in Hong Kong are, as the Indonesian consular officials noted, "very active." They have established many contacts over the years and their networks reach around the world, including many parts of Indonesia and other migrant worker destination countries in Europe, North and South America, and Asia. In 2016, faced with the passport problems in Hong Kong, they drew on their contacts and allies in Indonesia and approached top ministers and officials to bring attention to the passport problems that were not being satisfactorily resolved in Hong Kong. Their approach was based—impressively—on a network of citizens, migrant worker family members, current and former migrant workers, and sympathetic politicians and lawyers in Indonesia. They were supported by advocate NGOs in Hong Kong and Indonesia, and they successfully advocated for top Indonesian ministers to come to Hong Kong and negotiate with government officials on their behalf. Domestic worker activists conducted research and communicated openly with consular officials, and they were well respected by the consul general—and, perhaps with some misgiving,

10. At first the e-KTP program looked promising in Indonesia, but at the time of my research a significant corruption scandal broke, in which US$172 million was misappropriated (Datarama 2017). House Speaker Setya Novanto was charged with embezzlement and received a fifteen-year sentence (Varagur 2018).

by Mr. P and other consular officials—because they were "issue driven" and passionate but didn't personalize the issues. They worked to maintain communication and offer suggestions throughout the process (although the consulate did not always listen).

The activists mentioned in this book are not the only ones in Hong Kong or the only ones concerned about the passport project, but I was able to see up close how these particular activists continued, over decades, to build a wider base of advocates by developing connections with local Hong Kong citizens, young and old, with scholars, media, volunteers, and interns, and with a broader group of people in and well beyond Indonesia (Constable 2021a, 2021c). Communicating with the families of migrant workers is especially important. By activating such entanglements of care, activists continue to address issues that go far beyond passport problems. Today's brokers and sponsors are entangled with a wider global migration industry. Furthermore, as illustrated by Sura's story below, Indonesian passport problems will likely continue to produce problems for some time to come, a problem that I call the "afterlives of aspal documents."

SURA AND THE AFTERLIVES OF ASPAL DOCUMENTS

Sura, a former BMI in her early thirties, was married to a South Asian Hong Kong resident in 2005. They met in Hong Kong and married while she still had a domestic worker contract and lived with her employers.[11] They eventually had three children together. When I met them, the two youngest lived in Hong Kong with their parents, but the oldest, who was born in Indonesia when Sura had returned temporarily, lived there with his maternal grandmother. The two younger children are Hong Kong permanent residents (by virtue of being born there and having a Hong Kong permanent resident father), but Sura interrupted her stay each time she returned to Indonesia, and it was unclear whether the family had the required resources to apply for her permanent residency. When I met Sura in 2018, she was in crisis because of the aspal documents she had obtained

11. Unlike Singapore, Hong Kong does not prohibit FDWs from marrying locals (Constable 2020b).

about twenty years earlier, when she was two years under the legal age to work abroad.

Sura had only ever used one identity during her travels, and when she planned to marry, on advice of the Indonesian consulate (around 2005), she was advised to "accept" that identity (name, birth date, and place of origin) as her permanent ones, so she did (like some other women I knew). That identity appeared on all her Hong Kong documents, and on all three of her children's birth certificates. In 2018, Sura arranged to renew her passport and to obtain one for her two younger children at the Indonesian consulate in Hong Kong, so that they could travel to Indonesia together and visit the older child and bring him back to Hong Kong with them. Their passports were all renewed without a hitch. However, when the family returned to East Java they encountered numerous problems. First, Sura's husband was detained for many hours at the airport because officials claimed that the Indonesian visa in his passport was "fake" (although it had been issued by the Indonesian consulate in Hong Kong). As our mutual friend Indri said, clearly the officials saw them as "rich foreigners" and simply wanted a bribe, which they eventually paid. Then, when Suma tried to renew her older child's passport at the immigration office, she faced more problems. Anticipating the requirements, Suma had brought her marriage certificate, her child's Hong Kong birth certificate, and the Hong Kong Indonesian consulate's certified translation of both. But she was told that the Indonesian consulate's translations were unacceptable and that she had to have them translated locally (at further cost). She presented them with her son's expired passport and her current one, but was told that these were insufficient and that she needed to provide her Indonesian family card (KK), her birth certificate, and her Indonesian identity card (e-KTP), none of which she had under her current name. The officials at the immigration office would not back down, and she had neither the documents they required nor the time or money to obtain them, so she returned to Hong Kong without the older child.

Meanwhile, against her husband's better judgment and without his knowledge, given that their budget was extremely tight (and they needed to show evidence of sufficient resources for Sura's HK residency application), Sura went behind his back and arranged, through a former migrant worker contact, to get aspal documents from a local calo. Yet the promised date of delivery came and went, and Sura got in touch with her contact, who complained that the calo had said that the process was too risky, and that he required more money. Sura mistrusted her contact, but she eventually texted Sura a photo of the KK and told her she would send it after Sura sent more money. Ultimately, Sura spent thousands of Hong Kong dollars (partly borrowed from a friend). As of our last conversation in 2019, she was waiting for two more documents and her child was still in Indonesia.

As this story illustrates, passport problems are not just a onetime problem, and not only a problem for current migrant workers, but can stretch out and create ongoing problems across time and space, beyond a generation.

CONCLUSION

James Scott ends his otherwise very positive review of John Torpey's *The Invention of the Passport* with one criticism: "We are greatly enlightened by Torpey's book, but we would have been more enlightened if he had also turned his talents to explaining, systematically, the logic behind the huge chasm between facts on the ground and the administrative schemes of the nation-state" (Scott 2002, 144).

In this book, I have focused on passports and aspal documents and have sought to examine some of the entangled logics behind the "chasm between the facts on the ground" and the "administrative schemes of the nation-state." I have examined the multiple threads that entangle women migrant workers and their passports with consular officials, recruitment agencies and recruiters, and many other governmental and non-governmental actors and institutions, at and through different levels of society. This book has explored the temporalities and scales that problematize overly simplistic binaries of state and society, citizen and migrant, care and control, and real and fake. In so doing, it has also traced shifting ties between ethnographer and interlocutors, ethnographic research and writing.

On the ground, I have considered individual and collective experiences and actions of migrant workers, prospective migrant workers, consular officials, PLs and sub-PLs, local immigration staff, and agencies that produce and profit from aspal documents in Indonesia. At the level of the nation-state are the administrative schemes and policies that promote national development and transparent, responsive, and accountable "good governance" and anticorruption initiatives, aiming to modernize, while voicing ideals of protecting and caring for citizens, including migrant workers. Entangled with such proclaimed schemes and the realities on the ground are the multiple levels of bureaucracy—both governmental and in the wider migration industry—that seek to profit from migrant labor while promoting anticorruption, and that are often pulled toward licit but illegal practices.

Mr. P and his colleagues, responsible to supervisors in Jakarta, were "doing their jobs." Yet, in a sense, the immigration section of the consulate may have been "played"—performing the role of protector and reformer that was doomed to failure—because of the tremendous economic power of agencies on one hand, and the state's interest in maintaining migrant labor as a source of national (and sometimes personal) revenue on the other. Remittances are critically important to the state, as are the profits to the larger migration industry. In the name of "protection" of BMIs and their family members, mandatory programs increasingly siphon money from them to pay agencies, investors, banks, and insurance agencies for services that BMIs often do not want and cannot access. The complex and diverse administrative structures of the state and of agencies disguise their profit-driven collusion and corruption as "help and protection."

Passports play a key role in the administrative scheme of the nation-state, as Torpey argues, by facilitating the state's "embrace" of society and producing citizens with national and individual identities. Likewise, Scott has argued that states make society "legible"—and thus subject to identification and registration for state purposes such as taxation, corvée labor, and conscription. Following passports (rather than only following migrant workers with passport stories) through an "administrative scheme" of passport renewal that claimed to be transparent and accountable and to protect society revealed multiple disconnects between the accuracy, transparency, and protections that are supposedly facilitated by ever-newer global technologies and the actual well-being of migrant workers.

Examining the social lives and entanglements of passports reveals the inequalities and exclusions of migration. Today's BMIs sometimes resemble Javanese and Chinese coolies and indentured workers of the Dutch

East Indies in the nineteenth and early twentieth centuries, where poverty and lack of better work opportunities meant that their labor was arguably "unfree." Despite the abolition of slavery, that system was easily replaced by one of indenture, penal labor, and corvée labor. Travel passes and residential documents kept people in their place or facilitated moving them to where their labor was needed—like today's passports. Today's patterns of coercion and unfree labor—as well as forms of resistance and struggle—reappear in those spaces that exist in between the nation-state's schemes to control and protect citizens and their failures to do so.

Early passports were used in the late nineteenth and early twentieth centuries to exclude free Asians from settling in North American settler colonies or in the homelands of colonial powers, and today's passports serve similar purposes, allowing certain Asians to migrate to other countries temporarily as laborers, but not to settle there permanently. If insufficient work opportunities exist at home, are these workers "free" to choose to migrate? Passports help us see how both the state's gendered rhetoric of unity and protection and women activists' concerns about trafficking and debt bondage are now entangled with yet another "new" and ever-changing era of biometric technologies. Passports contain within them—figuratively if not literally—historical continuities regarding inequalities of class and gender upon which the production of cheap, flexible, and docile workers are reproduced through collaborations between multiple levels of state and non-state actors who stand to profit most from them. Passports, like earlier travel passes and residential permits, complicate the state logics of equal citizenship and protection and illustrate how they are deeply entangled with capital, inequality, surveillance, and control at multiple levels, all of which shapes the production and impact of aspal documents and the precarity of migrant workers.

References

Abu-Lughod, Lila. 1993. *Writing Women's Worlds: Bedouin Stories.* Berkeley: University of California Press.

Agar, Jon. 2001. Modern Horrors: British Identity and Identity Cards. In *Documenting Individual Identity: The Development of State Practices in the Modern World,* edited by Jane Caplan and John C. Torpey, 101–20. Princeton, NJ: Princeton University Press.

Agustinanto, Fatimana, and Jamie Davis. 2003. Domestic Workers. In *Trafficking of Women and Children in Indonesia,* edited by Ruth Rosenberg, 56–62. Jakarta: International Catholic Migration Commission.

Ahmat, Adam. 1995. *The Vernacular Press and the Emergence of Modern Indonesian Consciousness (1855–1913).* Ithaca, NY: Cornell University Press.

Aidit, D. N. 1958. *Indonesian Society and the Indonesian Revolution.* Jakarta: Jajasan "Pembaruan."

AIPJ (Australia-Indonesia Partnership for Justice). 2013. Baseline Study of Legal Identity: Indonesian's Missing Millions. https://puskapa.org/en /publication/782/.

Allerton, Catherine. 2020. Stuck in the Short Term: Immobility and Temporalities of Care among Florenese Migrants in Sabah, Malaysia. *Ethnos* 85, no. 2: 208–23.

Amrith, Megha. 2020. The Substance of Care: Ethical Dilemmas in Migrant Medical Labour. *Ethnos* 85, no. 2: 241–57.

Amrith, Sunil S. 2011. *Migration and Diaspora in Modern Asia.* Cambridge: Cambridge University Press.

———. 2013. *Crossing the Bay of Bengal: The Furies of Nature and the Fortunes of Migrants.* Cambridge, MA: Harvard University Press.

———. 2018. *Unruly Waters: How Rains, Rivers, Coasts and Seas Have Shaped Asia's History.* New York: Basic Books.

Ananta, Aris. 2009. Estimating the Value of the Business of Sending Low-Skilled Workers Abroad: An Indonesian Case. https://iussp2009.princeton .edu/papers/91804.

Anderson, Benedict. 1983. *Imagined Communities: Reflections on the Origin and Spread of Nationalism.* London: Verso.

———. 2006. *Language and Power: Exploring Political Cultures in Indonesia.* Jakarta: Equinox.

Anderson, Bridget. 2013. *Us and Them? The Dangerous Politics of Immigration Control.* New York: Oxford University Press.

Antons, Christoph, and Rosy Antons-Sutanto. 2017. The Construction of Ethnicity in Colonial Law and Its Legacy: The Example of the *Peranakan* Chinese in Indonesia. In *Routledge Handbook of Asian Law,* edited by Christoph Antons, 398–418. New York: Routledge.

Apakabar Online. 2017. Nama Nur Aini, Berkah Sekaligus Petaka bagi Dwi Murahati [The Name Nur Aini, Blessings and Disasters for Nur Murahati]. Apakabar: Indonesian Migrant Workers News Portal. http://apakabaronline .com/nama-nur-aini-berkah-sekaligus-petaka-bagi-dwi-murah-hati/.

Appadurai, Arjun. 1986. *The Social Life of Things: Commodities in Cultural Perspective.* New York: Cambridge University Press.

———. 1996. *Modernity at Large: Cultural Dimensions of Globalization.* Minneapolis: University of Minnesota Press.

Arendt, Hannah. 1968. *The Origins of Totalitarianism.* New York: Harcourt and Brace.

Arndt, H. W. 1983. Transmigration: Achievements, Problems, Prospects. *Bulletin of Indonesian Economic Studies* 19, no. 3: 50–73.

Baiocchi, Maria Lis. 2020. A Law of One's Own: Newfound Labor Rights, Household Workers' Agency, and Activist Praxis in Buenos Aires, Argentina. PhD dissertation, University of Pittsburgh.

Ball, Jessica, Leslie Butt, and Harriot Beazley. 2017. Birth Registration and Protection for Children of Transnational Labor Migrants in Indonesia. *Journal of Immigrant & Refugee Studies* 15, no. 3: 305–25.

Barker, Joshua. 1999. The Tattoo and the Fingerprint: Crime and Security in an Indonesian City. PhD dissertation, Cornell University.

Barter, Shane J., and Isabelle Côté. 2015. Strife of the soil? Unsettling Transmi-grant Conflicts in Indonesia. *Journal of Southeast Asian Studies* 46, no. 1: 60–85.

Basch, Linda G., Nina Glick Schiller, and Cristina Szanton Blanc. 1994. *Nations Unbound: Transnational Projects, Postcolonial Predicaments, and Deterritorialized Nation-States*. Amsterdam: Gordon and Breach.

Beck, Katie. 2017. Why Citizenship Is Now a Commodity. *BBC Worklife*, May 29, 2017. www.bbc.com/capital/story/20170530-why-citizenship-is-now-a-commodity.

Berlant, Lauren G. 2011. *Cruel Optimism*. Durham, NC: Duke University Press.

Blackburn, Susan. 2004. *Women and the State in Modern Indonesia*. New York: Cambridge University Press.

Blundy, Rachel. 2017. 'Little Progress since Erwiana': Activists Slam Lack of Government Action over Poor Sleeping Conditions for Domestic Workers. *South China Morning Post*, March 20. www.scmp.com/news/hong-kong/education-community/article/2096651/little-progress-erwiana-activists-slam-lack.

Boke, Charis. 2016. Care. From the Series: Lexicon for an Anthropocene Yet Unseen. Society for Cultural Anthropology, July 12. https://culanth.org/fieldsights/care?token=OuBjOnXZGwzoRCZiGbLaVI1WWXfcqA75.

Boris, Eileen, and Rhacel Salazar Parreñas. 2010. *Intimate Labors: Cultures, Technologies, and the Politics of Care*. Stanford, CA: Stanford University Press.

Borofsky, Robert. 2019. *An Anthropology of Anthropology: Is It Time to Switch Paradigms?* Center for a Public Anthropology. Open access: https://books.publicanthropology.org/an-anthropology-of-anthropology.html.

Borovoy, Amy, and Li Zhang. 2017. Between Biopolitical Governance and Care: Rethinking Health, Selfhood, and Social Welfare in East Asia. *Medical Anthropology* 36, no. 1: 1–5.

Bowles, Nellie. 2018. Silicon Valley Nannies Are Phone Police for Kids. *New York Times*, October 26. www.nytimes.com/2018/10/26/style/silicon-valley-nannies.html.

Brand, J. van den. 1904. *Nog eens: De Millioenen uit Deli* [The Millions from Deli]. Amsterdam: Höveker & Wormser.

Breckenridge, Keith D., and Simon Szreter. 2012. *Registration and Recognition: Documenting the Person in World History*. Oxford: Oxford University Press.

Breman, Jan. 2020. Colonialism and Its Racial Imprint. *Sojourn: Journal of Social Issues in Southeast Asia* 35, no. 3: 463–92.

Bruner, Edward M. 1986. Ethnography as Narrative. In *The Anthropology of Experience*, edited by Victor W. Turner and Edward M. Bruner, 139–55. Urbana: University of Illinois Press.

Bubandt, Nils. 2008. Rumors, Pamphlets, and the Politics of Paranoia in Indonesia. *Journal of Asian Studies* 67, no. 3: 789–817.

———. 2009. From the Enemy's Point of View: Violence, Empathy, and the Ethnography of Fakes. *Cultural Anthropology* 24, no. 3: 553–88.

Butt, Leslie, and Jessica Ball. 2017. Birth Registration in Southeast Asia: A Child's Foundation Right? *Asian Population Studies* 13, no. 3: 223–25.

———. 2018. Strategic Actions of Transnational Migrant Parents Regarding Birth Registration for Stay-Behind Children in Lombok, Indonesia. *Population, Space and Place* 25, no. 3: 1–9.

Buy Real and Fake Passports Online. n.d. Website. https://buyfakepassportsonline .com/ (accessed May 22, 2019).

Callon, Michel. 1998. Introduction: The Embeddedness of Economic Markets in Economies. In *The Laws of the Markets,* edited by Michel Callon, 1–57. Oxford: Blackwell.

Callon, Michel, and Vololona Rabeharisoa. 2004. Gino's Lesson on Humanity: Genetics, Mutual Entanglements and the Sociologist's Role. *Economy and Society* 33, no. 1: 1–27.

Caplan, Jane. 2001. "This or That Particular Person": Protocols of Identification in Nineteenth-Century Europe. In *Documenting Individual Identity: The Development of State Practices in the Modern World,* edited by Jane Caplan and John C. Torpey, 49–66. Princeton, NJ: Princeton University Press.

Caplan, Jane, and John C. Torpey, eds. 2001. *Documenting Individual Identity: The Development of State Practices in the Modern World.* Princeton, NJ: Princeton University Press.

Certeau, Michel de. 1984. *The Practice of Everyday Life.* Berkeley: University of California Press.

Chan, Carol. 2018. *In Sickness and in Wealth: Migration, Gendered Morality, and Central Java.* Bloomington: Indiana University Press.

Chang, Andy S. 2021. Selling a Resume and Buying a Job: Stratification of Gender and Occupation by States and Brokers in International Migration from Indonesia. *Social Problems* 68, no. 4: 903–24.

Chin, Christine B. N. 1998. *In Service and Servitude: Foreign Female Domestic Workers and the Malaysian "Modernity" Project.* New York: Columbia University Press.

Chiu, Peace. 2018. Record 1.37 Million People Living below Poverty Line in Hong Kong as Government Blames Rise on Ageing Population and City's Improving Economy. *South China Morning Post,* November 19. www.scmp .com/news/hong-kong/society/article/2174006/record-13-million-people- living-below-poverty-line-hong-kong.

Chow, Rey. 2012. *Entanglements, or Transmedial Thinking about Capture.* Durham, NC: Duke University Press.

Clifford, James, and George E. Marcus, eds. 1986. *Writing Culture: The Poetics and Politics of Ethnography.* Berkeley: University of California Press.

Cohen, Lawrence. 2019. The 'Social' De-Duplicated: On the Aadhaar Platform and the Engineering of Service. *South Asia: Journal of South Asian Studies* 42, no. 3: 482–500.

Cole, Simon A. 2002. *Suspect Identities: A History of Fingerprinting and Criminal Identification*. Cambridge, MA: Harvard University Press.

Collier, Stephen J. 2006. Global Assemblages. *Theory, Culture & Society* 23, no. 2–3: 399–401.

Constable, Nicole. 2003. *Romance on a Global Stage: Pen Pals, Virtual Ethnography, and "Mail-Order" Marriages*. Berkeley: University of California Press.

———. 2007. *Maid to Order in Hong Kong: Stories of Migrant Workers*, 2nd ed. Ithaca, NY: Cornell University Press.

———. 2009a. The Commodification of Intimacy: Marriage, Sex, and Reproductive Labor. *Annual Review of Anthropology* 38: 49–64.

———. 2009b. Migrant Workers and the Many States of Protest in Hong Kong. *Critical Asian Studies* 41, no. 1: 143–64.

———. 2010. Telling Tales of Migrant Workers in Hong Kong: Transformations of Faith, Life Scripts, and Activism. *Asia Pacific Journal of Anthropology* 11, no. 3–4: 311–29.

———. 2011. *Migrant Workers in Asia: Distant Divides, Intimate Connections*. London: New York: Routledge.

———. 2014. *Born Out of Place: Migrant Mothers and the Politics of International Labor*. Berkeley: University of California Press.

———. 2015. Migrant Motherhood, 'Failed Migration', and the Gendered Risks of Precarious Labour. *TRaNS: Trans-Regional & -National Studies of Southeast Asia* 3, no. 1: 135–51.

———. 2016. Obstacles to Claiming Rights: Migrant Domestic Workers in Asia's World City, Hong Kong. In *Care, Migration and Human Rights: Law and Practice*, edited by Siobhán Mullally, 96–115. London: Routledge.

———. 2018a. Assemblages and Affect: Migrant Labour and the Varieties of Absent Children. *Global Networks* 18, no. 1: 168–85.

———. 2018b. Temporary Intimacies, Incipient Transnationalism, and Failed Cross-Border Marriages. In *Intimate Mobilities: Sexual Economies, Marriage and Migration in a Disparate World*, edited by C. Groes and N. Fernandez, 52–73. New York: Berghahn.

———. 2020a. Afterword: Rethinking Ethnographic Entanglements of Care and Control. *Ethnos* 85, no. 2: 327–34.

———. 2020b. Tales of Two Cities: Legislating Pregnancy and Marriage among Foreign Domestic Workers in Singapore and Hong Kong. *Journal of Ethnic and Migration Studies* 46, no. 16: 3491–507.

———. 2021a. Continual Arrival and the Longue Durée: Emplacement as Activism among Migrant Workers in Hong Kong. *Migration Studies*, mnab034.

———. 2021b. Migrant Mothers, Rejected Refugees and Excluded Belonging in Hong Kong. *Population, Space and Place* 27, no. 5: e2475

———. 2021c. Simultaneous Citizen and Noncitizen: Displacement, Precarity, and Passports in Hong Kong. *Humanity* 12, no. 3: 324–38.

———. n.d. Human Trafficking in Hong Kong. Unpublished manuscript.

Crapanzano, Vincent. 1980. *Tuhami: Portrait of a Moroccan.* Chicago: University of Chicago Press.

Cribb, R. B., and Audrey Kahin. 2004. *Historical Dictionary of Indonesia.* Lanham, MD: Scarecrow Press.

Dahinden, Janine. 2016. A Plea for the "De-migranticization" of Research on Migration and Integration. *Ethnic and Racial Studies* 39, no. 13: 2207–25.

Dahinden, Janine, Carolin Fischer, and Joanna Menet. 2021. Knowledge Production, Reflexivity, and the Use of Categories in Migration Studies: Tackling Challenges in the Field. *Ethnic and Racial Studies* 44, no. 4: 535–54.

Datarama. 2017. Indonesia's e-KTP Scandal and Implications for Investment. *Medium,* September 14. https://medium.com/@dataramatech/indonesias-e-ktp-scandal-and-implications-for-investment-7838183c64f5.

Davis, Jamie. 2003. Lack of Birth Registry. In *Trafficking of Women and Children in Indonesia,* edited by Ruth Rosenberg, 120–21. Jakarta: International Catholic Migration Commission.

De-Yuan.com. 2016. Dwi Murahati, TKW Hong Kong Single Mother yang Terkena Koreksi Data [Dwi Murahati, Hong Kong FDW Single Mother Affected by Data Correction], April 25. www.de-yuan.com/2016/04/dwi-murahati-tkw-hong-kong-single.html.

Duara, Prasenjit. 2013. *Asia Redux: Conceptualizing a Region for Our Times.* Singapore: ISEAS, Yusof Ishak Institute.

———. 2019. Circulatory and Competitive Histories. In *China, India and Alternative Asian Modernities,* edited by Sanjay Kumar, Satya P. Mohanty, Archana Kumar, and Raj Kumar, 18–41. New York: Taylor & Francis.

Ehrenreich, Barbara, and Arlie Russell Hochschild. 2003. *Global Woman: Nannies, Maids, and Sex Workers in the New Economy.* New York: Metropolitan/Owl Books.

Enrich/Experion. 2019. The Value of Care: Key Contributions of Migrant Domestic Workers to Economic Growth and Family Well-Being in Asia. https://enrichhk.org/sites/default/files/2019–09/Final_The-Value-of-Care_Full-Report.pdf.

Fabian, Johannes. 1983. *Time and the Other: How Anthropology Makes Its Object.* New York: Columbia University Press.

Fahrmeir, Andreas. 2001. Governments and Forgers: Passports in Nineteenth-Century Europe. In *Documenting Individual Identity: The Development of State Practices in the Modern World,* edited by Jane Caplan and John C. Torpey, 218–34. Princeton, NJ: Princeton University Press.

Falcone, Jessica. 2012. Maitreya, or the Love of Buddhism: The Non-event of Bodh Gaya's Giant Statue. In *Cross-Disciplinary Perspectives on a Contested*

Buddhist Site: Bodhgaya Jataka, edited by David Geary, Matthew R. Sayers, and Abhishek Singh Amar, 153–71. New York: Routledge.

Fatharini, Anjani Tri. 2018. Indonesian Migrant Workers Activism in Hong Kong. *Journal of Advanced Research in Social Sciences and Humanities 3,* no. 3: 102–09.

Fearon, James D., and David D. Laitin. 2011. Sons of the Soil, Migrants, and Civil War. *World Development 39,* no. 2: 199–211.

Feldman, Gregory. 2012. *The Migration Apparatus: Security, Labor, and Policy-making in the European Union.* Stanford, CA: Stanford University Press.

Ferguson, James. 2012. What Comes after the Social? Historicizing the Future of Social Assistance and Identity Registration in Africa. In *Registration and Recognition: Documenting the Person in World History,* edited by Keith D. Breckenridge and Simon Szreter, 496–516. Oxford: Oxford University Press.

Ford, Michelle, and Lenore Lyons. 2011. Travelling the Aspal Route: Grey Labor Migration through an Indonesian Town. In *The State and Illegality in Indonesia,* edited by Edward Aspinall and Gerry van Klinken, 108–22. Leiden, The Netherlands: Brill.

Foucault, Michel. 1977. *Discipline and Punish: The Birth of the Prison.* London: Penguin.

———. 1991. Governmentality. Translated by Rosi Braidotti and Colin Gordon. In *The Foucault Effect: Studies in Governmentality,* edited by Graham Burchell, Colin Gordon, and Peter Miller, 87–104. Chicago: University of Chicago Press.

Freeman, Caren. 2011. *Making and Faking Kinship: Marriage and Labor Migration between China and South Korea.* Ithaca, NY: Cornell University Press.

Friedman, Sara L. 2015. *Exceptional States: Chinese Immigrants and Taiwanese Sovereignty.* Oakland: University of California.

Ghosh, Amitav. 2008. *Sea of Poppies.* New York: Farrar, Straus and Giroux.

———. 2011. *River of Smoke.* New York: Farrar, Straus and Giroux.

———. 2015. *Flood of Fire: A Novel.* New York: Farrar, Straus and Giroux.

Global Compact for Migration. 2018. Global Compact for Safe, Orderly and Regular Migration. https://refugeesmigrants.un.org/sites/default/files/180711_final_draft_0.pdf.

Global Forum on Migration and Development. n.d. Website. Process and Background. www.gfmd.org/process/background.

Goffman, Erving. 1959. *The Presentation of Self in Everyday Life.* New York: Anchor Books.

Groebner, Valentin. 2007. *Who Are You? Identification, Deception, and Surveillance in Early Modern Europe.* Brooklyn, NY: Zone Books.

Gupta, Akhil. 1995. Blurred Boundaries: The Discourse of Corruption, the Culture of Politics, and the Imagined State. *American Ethnologist 22,* no. 2: 375–402.

Gupta, Akhil, and James Ferguson. 1992. Beyond "Culture": Space, Identity, and the Politics of Difference. *Cultural Anthropology* 7, no. 1: 6–23.

Gupta, Akhil, David Nugent, and Shreyas Sreenath. 2015. State, Corruption, Postcoloniality: A Conversation with Akhil Gupta on the 20th Anniversary of "Blurred Boundaries." *American Ethnologist* 42, no. 4: 581–91.

Ham, Julie. 2016. Opinion: Indonesian Domestic Workers Preventing Criminalization of Identification. University of Hong Kong, Department of Sociology, August 16. https://sociology.hku.hk/news/2016/08/indonesian-domestic-workers-preventing-criminalization-identification/.

Hamin, Anis. 2003. The Impact of Corruption on Trafficking. In *Trafficking of Women and Children in Indonesia*, edited by Ruth Rosenberg, 145–50. Jakarta: International Catholic Migration Commission.

Haraway, Donna. 1988. Situated Knowledges: The Science Question in Feminism and the Privilege of Partial Perspective. *Feminist Studies* 14, no. 3: 575–99.

Hardjono, J. M. 1977. *Transmigration in Indonesia*. Oxford: Oxford University Press.

Hardt, Michael. 1999. Affective Labor. *Boundary 2* 26, no. 2: 89–100.

Hincks, Joseph. 2017. In the World's Most Expensive City, 1 in 10 Maids Sleeps in a Kitchen, Toilet, or Corner of the Living Room. *Time*, May 19. https://time.com/4775376/hong-kong-migrant-workers-maids-helpers-conditions/.

Ho, Engseng. 2006. *The Graves of Tarim: Genealogy and Mobility across the Indian Ocean*. Berkeley: University of California Press.

Hochschild, Arlie R. 1983. *The Managed Heart: Commercialization of Human Feeling*. Berkeley: University of California Press.

———. 2000. Global Care Chains and Emotional Surplus Value. In *On the Edge: Living with Global Capitalism*, edited by Will Hutton and Anthony Giddens. London: Jonathan Cape.

Hollingsworth, Julia. 2017. Sleepless in Hong Kong . . . on Fridges and in Toilets: Worst Places City's Domestic Helpers Have Called a Bed. *South China Morning Post*, June 3. www.scmp.com/news/hong-kong/education-community/article/2096697/sleepless-hong-kong-fridges-and-toilets-worst.

Hong Kong Immigration Department. 2013. Annual Report, 2013. Appendix 16: Statistics on Forged Travel Documents Detected in Hong Kong. www.immd.gov.hk/publications/a_report_2013/pdf/appendix_16_en.pdf.

———. 2014. Annual Report, 2014. Appendix 16: Statistics on Forged Travel Documents Detected in Hong Kong. www.immd.gov.hk/publications/a_report_2014/pdf/appendix_16_en.pdf.

———. 2015. Annual Report, 2015. Appendix 16: Statistics on Forged Travel Documents Detected in Hong Kong. www.immd.gov.hk/publications/a_report_2015/pdf/appendix_16_en.pdf.

———. 2016. Annual Report, 2016. Appendix 17: Statistics on Forged Travel Documents Detected in Hong Kong. www.immd.gov.hk/publications/a_report_2016/pdf/appendix_17_en.pdf.

———. 2017. Annual Report, 2017. Appendix 17: Statistics on Forged Travel Documents Detected in Hong Kong. www.immd.gov.hk/publications/a_report_2017/pdf/appendix_17_en.pdf.

Horton, Sarah. 2015. Identity Loan: The Moral Economy of Migrant Document Exchange in California's Central Valley. *American Ethnologist* 42, no. 1: 55–67.

Hsia, Hsiao-Chuan. 2009. The Making of a Transnational Grassroots Migrant Movement: A Case Study of Hong Kong's Asian Migrants Coordinating Body. *Critical Asian Studies* 41, no. 1: 113–41.

Hugo, Graeme. 2005. Indonesian International Domestic Workers: Contemporary Developments and Issues. In *Asian Women as Transnational Domestic Workers,* edited by Shirlena Huang, Brenda S. A. Yeoh, and Noor Abdul Rahman, 54–91. Singapore: Marshall Cavendish.

———. 2007. Indonesia's Labor Looks Abroad. Migration Policy Institute, April 1, 2007. www.migrationpolicy.org/article/indonesias-labor-looks-abroad.

Hull, Matthew. 2012. *Government of Paper: The Materiality of Bureaucracy in Urban Pakistan.* Berkeley: University of California Press.

Hwang, Maria C. 2018. Gendered Border Regimes and Displacements: The Case of Filipina Sex Workers in Asia. *Signs* 43, no. 3: 515–37.

Imigrasi. 2010. Surat Perjalanan Republik Indonesia/Paspor berdasarkan jenis, masa berlaku, dan kegunaannya [Travel Letter of the Republic of Indonesia /Passport based on type, validity period, and use]. May 26. www.imigrasi .go.id/ (accessed August 8, 2018).

———. 2012. History [Longer version]. www.imigrasi.go.id/index.php/en/profile /history (last accessed August 20, 2018).

———. 2018. Bengkulu Immigration Rejected Passport Issuance for 44 Prospective Indonesian Migrant Workers, Why? August 8. www.imigrasi.go. id/index.php/en/news/headlines/1771-bengkulu-immigration-rejected-passport-issuance-for-44-prospective-indonesian-migrant-workers,-why.

———. n.d.a. History [Sejarah]. www.imigrasi.go.id/profil/sejarah (accessed August 5, 2020).

———. n.d.b. Mars Imigrasi. www.imigrasi.go.id/profil/mars-imigrasi (accessed July 6, 2021).

Indonesian Consulate General, Hong Kong. 2016. The Indonesian Minister of Foreign Affairs and the Indonesian Minister of Law and Human Rights Visit Hong-Kong. www.kemlu.go.id/hongkong/id/berita-agenda/berita-perwakilan /Pages/Kunjungan-Bu-Menlu-RI-dan-Menkumham-RI-ke-Hong-Kong.aspx.

Indonesian Government. n.d. Profil BP2MI. https://bp2mi.go.id/profil-sejarah for the history of BP2MI.

IOM (International Organization for Migration). 2005. The Role of IOM in the
Improvement of Travel Documents and Issuance Systems. www.iom.int
/jahia/webdav/site/myjahiasite/shared/shared/mainsite/activities/tcm/IOM_
Kesing_Symposium_Notes_2_ENG.pdf.

Jakarta Post. 2017. Indonesian Passport among World's Weakest; Expert
Weighs in on Why. Asia News Network, October 27. www.asiaone.com/asia
/indonesian-passport-among-worlds-weakest-expert-weighs-why.

JBMI. 2016a. Press Release: Victim of Data Correction by Indonesian Consulate Is Not Given Maximum (Sentence) [Press Rilis: Korban Koreksi Data
Didampingi KJRI, Namun Tidak Maksimal], May 26. https://fendyrahayu
.wordpress.com/2016/05/26/korban-koreksi-data-didampingi-kjri-namun-
tidak-maksimal.

———. 2016b. Press Release: Save SIMKIM Passport Victims [Press Rilis:
Selamatkan Korban Paspor SIMKIM], June 16. https://fendyrahayu
.wordpress.com/2016/06/16/selamatkan-korban-paspor-simkim/.

———. 2016c. Victims of Data Correction Get Free from Jail [Korban Koreksi
Data Terbebas Dari Hukuman Penjara], August 25. https://fendyrahayu
.wordpress.com/2016/08/25/.

JBMI and KABAR BUMI. 2016. Save Victims of Passport Data Correction
from Prison and Deportation [Selamatkan Korban Koreksi Data Paspor
Dari Penjara dan Deportasi], May 20. www.petisionline.net/selamatkan_
korban_koreksi_data_paspor_dari_penjara_dan_deportasi.

Johnson, Mark, Maggy Lee, Michael McCahill, and Rosalyn Mesina. 2020.
Beyond the 'All Seeing Eye': Filipino Migrant Domestic Workers' Contestation of Care and Control in Hong Kong. *Ethnos* 85, no. 2: 276–92.

Johnson, Mark, and Johan Lindquist. 2020. Care and Control in Asian Migrations. *Ethnos* 85, no. 2: 195–207.

Juwita, Etik. 2019. I'm Not Yem. In *At a Moment's Notice: Indonesian Maids
Write Their Lives Abroad,* edited by Jafar Suryomenggolo, 169–78. Copenhagen: NIAS Press.

Kearney, Michael. 1995. The Local and the Global: The Anthropology of
Globalization and Transnationalism. *Annual Review of Anthropology* 24:
547–65.

Keshavarz, Mahmoud. 2015. Material Practices of Power—Part I: Passports
and Passporting. *Design Philosophy Papers* 13, no. 2: 97–113.

———. 2016. Material Practices of Power—Part II: Forged Passports as
Material Dissents. *Design Philosophy Papers* 14, no. 1–2: 3–18.

———. 2019. *The Design Politics of the Passport: Materiality, Immobility, and
Dissent.* London: Bloomsbury.

Khaerudina, Ratna. 2019. Susi. In *At a Moment's Notice: Indonesian Maids
Write Their Lives Abroad,* edited by Jafar Suryomenggolo, 32–38. Copenhagen: NIAS Press.

Killias, Olivia. 2018. *Follow the Maid: Domestic Worker Migration in and from Indonesia.* Copenhagen: NIAS Press.

Klinken, Gerry van, and Joshua Barker. 2009. *State of Authority: The State in Society in Indonesia.* Ithaca, NY: Cornell University.

Kloppenburg, Sanneke. 2013. Tracing Mobilities Regimes: The Regulation of Drug Smuggling and Labour Migration at Two Airports in the Netherlands and Indonesia. PhD dissertation, University of Amsterdam.

Kondo, Dorinne. 1986. Dissolution and Reconstitution of Self: Implications for Anthropological Epistemology. *Cultural Anthropology* 1, no. 1: 74–88.

Konsulat Jenderal Republik Indonesia. 2018. Penerapan Sistem Informasi Manajemen Keimigrasian (SIMKIM) Dalam Pelayanan Penerbitan Paspor Di KJRI Frankfurt. www.indonesia-frankfurt.de/penerapan-sistem-informasi-manajemen-keimigrasian-simkim-dalam-pelayanan-penerbitan-paspor-di-kjri-frankfurt/ (accessed April 9, 2022).

Kuipers, Joel C., and Askuri. 2017. Islamization and Identity in Indonesia: The Case of Arabic Names in Java. *Indonesia* 103: 26–49.

Lan, Pei-Chia. 2006. *Global Cinderellas: Migrant Domestics and Newly Rich Employers in Taiwan.* Durham, NC: Duke University Press.

Latour, Bruno. 1993. *We Have Never Been Modern.* Translated by C. Porter. Cambridge, MA: Harvard University Press.

LegCo (Legislative Council). 2017. Foreign Domestic Helpers and Evolving Care Duties in Hong Kong. *Research Brief* no. 4. www.legco.gov.hk/researchpublications/english/1617rb04-foreign-domestic-helpers-and-evolving-care-duties-in-hong-kong-20170720-e.pdf (accessed June 6, 2021).

Liebelt, Claudia. 2008. On Sentimental Orientalists, Christian Zionists, and "Working Class Cosmopolitans": Filipina Domestic Workers' Journeys to Israel and Beyond. *Critical Asian Studies* 40, no. 4: 567–85.

Lin, Weiqiang, Johan Lindquist, Biao Xiang, and Brenda S. A. Yeoh. 2017. Migration Infrastructures and the Production of Migrant Mobilities. *Mobilities* 12, no. 2: 167–74.

Lindquist, Johan A. 2009. *The Anxieties of Mobility: Migration and Tourism in the Indonesian Borderlands.* Honolulu: University of Hawaii Press.

———. 2010. Labour Recruitment, Circuits of Capital and Gendered Mobility: Reconceptualizing the Indonesian Migration Industry. *Pacific Affairs* 83, no. 1: 115–32.

———. 2012. The Elementary School Teacher, the Thug and His Grandmother: Informal Brokers and Transnational Migration from Indonesia. *Pacific Affairs* 85, no. 1: 69–89.

———. 2015. Of Figures and Types: Brokering Knowledge and Migration in Indonesia and Beyond. *Journal of the Royal Anthropological Institute* 21, Supplement 1: 162–77.

———. 2017. Brokers, Channels, Infrastructure: Moving Migrant Labor in the Indonesian-Malaysian Oil Palm Complex. *Mobilities* 12, no. 2: 213–26.

———. 2018a. Infrastructures of Escort: Transnational Migration and Economies of Connection in Indonesia. *Indonesia,* no. 105: 77–95.

———. 2018b. Reassembling Indonesian Migration: Biometric Technology and the Licensing of Informal Labour Brokers. *Ethnos* 83, no. 5: 832–49.

Lindquist, Johan A., Biao Xiang, and Brenda S. A. Yeoh. 2012. Opening the Black Box of Migration: Brokers, the Organization of Transnational Mobility and the Changing Political Economy in Asia. *Pacific Affairs* 85, no. 1: 7–19.

Lo, Clifford. 2018. Man Arrested over High-Interest Loans to Helpers. *South China Morning Post,* July 6, City News, Crime, 3.

Lukacs, Gabriella. 2020. *Invisibility by Design: Women and Labor in Japan's Digital Economy.* Durham, NC: Duke University Press.

Lyon, David. 2001. Under My Skin: From Identification Papers to Body Surveillance. In *Documenting Individual Identity: The Development of State Practices in the Modern World,* edited by Jane Caplan and John C. Torpey, 291–310. Princeton, NJ: Princeton University Press.

MacAndrews, Colin. 1978. Transmigration in Indonesia: Prospects and Problems. *Asian Survey* 18, no. 5: 458–72.

Madianou, Mirca, and Daniel Miller. 2012. *Migration and New Media: Transnational Families and Polymedia.* New York: Routledge.

Magramo, Kathleen. 2022. Helpers "Denied Treatment, Forced to Sleep Rough." *South China Morning Post,* February 19, News, 12.

Mani, Lata. 1987. Contentious Traditions: The Debate on Sati in Colonial India. *Cultural Critique* 7: 119–56.

Marcus, George E., and D. Cushman. 1982. Ethnographies as Texts. *Annual Review of Anthropology* 11: 25–69.

Marcus, George E., and Michael M. J. Fischer. 1986. *Anthropology as Cultural Critique: An Experimental Moment in the Human Sciences.* Chicago: University of Chicago Press.

McKay, Deirdre. 2012. *Global Filipinos: Migrants' Lives in the Virtual Village.* Bloomington: Indiana University Press.

———. 2016. *An Archipelago of Care: Filipino Migrants and Global Networks.* Bloomington: Indiana University Press.

McKeown, Adam. 2008. *Melancholy Order: Asian Migration and the Globalization of Borders.* New York: Columbia University Press.

———. 2012. How the Box Became Black: Brokers and the Creation of the Free Migrant. *Pacific Affairs* 85, no. 1: 21–45.

MFMW (Mission for Migrant Workers). 2017. *Pictures from The Inside: Investigating Living Accommodation of Women Migrant Domestic Workers toward Advocacy and Action.* Hong Kong: Mission for Migrant Workers.

Migdal, Joel S. 2001. *State in Society: Studying How States and Societies Transform and Constitute One Another.* Cambridge: Cambridge University Press.

Milone, Pauline Dublin. 1966. *Urban Areas in Indonesia; Administrative and Census Concepts.* Berkeley, CA: Institute of International Studies.

Misra, Neha, and Ruth Rosenberg. 2003. Migrant Workers. In *Trafficking of Women and Children in Indonesia,* edited by Ruth Rosenberg, 38–55. Jakarta: International Catholic Migration Commission.

Missbach, Antje, and Wayne Palmer. 2018. Indonesia: A Country Grappling with Migrant Protection at Home and Abroad. Migration Policy Institute, September 19. www.migrationpolicy.org/article/indonesia-country-grappling-migrant-protection-home-and-abroad.

Mobini-Kesheh, Natalie. 1999. *The Hadrami Awakening: Community and Identity in the Netherlands East Indies, 1900–1942.* Ithaca, NY: Southeast Asia Program, Cornell University.

Mohanty, Chandra Talpade, Ann Russo, and Lourdes Torres. 1991. *Third World Women and the Politics of Feminism.* Bloomington: Indiana University Press.

Mol, Annemarie. 2008. *The Logic of Care: Health and the Problem of Patient Choice.* New York: Routledge.

Mongia, Radhika Viyas. 1999. Race, Nationality, Mobility: A History of the Passport. *Public Culture* 11, no. 3: 527–55.

———. 2018. *Indian Migration and Empire: A Colonial Genealogy of the Modern State.* Durham, NC: Duke University Press.

Muir, Sarah, and Akhil Gupta. 2018. Rethinking Anthropology of Corruption: An Introduction to Supplement 18. *Current Anthropology* 59, Supplement 18: S4–S15.

Mulla, Sameena. 2014. *The Violence of Care: Rape Victims, Forensic Nurses, and Sexual Assault Intervention.* New York: New York University Press.

Narayan, Kirin. 1993. How Native Is a "Native" Anthropologist? *American Anthropologist* 95, no. 3: 671–86.

Nash, Jim. 2021. Scattershot ID Techniques in Passports Are Not Catching Fraudsters. *Biometric Update,* May 7. www.biometricupdate.com/202105/scattershot-id-techniques-in-passports-are-not-catching-fraudsters.

Ng, Kang-Chung. 2018. Act against Loan Sharks Who Target Maids, Jakarta Envoy Urges HK Officials. *South China Morning Post,* October 22, City News, Crime, 1.

Niok, Maria Bo. 2019. A, Ne, Ge. In *At a Moment's Notice: Indonesian Maids Write Their Lives Abroad,* edited by Jafar Suryomenggolo, 18–31. Copenhagen: NIAS Press.

Noiriel, Gérard. 2001. The Identification of the Citizen: The Birth of Republican Civil Service in France. In *Documenting Individual Identity: The*

Development of State Practices in the Modern World, edited by Jane Caplan and John C. Torpey, 28–48. Princeton, NJ: Princeton University Press.

O'Connor, C. M. 2004. Effects of Central Decisions on Local Livelihoods in Indonesia: Potential Synergies between the Programs of Transmigration and Industrial Forest Conversion. *Population and Environment* 25, no. 4: 319–33.

Ong, Aihwa. 1999. *Flexible Citizenship: The Cultural Logics of Transnationality.* Durham, NC: Duke University Press.

Ong, Aihwa, and Stephen J. Collier, eds. 2005. *Global Assemblages: Technology, Politics, and Ethics as Anthropological Problems.* Malden, MA: Blackwell.

Palmer, Wayne. 2010. Costly Inducements: Pocket Money Given to Intending Migrant Domestic Workers Comes at a Price. *Inside Indonesia,* April 24. www.insideindonesia.org/feature-editions/costly-inducements.

———. 2012. Discretion and the Trafficking-Like Practices of the Indonesian State. In *Labour Migration and Human Trafficking in Southeast Asia: Critical Perspectives,* edited by Michele Ford, Lenore Lyons, and Willem van Schendel, 149–66. London: Routledge.

———. 2013. Public-Private Partnerships in the Administration and Control of Indonesian Temporary Migrant Labour in Hong Kong. *Political Geography* 34.

———. 2016. *Indonesia's Overseas Labour Migration Programme, 1969–2010.* Leiden, The Netherlands: Brill.

———. 2020a. International Migration and Stereotype Formation: Indonesian Migrants in Hong Kong. *Journal of International Migration and Integration* 21: 731–44.

———. 2020b. Prosecuting Corporate Crime in Indonesia: Recruitment Agencies That Traffic Migrant Workers. *Asian Journal of Comparative Law* 15, no. 1: 23–44.

Parreñas, Rhacel Salazar. 2001. *Servants of Globalization: Women, Migration and Domestic Work.* Stanford, CA: Stanford University Press.

———. 2008. *The Force of Domesticity: Filipina Migrants and Globalization.* New York: NYU Press.

———. 2011. *Illicit Flirtations: Labor, Migration, and Sex Trafficking in Tokyo.* Stanford, CA: Stanford University Press

Pascu, Luana. 2019. Biometric Passports in Indonesia Now PKD-Certified by ICAO. *Biometric Update,* October 2. www.biometricupdate.com/201910 /biometric-passports-in-indonesia-now-pkd-certified-by-icao.

Passport Index. n.d. Passe/Port (website). https://discover.passportindex.org /security/what-secrets-is-your-passport-hiding/ (accessed May 19, 2021).

Patico, Jennifer. 2018. Awkward Sincerity and Critical Empathy: Encounters in "International Marriage Brokering" and Feminist Anthropology. *Critique of Anthropology* 38, no. 1: 75–95.

Pels, Peter. 2018. Anthropology Should Never Be Fully Decolonized. *Etnofoor* 30, no. 2: 71–76.

Puig de la Bellacasa, Maria. 2017. *Matters of Care: Speculative Ethics in More Than Human Worlds*. Minneapolis: University of Minnesota Press.

Rabinow, Paul. 1977. *Reflections on Fieldwork in Morocco*. Berkeley: University of California Press.

Rao, Ursula, and Vijayanka Nair. 2019. Aadhaar: Governing with Biometrics. *South Asia: Journal of South Asian Studies* 42, no. 3: 469–81.

Reid, Anthony. 1993. The Decline of Slavery in Nineteenth-Century Indonesia. In *Breaking the Chains: Slavery, Bondage, and Emancipation in Modern Africa and Asia*, edited by Martin A. Klein, 64–82. Seattle: University of Washington Press.

Renaldi, Erwin. 2018. Proses Awal Pembuatan Paspor RI di Melbourne Masih Terhambat. www.abc.net.au/indonesian/2018-02-15/proses-registrasi-online-simkim/9449894?utm_campaign=abc_news_web&utm_content=link&utm_medium=content_shared&utm_source=abc_news_web (accessed April 9, 2022).

Republika. 2013. Building a Transparent, Accountable and Responsive Immigration System [Membangun Sistem Keimigrasian yang Transparan, Akuntabel, dan Responsif], January 26. www.republika.co.id/berita/nasional/hukum/13/01/25/mh6m69-membangun-sistem-keimigrasian-yang-transparan-akuntabel-dan-responsif.

Rigg, Jonathan. 1991. *Southeast Asia: A Region in Transition*. Boston: Unwin Hyman.

Riles, Annelise. 2006. *Documents: Artifacts of Modern Knowledge*. Ann Arbor: University of Michigan Press.

Robertson, Craig. 2010. *The Passport in America: The History of a Document*. New York: Oxford University Press.

Robinson, Kathryn. 2000. Gender, Islam, and Nationality: Indonesian Domestic Servants in the Middle East. In *Home and Hegemony: Domestic Service and Identity Politics in South and Southeast Asia*, edited by Kathleen M. Adams and Sara Dickey, 249–82. Ann Arbor: University of Michigan Press.

Rodriguez, Robyn Magalit. 2010. *Migrants for Export: How the Philippine State Brokers Labor to the World*. Minneapolis: University of Minnesota Press.

Rosaldo, Renato. 1986. From the Door of His Tent: The Fieldworker and the Inquisitor. In *Writing Culture: The Poetics and Politics of Ethnography*, edited by James Clifford and George E. Marcus, 77–97. Berkeley: University of California Press.

Rosenberg, Ruth, ed. 2003. *Trafficking of Women and Children in Indonesia*. Jakarta: International Catholic Migration Commission.

Rossum, Mattias van. 2018. The Carceral Colony: Colonial Exploitation, Coercion, and Control in the Dutch East Indies, 1810s–1940s. *International Review of Social History* 63: 65–88.

Rudnyckyj, Daromir. 2004. Technologies of Servitude: Governmentality and Indonesian Transnational Labor Migration. *Anthropological Quarterly* 77, no. 3: 407–34.

Sadiq, Kamal. 2009. *Paper Citizens: How Illegal Immigrants Acquire Citizenship in Developing Countries.* New York: Oxford University Press.

Salim, Tama. 2016a. RI Seeks Deal with HK to Prevent Falsified Document Cases. *Jakarta Post,* June 9. www.thejakartapost.com/news/2016/06/09 /ri-seeks-deal-with-hk-prevent-falsified-document-cases.html.

———. 2016b. RI Workers in HK Jailed for Overstaying. *Jakarta Post,* June 13. www.thejakartapost.com/news/2016/06/13/ri-workers-hk-jailed-overstaying.html.

Salter, Mark B. 2015. Passport Photos. In *Making Things International 1: Circuits in Motion,* edited by Mark B. Salter, 18–32. Minneapolis: University of Minnesota Press.

Scott, James C. 1987. *Weapons of the Weak.* New Haven, CT: Yale University Press.

———. 1998. *Seeing Like a State: How Certain Schemes to Improve the Human Condition Have Failed.* New Haven, CT: Yale University Press.

———. 2002. Review of *The Invention of the Passport: Surveillance, Citizenship, and the State* by John C. Torpey. *Journal of Modern History* 74, no. 1: 142–44.

Scott, James C., John Tehranian, and Jeremy Mathias. 2002. The Production of Legal Identities Proper to States: The Case of the Permanent Family Surname. *Comparative Studies in Society and History* 44, no. 1: 4–44.

Sengoopta, Chandak. 2003. *Imprint of the Raj: How Fingerprinting Was Born in Colonial India.* London: Macmillan.

Silvey, Rachel. 2004. Transnational Domestication: State Power and Indonesian Migrant Women in Saudi Arabia. *Political Geography* 23: 245–64.

———. 2007. Unequal Borders: Indonesian Transnational Migrants at Immigration Control. *Geopolitics* 12, no. 2: 265–79.

———. 2018. From Java to Saudi Arabia and Dubai: Precarious Itineraries of Indonesian Domestic Workers. In *Departing from Java: Javanese Labour, Migration, and Diaspora,* edited by Rosemarijn Hoefte and Peter Meel. Copenhagen: NIAS Press.

Singha, Radhika. 2000. Settle, Mobilize, Verify: Identification Practices in Colonial India. *Studies in History* 16, no. 2: 151–98.

———. 2013. The Great War and a 'Proper' Passport for the Colony: Border-Crossing in British India, c. 1882–1922. *Indian Economic and Social History Review* 50, no. 3: 289–315.

Spaan, Ernst. 1994. Taikongs and Calos: The Role of Middlemen and Brokers in Javanese International Migration. *International Migration Review* 28, no. 1: 93–113.

Spivak, Gayatri C., and S. Gunew. 1990. Questions of Multiculturalism. In *The Post-colonial Critic: Interviews, Strategies, Dialogues,* edited by Sarah Harasym, 59–66. London: Routledge.

Stacey, Judith. 1988. Can There Be a Feminist Ethnography? *Women's Studies International Forum* 11, no. 1: 21–27.

Stoler, Ann L. 1985. *Capitalism and Confrontation in Sumatra's Plantation Belt, 1870–1979.* New Haven, CT: Yale University Press.

———. 1989. Making Empire Respectable: The Politics of Race and Sexual Morality in 20th-Century Colonial Cultures. *American Ethnologist* 16, no. 4: 634–60.

———. 1992. Sexual Affronts and Racial Frontiers: European Identities and the Cultural Politics of Exclusion in Colonial Southeast Asia. *Comparative Studies in Society and History* 34, no. 3: 514–51.

———. 2002. Colonial Archives and the Arts of Governance. *Archival Science* 2: 87–109.

———. 2009. *Along the Archival Grain: Epistemic Anxieties and Colonial Common Sense.* Princeton, NJ: Princeton University Press.

———. 2016. *Duress: Imperial Durabilities in Our Times.* Durham, NC: Duke University Press.

Strassler, Karen. 2010. *Refracted Visions: Popular Photography and National Modernity in Java.* Durham, NC: Duke University Press.

Strathern, Marilyn. 1987. An Awkward Relationship: The Case of Feminism and Anthropology. *Signs* 12, no. 2: 276–92.

Suara. 2016a. 18 Indonesian Citizens Checked in Hong Kong Allegedly Falsified Passport Data [18 WNI Diperiksa di Hongkong Diduga Palsukan Data Paspor]. *Suara,* June 6.

———. 2016b. Indonesia Asks for 3 Years Amnesty [Indonesia Minta Amnesti 3 Tahun]. *Suara,* June 24, 2016, 1–2 [print copy].

Sumner, Cate. 2015. Indonesia's Missing Millions: Erasing Discrimination in Birth Certification in Indonesia. *Center for Global Development Policy Paper 064,* June. www.cgdev.org/sites/default/files/CGD-Policy-Paper-64-Sumner-Missing-Millions.pdf.

Suryadinata, Leo. 1979. *Political Thinking of the Indonesian Chinese, 1900–1977: A Sourcebook.* Singapore: Singapore University Press.

Sutherland, Heather. 1979. *The Making of a Bureaucratic Elite: The Colonial Transformation of the Javanese Priyayi.* Singapore: Heinemann.

Syahrin, M. Alvi. 2013. Returning Immigration Times. *Norms: An Anthology of Articles on Legal, Social, Political, and Humanities [Issues] (Petak Norma: Bunga Rampai Tulisan Seputar (Isu) Hukum, Sosial, Politik, dan Humaniora),* November 13. www.petaknorma.com/2013/11/mengembalikan-wibawa-imigrasi.html.

————. 2014. Bhumi Pura. . . . *Norms: An Anthology of Articles on Legal, Social, Political, and Humanities [Issues] (Petak Norma: Bunga Rampai Tulisan Seputar (Isu) Hukum, Sosial, Politik, dan Humaniora)*, May 22. http:// muhammadalvisyahrin.blogspot.com/2014/05/bhumi-pura.html.

————. 2018. Menakar Kedaulatan Negara dalam Perspektif Keimigrasian [Assessing State's Sovereignty from the Perspective of Immigration Affairs]. *Jurnal Penelitian Hukum: De Jure* 18: 43–57.

Tempo. 2016. Many Indonesian Migrant Workers Affected by Cases in Hong Kong, Consulate Denies Not Defending [Banyak TKI Kena Kasus di Hong Kong, KJRI Bantah Tak Membela], June 8. https://nasional.tempo.co /read/777739/banyak-tki-kena-kasus-di-hong-kong-kjri-bantah-tak-membela/full&view=ok.

Thomas, Nicholas. 1991. *Entangled Objects: Exchange, Material Culture and Colonialism in the Pacific*. Cambridge, MA: Harvard University Press.

Thufail, Fadjar I. 2005. Ninjas in Narratives of Local and National Violence in Post-Suharto Indonesia. In *Beginning to Remember: The Past in the Indonesian Present*, edited by Mary S. Zurbuchen, 150–67. Singapore: Singapore University Press.

Ticktin, Miriam. 2011. *Casualties of Care: Immigration and the Politics of Humanitarianism in France*. Berkeley: University of California Press.

Tidey, Sylvia. 2016. Between the Ethical and the Right Thing: How (Not) to Be Corrupt in Indonesian Bureaucracy in an Age of Good Governance. *American Ethnologist* 43, no. 4: 663–76.

————. 2018. A Tale of Two Mayors: Configurations of Care and Corruption in Eastern Indonesian Direct District Head Elections. *Current Anthropology* 59, Supplement 18: S117–27.

Tirtosudarmo, Riwanto. 2018. *The Politics of Migration in Indonesia and Beyond*. Singapore: Springer.

Torpey, John C. 2000. *The Invention of the Passport: Surveillance, Citizenship, and the State*. New York: Cambridge University Press.

Tosoni, Simone, and Trevor Pinch. 2017. *Entanglements—Conversations on the Human Traces of Science, Technology and Sound*. Cambridge, MA: MIT Press.

Tyner, James A. 2004. *Made in the Philippines: Gendered Discourses and the Making of Migrants*. New York: Routledge Curzon.

UN (United Nations). 2018. Global Compact for Safe, Orderly and Regular Migration, July 11. www.un.org/pga/72/wp-content/uploads/sites/51/2018 /07/migration.pdf.

U.S. Department of State. 2006. *Visa and Passport Security*. Appendix [Operation Triple X (Surabaya)]. U.S. Department of State, Washington, D.C.

Utami, Ayu. 2005. *Saman: A Novel*. Jakarta: Equinox.

Vandenbosch, Amry. 1942. *The Dutch East Indies: Its Government, Problems, and Politics.* Berkeley: University of California Press.

Varagur, Krithika. 2018. Indonesian Corruption Sentence Hailed as Turning Point. *VOA News,* April 27. www.voanews.com/east-asia-pacific/indonesian-corruption-sentence-hailed-turning-point.

Verdery, Katherine. 2018. *My Life as a Spy: Investigations in a Secret Police File.* Durham, NC: Duke University Press.

Vertovec, Steven. 1999. Conceiving and Researching Transnationalism. *Ethnic and Racial Studies* 22, no. 2: 447–62.

Vismann, Cornelia. 2008. *Files: Law and Media Technology.* Translated by Geoffrey Winthrop-Young. Stanford, CA: Stanford University Press.

Visweswaran, Kamala. 1994. *Fictions of Feminist Ethnography.* Minneapolis: University of Minnesota Press.

Voice of Migrants. 2015. Sistem Online Merugikan BMI/TKI Hong Kong [Online System Has Disadvantages for Hong Kong TKI/BMIs]. https://buruhmigran.or.id/2015/01/22/sistem-online-merugikan-bmitki-hong-kong/.

———. 2016. Janji Palsu KJRI Hong Kong: Kasus Koreksi Paspor SI, Berujung Penjara dan Deportasi [Fake Promise from Hong Kong Consulate: Case of Passport Correction, Ends in Prison and Deportation]. https://buruhmigran.or.id/2016/08/18/janji-palsu-kjri-hong-kong-kasus-koreksi-paspor-si-berujung-penjara-dan-deportasi/.

Walters, William, and Daniel Vanderlip. 2015. Electronic Passports. In *Making Things International 1: Circuits in Motion,* edited by Mark B. Salter, 3–17. Minneapolis: University of Minnesota Press.

Ward, Kerry. 2009. *Networks of Empire: Forced Migration in the Dutch East India Company.* New York: Cambridge University Press.

Watson, Rubie S. 1986. The Named and the Nameless: Gender and Person in Chinese Society. *American Ethnologist* 13, no. 4: 619–31.

Weeks, Kathi. 2011. *The Problem with Work: Feminism, Marxism, Antiwork Politics, and Postwork Imaginaries.* Durham, NC: Duke University Press.

Widodo, Sahid Teguh. 2014. The Development of Personal Names in Kudus, Central Java, Indonesia. *Procedia—Social and Behavioral Sciences* 134: 154–60.

Widodo, Sahid Teguh, and Kundharu Saddhono. 2012. Petangan Tradition in Javanese Personal Naming Practice: An Ethnoliguistic Study. *GEMA Online Journal of Language Studies* 12, no. 4: 1165–77.

Williams, Shiela, ed. 2020. *Entanglements: Tomorrow's Lovers, Families and Friends. New Science Fiction Inspired by Today's Emerging Technologies.* Cambridge, MA: MIT Press.

Wolf, Eric R. 1982. *Europe and the People without History.* Berkeley: University of California Press.

Xiang, Biao, and Johan Lindquist. 2014. Migration Infrastructure. *International Migration Review* 48, Supplement 1: 122–48.

Yamamoto, Takahiro. 2017. Japan's Passport System and the Opening of Borders, 1866–1878. *Historical Journal* 60, no. 4: 997–1021.

Yates-Doerr, Emily. 2014. Care: Provocation. From the Series: Care. Society for Cultural Anthropology, March 17. https://culanth.org/fieldsights/care-provocation.

Yosephine, Liza. 2016a. Govt to Improve System for Indonesian Migrant Workers in Hong Kong. *Jakarta Post,* June 17. www.thejakartapost.com/news/2016/06/17/govt-to-improve-system-for-indonesian-migrant-workers-in-hong-kong.html.

———. 2016b. Indonesia, Hong Kong to Cooperate on Migrant Workers' Problems. *Jakarta Post,* June 17. www.thejakartapost.com/news/2016/06/17/indonesia-hong-kong-to-cooperate-on-migrant-workers-problems.html.

YouTube. 2016. Mars Imigrasi Remix Edition, September 2. www.youtube.com/watch?v=u89aM59KNBk.

———. 2017. Mars Imigrasi Indonesia (with Lyrics), July 23. www.youtube.com/watch?v=KL1-eUU5F8c.

Yu, Sylvia. 2017. The Indonesian Child Maids of Hong Kong, Singapore: Why They're Suffering in Silence. *South China Morning Post,* March 25. www.scmp.com/week-asia/society/article/2081823/indonesian-child-maids-hong-kong-singapore-why-theyre-suffering.

Zelizer, Viviana A. Rotman. 2005. *The Purchase of Intimacy.* Princeton, NJ: Princeton University Press.

Index

Abdon-Tellez, Cynthia, 164, 173
abolition, 124, 132, 145, 146, 147n24, 150.
    See also slavery
Abu-Lughod, Lila, 23, 48
abuse. *See* FDW, abuse of; violence
activists, 169, 170–175. *See also* ATKI;
    BMI, activism; IMWU; JBMI; KABAR
    BUMI
actor-network theory, 12
age: "real," 19, 92; changed, 68, 110, 115–116;
    legal, 1, 64, 208; minimum, 15, 63, 126,
    199–200. *See also* identity
Anderson, Bridget, 154–155
Andry Indrady, 38, 39, 40, 41, 52, 99
anthropology: and colonialism, 33; decoloniz-
    ing of, 48; evolutionary, 190; and racism,
    190
anthropology of entanglement, 12, 21, 190.
    See also Callon, Michel
anti-terrorism, 20, 60, 187
anti-trafficking, 9, 15, 20, 60, 125, 127, 152;
    discourse, 206; in Hong Kong, 204–205;
    policies, 46, 187, 198. *See also* labor,
    forced; trafficking; Trafficking in Persons
    Report
Antonio-Santoyo, Edwina, 172
Appadurai, Arjun, 11–13

Asian: "economic tigers," 167; exclusion,
    211; Financial Crisis, 60, 138, 193. *See
    also* migration
asli (real), 1, 10; ages, 19; names, 19, 86–87,
    200
Asia Pacific Mission of Migrants (APMM),
    170
aspal (asli tapi palsu), 3, 86–87, 96; docu-
    ments, 25, 91, 207–209; passports,
    89–92
"aspal route," 89–92, 158; as illegal but licit,
    89
asylum seekers: in Hong Kong, 11, 30, 44,
    72, 80; in Indonesia, 139n20; and locals,
    155
ATKI (association of Indonesian Migrant
    Workers), 8, 36, 45, 104, 170 173
"awkward relationships," 47–48

Barker, Joshua, 119, 120
Bethune House, 170, 173
Bhumi Pura Wira Wibaya (guardians of the
    gate), 141
binaries: care-control, 23, 54–59; citizen-
    migrant, 17, 24, 154–157, 185–187;
    consular officials-BMI, 26–27; critiques
    of, 12, 21, 22, 197, 209; as entangled,

Founded in 1893,
UNIVERSITY OF CALIFORNIA PRESS
publishes bold, progressive books and journals
on topics in the arts, humanities, social sciences,
and natural sciences—with a focus on social
justice issues—that inspire thought and action
among readers worldwide.

The UC PRESS FOUNDATION
raises funds to uphold the press's vital role
as an independent, nonprofit publisher, and
receives philanthropic support from a wide
range of individuals and institutions—and from
committed readers like you. To learn more, visit
ucpress.edu/supportus.